A 1997 HOMETOWN COLLECTION

America's Best Recipes

Oxmoor
House ®

©1997 by Oxmoor House, Inc.
Book Division of Southern Progress Corporation
P.O. Box 2463, Birmingham, Alabama 35201

ISBN: 0-8487-1545-4
ISSN: 0898-9982

Manufactured in the United States of America
First Printing 1997

Editor-in-Chief: Nancy Fitzpatrick Wyatt
Senior Foods Editor: Susan Carlisle Payne
Senior Editor, Editorial Services: Olivia Kindig Wells
Art Director: James Boone

America's Best Recipes: A 1997 Hometown Collection

Editor: Whitney Wheeler Pickering
Copy Editor: Donna Baldone
Editorial Assistants: Stacey Geary, Catherine S. Ritter
Designer: Rita Yerby
Director, Test Kitchens: Kathleen Royal Phillips
Assistant Director, Test Kitchens: Gayle Hays Sadler
Test Kitchens Home Economists: Molly L. Baldwin,
    Susan Hall Bellows, Julie Christopher, Michele Brown Fuller,
    Natalie E. King, Elizabeth Tyler Luckett, Jan Jacks Moon,
    Iris Crawley O'Brien, Jan A. Smith
Photographers: Brit Huckabay, Randy Mayor
Photo Stylists: Virginia R. Cravens, Iris Crawley O'Brien
Indexer: Mary Ann Laurens
Production and Distribution Director: Phillip Lee
Associate Production Manager: Theresa L. Beste
Production Assistant: Faye Porter Bonner
Project Consultants: Meryle Evans, Audrey P. Stehle

Cover: *Chicken Pie (page 241)*

WE'RE HERE FOR YOU!
    We at Oxmoor House are dedicated to serving you with
reliable information that expands your imagination and
enriches your life. We welcome your comments and
suggestions. Please write to us at:
    Oxmoor House, Inc.
    Editor, *America's Best Recipes*
    2100 Lakeshore Drive
    Birmingham, AL 35209

To order additional publications, call 1-205-877-6560.

Contents

Introduction

Across America proud cooks preserve treasured family recipes and regional cuisines in quality community cookbooks. And *America's Best Recipes* brings you nearly 400 of the highest-rated community cookbook recipes from across the U.S., all rigorously taste-tested by our Test Kitchens staff. You'll find the best of regional cuisines as well as cherished family fare in these fund-raising cookbooks compiled by some of America's best cooks. These are the recipes that are swapped and shared with family and friends in hometowns throughout our land.

We also bring you the country's prized grilling recipes in our special chapter, "Favorite Recipes from the Grill." From tender steaks and tasty ribs to bountiful salads and homemade soups (yes, salads and soups), our outdoor cooking suggestions are big on taste. You'll find

- Recipes for any occasion, from cookouts and barbecues to easy family fare
- Answers to your most frequently asked questions about grilling such as "Should I buy a gas or charcoal grill?"
- An easy-to-follow grilling chart complete with kitchen-tested times and temperatures

In addition, don't miss our "Quick and Easy" chapter beginning on page 45. This chapter features timesaving recipes that are easy to prepare (just 45 minutes or less) and use only a handful of common ingredients.

We're proud to bring you this stellar collection of recipe winners. If a particular book sparks your interest and you'd like to order a copy, you'll find an alphabetical listing of these books, along with mailing addresses in the Acknowledgments beginning on page 320. When you order copies, you'll receive great recipes and the satisfaction of knowing that you're helping support the local communities and their charitable causes with the monies raised from the sale of these outstanding cookbooks.

The Editors

Favourites from the Grill

Hickory Ribs, page 25

Top 5 Grilling Questions

Slip on an apron and grab some tongs–grilling isn't just for hot dogs and hamburgers anymore. Here, we give you answers to some commonly asked questions to help make grilling fun and easy.

1. Should I buy a gas or charcoal grill?

Your choice depends not only on your pocketbook, but also where you grill, your flavor preferences, how much time you have to cook, and the time of year you cook out. More expensive than its charcoal counterpart, a gas grill offers fast start-up, adjustable heat control, and the most convenient year-round cooking. Many charcoal grill purists insist that charcoal gives superior flavor though, and that a charcoal grill offers more portability and ambiance, despite taking longer to heat up. Whichever type you choose, make sure it has a cover to afford you maximum flexibility.

2. I tried to cook a whole chicken on the grill, but it burned on the outside and was raw on the inside. What's the solution?

It sounds like you grilled your chicken directly over hot coals when you would have been more successful grilling it indirectly. Direct heat results in quick cooking with more surface browning. It's best for small cuts of meat like chops, steaks, kabobs, and hamburgers. Large cuts of meat such as whole chickens, tenderloins, and roasts require the slow, even cooking of indirect heat.

Indirect grilling is quite simple. When using a gas grill, light one burner, and place a disposable aluminum foil pan on the opposite side. Place the meat over the pan, and close the lid. The heat from the burner warms the grill like an oven—this prevents flare-ups and ensures juicier meats. Turning isn't necessary unless you're basting with a sauce.

For a charcoal grill, arrange the coals at the sides of the grill or around the foil pan, making sure the pan is slightly larger than the food. Place the meat over the pan, and close the lid. Lift the lid only to add coals as needed to maintain a constant temperature.

Our chart at the right clarifies which type of heat is best for different meats, as well as correct cooking times and temperatures.

3. How do I use the different wood chips and chunks for grilling that I see at my supermarket?

For subtle wood-smoke flavor, experiment with the many aromatic wood chips and chunks available like mesquite, maple, hickory, oak, and fruitwoods. Wood chips are recommended for foods that cook in an hour or less; chunks burn slower and are better for longer cooking.

For best results from chips or chunks, first soak them in water for 30 minutes. Drain them, and add directly to the hot coals of a charcoal grill. For a gas grill, wrap the soaked wood in aluminum foil, leaving the ends open, and place them on the hot lava rocks.

4. A friend told me I shouldn't baste meats with any leftover marinade. Why not?

Cross-contamination (uncooked meat juices spreading bacteria to cooked meat) is the biggest concern when it comes to basting meats as they cook or serving leftover marinade at the table. When you want to use some of the marinade to baste meat or to serve on the side, pour off a portion to reserve for that. Discard the marinade that was in contact with the raw meat. Or, after marinating the meat, drain the marinade and bring it to a boil to destroy any bacteria from uncooked meat juices.

5. I lost an orange roughy fillet through the grill rack recently. Is there anything I can do to make sure another fish doesn't get away?

Avoid the problem of losing fish, shellfish, and vegetables to the grill by enclosing them in a greased grilling basket. That way, you can turn the basket over without any food sticking to or falling through the rack.

GROUND RULES FOR GRILLING MEAT

MEAT	COOKING TIME	METHODS	INSTRUCTIONS
BEEF			
Ground beef patties	8 to 12 minutes	Direct	Grill, uncovered, until no longer pink.
Steaks (1 to 1½ inches thick)	8 to 10 minutes	Direct	Grill, uncovered, to at least 145°.
Tenderloin	30 to 45 minutes	Indirect	Grill, covered, to at least 145°.
Brisket (6 pounds)	3 to 4 hours	Indirect	Grill, covered, to at least 145°.
FISH			
Whole fish (per inch of thickness)	10 to 12 minutes	Direct	Grill, covered.
Fish fillets (per inch of thickness)	10 minutes	Direct	Grill, uncovered.
LAMB			
Chops or steaks (1 inch thick)	10 to 12 minutes	Direct	Grill, uncovered, to at least 150°.
Leg (boneless or butterflied)	40 to 50 minutes	Indirect	Grill, covered, to at least 150°.
PORK			
Chops (¾ inch thick)	10 to 12 minutes	Direct	Grill, covered, to 160°.
Tenderloin (½ to 1½ pounds)	16 to 21 minutes	Direct	Grill, covered, to 160°.
Ribs	1½ to 2 hours	Indirect	Grill, covered, to 160°.
POULTRY			
Chicken (thighs, quarters, halves, and whole)	30 to 60 minutes	Indirect	Grill, covered, to 180°.
Chicken (bone-in breasts)	30 minutes	Indirect	Grill, covered, to 170°.
Chicken (boneless breasts)	10 to 12 minutes	Direct	Grill, uncovered.
Turkey (bone-in breast, cut lengthwise in half)	45 minutes	Indirect	Grill, covered, to 170°.

* All times given are based on medium-hot coals (350° to 400°).

Bombay Fish

We gave this classic curry our highest rating–it's worth the effort!

3 pounds halibut fillets, cut into 1-inch cubes
1 cup peanut oil
¼ cup fresh lime juice
3 tablespoons soy sauce
14 (12-inch) wooden skewers
1 pound unpeeled large fresh shrimp
1 large cucumber, cut into ½-inch-thick slices
14 green onions, cut into 2-inch pieces
Vegetable cooking spray
Hot cooked rice
Curry Sauce
Assorted condiments: toasted flaked coconut, chopped peanuts, chutney, raisins

Place fish in a large heavy-duty, zip-top plastic bag. Combine peanut oil, lime juice, and soy sauce; stir well. Pour over fish; seal bag. Marinate in refrigerator 1 hour.

Soak wooden skewers in water 30 minutes.

Peel shrimp, and devein, if desired.

Remove fish from marinade, reserving marinade. Place marinade in a small saucepan. Bring to a boil; set aside.

Alternately thread fish, shrimp, cucumber, and onions onto skewers. Coat food rack with cooking spray; place on grill over medium-hot coals (350° to 400°). Place skewers on rack, and grill, covered, 10 minutes or until fish flakes easily when tested with a fork and shrimp turn pink, turning and basting occasionally with reserved marinade. Serve over rice with Curry Sauce and condiments. Yield: 7 servings.

Curry Sauce

1 medium onion, minced
1 medium cooking apple, peeled, cored, and minced
1 stalk celery, minced
¼ cup plus 1 tablespoon butter or margarine, melted
¼ cup all-purpose flour
2½ tablespoons curry powder
3 cups chicken broth
½ cup half-and-half
1 tablespoon lemon juice
¼ teaspoon salt
¼ teaspoon freshly ground pepper
2 tablespoons mango chutney

Cook onion, apple, and celery in butter in a large saucepan over medium-high heat, stirring constantly, until tender. Sprinkle with flour and curry powder, stirring constantly. Gradually add chicken broth, stirring constantly. Bring to a boil; reduce heat, and simmer 45 minutes. Stir in half-and-half, lemon juice, salt, and pepper. Just before serving, stir in chutney. Yield: 3 cups.

Seaport Savories
TWIG Junior Auxiliary of Alexandria Hospital
Alexandria, Virginia

Lime- and Ginger-Grilled Salmon

This marinade has pucker power. It gets its kick from the tangy lime.

2 tablespoons grated fresh
  ginger
2 tablespoons grated lime rind
½ teaspoon sea salt
¼ teaspoon ground white
  pepper
¼ teaspoon freshly ground
  black pepper

4 (8-ounce) salmon fillets
  (1 inch thick), skinned
2 tablespoons butter or
  margarine, melted
2 teaspoons lime juice
Garnish: fresh lime slices

Combine first 5 ingredients. Press ginger-lime mixture onto both sides of salmon fillets. Cover and marinate in refrigerator 45 minutes. Gently scrape ginger-lime mixture from fillets with back of a knife.

Combine butter and lime juice. Baste salmon fillets with butter mixture.

Place salmon fillets in a greased grilling basket. Grill, uncovered, over medium-hot coals (350° to 400°) about 5 minutes on each side or until fish flakes easily when tested with a fork. Transfer fillets to individual serving plates. Garnish, if desired. Yield: 4 servings.

Note: We recommend using a grilling basket for these tangy salmon fillets. Even though we used vegetable cooking spray, we found the fillets stuck slightly when cooked directly on the grill rack.

Emory Seasons, Entertaining Atlanta Style
Emory University Woman's Club
Atlanta, Georgia

Caribbean Snapper

Crusty French bread or rice makes the perfect accompaniment with these fillets to soak up the rich rum sauce.

6 (8-ounce) red snapper fillets
1 cup dry white wine
1 cup orange juice
½ cup chopped shallots
¼ cup chopped fresh parsley
¼ cup dark rum
¼ cup fresh lime juice

¼ cup soy sauce
4 cloves garlic, minced
2 teaspoons dried rosemary
¼ teaspoon ground white
  pepper
¼ teaspoon salt
Vegetable cooking spray

Place fillets in a large heavy-duty, zip-top plastic bag. Combine wine and next 10 ingredients; pour over fish. Seal bag; marinate in refrigerator 2 hours.

Remove fillets from marinade, reserving marinade. Pour marinade into a medium saucepan; bring to a boil. Reduce heat to medium and cook 12 minutes or until mixture is reduced by half; set aside, and keep warm.

Coat food rack with cooking spray; place on grill over medium-hot coals (350° to 400°). Place fillets on rack; grill, covered, 4 to 5 minutes on each side or until fish flakes easily when tested with a fork. Remove from grill. Serve with reserved marinade. Yield: 6 servings.

Gold'n Delicious
The Junior League of Spokane, Washington

Tandoori Swordfish Steaks

The tandoori nomenclature traditionally refers to an Indian cooking technique, but it's becoming more commonly used to describe the earthy Indian flavors of curry, coriander, and ginger permeating this fish.

4 (4-ounce) swordfish steaks
½ cup plain yogurt
3 tablespoons lime juice
1 teaspoon minced garlic
¾ teaspoon grated fresh ginger
½ teaspoon ground cumin
½ teaspoon chili powder

¼ teaspoon salt
¼ teaspoon dried crushed red
  pepper
¼ teaspoon curry powder
⅛ teaspoon ground coriander
Vegetable cooking spray

Place swordfish steaks in a heavy-duty, zip-top plastic bag. Combine yogurt and next 9 ingredients in a small bowl, stirring well. Reserve half of marinade; pour remaining marinade over steaks. Seal bag, and shake gently until steaks are well coated. Marinate in refrigerator 2 hours, turning bag occasionally.

Remove steaks from marinade, discarding marinade. Coat grill rack with cooking spray; place on grill over medium-hot coals (350° to 400°). Place steaks on rack, and grill 10 minutes on each side or until fish flakes easily when tested with a fork. Serve with reserved marinade. Yield: 4 servings.   Julie Lampie

A Celebration of Food
Sisterhood Temple Beth David
Westwood, Massachusetts

Grilled Fresh Tuna

A sassy marinade of citrus juices and soy sauce flatters the thick tuna steaks.

4 (4- to 5-ounce) yellowfin tuna
   steaks (¾ inch thick)
¼ cup orange juice
¼ cup soy sauce
2 tablespoons ketchup
2 tablespoons chopped fresh
   parsley

1 tablespoon lemon juice
1 clove garlic, minced
½ teaspoon dried oregano
⅛ teaspoon ground white
   pepper
Vegetable cooking spray

Place tuna in a large heavy-duty, zip-top plastic bag. Combine orange juice and next 7 ingredients; pour over tuna. Seal bag; marinate in refrigerator 1 hour.

Remove tuna from marinade, reserving marinade. Pour marinade into a small saucepan; bring to a boil.

Coat food rack with cooking spray; place on grill over medium-hot coals (350° to 400°). Place steaks on rack; grill, covered, 3 to 4 minutes on each side or until fish flakes easily when tested with a fork, turning and basting with reserved marinade. Yield: 4 servings.   Pat Chitty

Timeless Treasures
The Junior Service League of Valdosta, Georgia

Scallops with Orange-Butter Sauce

You'll reel in the compliments with these tangy scallops that can also be served as an appetizer for 8.

2 tablespoons chopped fresh thyme
2 tablespoons olive oil
2 tablespoons lemon juice
1 tablespoon chopped fresh rosemary
2 cloves garlic, minced
½ teaspoon salt
¼ teaspoon ground white pepper
⅛ teaspoon dried crushed red pepper

1½ pounds fresh sea scallops
½ cup fresh orange juice with pulp
¼ cup butter, softened
¾ cup seeded and diced tomato
¼ cup chopped fresh parsley
Salt and pepper to taste
Vegetable cooking spray

Combine first 8 ingredients in a medium bowl; add scallops, and toss well. Cover and marinate in refrigerator 1 hour.

Place orange juice in a medium saucepan. Bring to a boil, reduce heat, and simmer, uncovered, 10 minutes or until reduced by half. Gently stir in butter, tomato, and parsley, stirring constantly. Cook until thoroughly heated; add salt and pepper to taste. Set aside, and keep warm.

Remove scallops from marinade, discarding marinade; thread scallops onto four 12-inch skewers. Coat food rack with cooking spray; place on grill over medium-hot coals (350° to 400°). Place skewers on rack; grill, covered, 4 to 5 minutes on each side or until scallops turn white. Serve with orange sauce. Yield: 4 servings.   Mary McKenney

Cooks by the Yard
Harvard Neighbors, Harvard University
Cambridge, Massachusetts

Grilled Asian Pesto Shrimp

The longer you marinate the shrimp, the more fresh herb impact you'll enjoy.

2 pounds unpeeled medium-size fresh shrimp
⅓ cup olive oil
1 teaspoon sesame oil
3 tablespoons minced garlic
2 tablespoons chopped fresh basil
1 tablespoon chopped fresh chives
1 tablespoon dry sherry
1 teaspoon chopped fresh thyme
1 teaspoon chopped fresh rosemary
1 teaspoon salt
2 teaspoons dried crushed red pepper
½ teaspoon freshly ground pepper
Vegetable cooking spray

Peel shrimp, and devein, if desired; set aside.

Combine olive oil and next 10 ingredients in container of an electric blender; process until smooth, stopping once to scrape down sides. Place in a large heavy-duty, zip-top plastic bag. Add shrimp; seal bag securely, and shake until shrimp are coated. Marinate in refrigerator 1 to 3 hours, turning bag occasionally.

Remove shrimp from marinade, discarding marinade; thread shrimp onto 12 (10-inch) skewers. Coat food rack with cooking spray, and place on grill over medium-hot coals (350° to 400°). Place skewers on rack, and grill, uncovered, 3 minutes on each side or until done. Yield: 4 servings.

Take the Tour
St. Paul's Episcopal Church Women
Edenton, North Carolina

Barbecue Beef Brisket

The slow cooking of the meat made this barbecue melt in our mouth and get our best rating.

1 (5- to 6-pound) boneless beef brisket
2 teaspoons paprika
½ teaspoon pepper
1 (11- x 9- x 2-inch) disposable aluminum roasting pan

Hickory chunks
1 cup water
Vegetable cooking spray
Sauce

Sprinkle brisket with paprika and pepper; rub over surface of roast. Place roast in disposable pan; add 1 cup water, and cover with aluminum foil.

Soak hickory chunks in water to cover 30 minutes; drain. Wrap chunks in heavy-duty foil, and make several holes in foil. Light gas grill on one side; place foil-wrapped chunks directly on hot coals. Let grill preheat 10 to 15 minutes. Place pan with brisket on rack opposite hot coals; cover and grill 3½ to 4 hours or until tender. Turn brisket every hour, adding water as needed. Remove brisket from pan, reserving 1 cup pan drippings for sauce.

Coat grill rack with cooking spray; place rack over hot coals. Place brisket on rack; cover and grill 10 to 15 minutes on each side. Slice against grain into thin slices. Serve with Sauce. Yield: 12 servings.

Sauce

1 onion, finely chopped
1 tablespoon butter or margarine, melted
1 cup reserved pan drippings
½ teaspoon pepper

1½ cups ketchup
1 tablespoon lemon juice
1 tablespoon Worcestershire sauce
1 teaspoon hot sauce

Cook onion in butter in a large skillet over medium-high heat, stirring constantly, until tender. Stir in drippings and remaining ingredients. Bring to a boil; reduce heat, and simmer 15 minutes, stirring occasionally. Yield: 3 cups.

Ann Woolley

Discover Oklahoma Cookin'
Oklahoma 4-H Foundation
Stillwater, Oklahoma

Cajun Grilled Tenderloin with Mustard-Horseradish Cream

For appetizers instead of entrées, thinly slice the tenderloin and serve on cocktail buns with Mustard-Horseradish Cream. It'll serve about 24 lucky people.

1 (3½-pound) beef tenderloin
¼ cup hot sauce
¼ cup teriyaki sauce
2 tablespoons Worcestershire
  sauce

1 tablespoon Creole seasoning
Vegetable cooking spray
Mustard-Horseradish Cream

Place tenderloin in a large heavy-duty, zip-top plastic bag. Combine hot sauce and next 3 ingredients. Pour over tenderloin. Seal bag; marinate in refrigerator 1½ hours, turning occasionally.

Remove tenderloin from marinade, discarding marinade.

Light gas grill on one side. Coat grill rack on opposite side with cooking spray. Place rack over cool lava rocks; let grill preheat 10 to 15 minutes. Place tenderloin on rack opposite hot coals; cover and grill 30 to 40 minutes or until meat thermometer inserted in thickest part of tenderloin registers 145° (medium-rare) or 160° (medium). Let stand 10 minutes before slicing. Serve with Mustard-Horseradish Cream. Yield: 8 servings.

Mustard-Horseradish Cream

¼ cup prepared horseradish
1 cup whipping cream

¼ cup Dijon mustard
1 tablespoon fresh lemon juice

Place horseradish in a fine wire-mesh strainer; press with back of a spoon against sides of strainer to squeeze out juice. Discard juice. Set horseradish aside.

Beat whipping cream at high speed of an electric mixer until soft peaks form. Fold in horseradish, mustard, and lemon juice. Cover and chill thoroughly. Yield: 2½ cups.

The Artful Table
Dallas Museum of Art League
Dallas, Texas

Prime Strip Steaks à la Allen III's Green Peppercorn Wine Sauce

The secret to this recipe lies in the green peppercorns. The peppercorns add a fresh, mild accent to the steaks.

1 cup port wine
1 cup dry red wine
¼ cup Worcestershire sauce
1 (.25-ounce) jar dried whole green peppercorns

Vegetable cooking spray
6 (8-ounce) New York strip steaks, (about 1¼ inches thick)

Combine first 4 ingredients in a small saucepan. Bring to a boil; reduce heat, and simmer, uncovered, 5 minutes. Set aside.

Coat grill rack with cooking spray; place on grill over medium-hot coals (350° to 400°). Place steaks on rack, and grill, uncovered, 5 minutes on each side or to desired degree of doneness, basting frequently with ¾ cup sauce. Reserve remaining sauce to serve with steaks. Yield: 6 servings.

Appealing Fare
Frost & Jacobs
Cincinnati, Ohio

Grilled Sirloin Steak with Elephant Garlic Crust

Mellow elephant garlic crowns mouthwatering sirloin for a surprising nuance.

¼ teaspoon salt
¼ teaspoon black pepper
4 (8-ounce) lean sirloin steaks (about 1-inch thick)
3 tablespoons olive oil, divided
½ cup chopped onion

1 head elephant garlic, peeled and diced
1 cup soft breadcrumbs
⅛ teaspoon dried crushed red pepper

Sprinkle salt and black pepper evenly over steaks. Grill, covered, over medium-hot coals (350° to 400°) 4 minutes on each side or to desired degree of doneness. Keep warm.

Heat 1 tablespoon oil in a large skillet. Add onion; cook, stirring constantly, 1 minute over medium-high heat. Add garlic; cook, stirring constantly, 3 minutes over medium heat.

Position knife blade in food processor bowl; add garlic mixture, breadcrumbs, remaining 2 tablespoons olive oil, and red pepper. Process until smooth, stopping once to scrape down sides.

Spread garlic mixture evenly over top of grilled steaks. Broil 5½ inches from heat (with electric oven door partially opened) 5 minutes or until topping is golden. Yield: 4 servings.

Cooking Atlanta Style
Atlanta Community Food Bank
Marietta, Georgia

Grilled Teriyaki Flank Steak

Robust beef consommé, red wine, and soy sauce impart their assertiveness in the paper-thin slices of steak.

2 **pounds flank steak**	3 **tablespoons lime juice**
1 **cup canned beef consommé**	2 **tablespoons brown sugar**
½ **cup dry red wine**	2 **teaspoons ground ginger**
¼ **cup sliced green onions**	1 **clove garlic, minced**
⅓ **cup soy sauce**	½ **teaspoon salt**

Cut flank steak into 1½-inch strips diagonally across the grain. Place steak in a large heavy-duty, zip-top plastic bag. Combine consommé and remaining 8 ingredients; stir well. Pour marinade over steak. Seal bag securely; marinate in refrigerator 8 hours, turning occasionally.

Remove steak from marinade, discarding marinade. Grill, covered, over medium-hot coals (350° to 400°) 5 minutes on each side or to desired degree of doneness. Yield: 6 servings.   Rochelle Hicks

Note: The flank steak will be easier to slice if you first partially freeze it.

Plain & Fancy Favorites
Montgomery Woman's Club
Cincinnati, Ohio

Pronto Spicy Beef and Black Bean Salsa

A homemade blend of chili powder, cumin, salt, and red pepper pulls double duty as a spicy rub for the thinly sliced beef and a cheeky seasoning to the salsa.

1 tablespoon chili powder
1 teaspoon ground cumin
1 teaspoon salt
½ teaspoon ground red pepper
1 (15-ounce) can black beans, rinsed and drained
1 medium tomato, chopped
1 small purple onion, finely chopped
3 tablespoons coarsely chopped fresh cilantro
1 pound lean boneless top sirloin steak (1 inch thick)
Vegetable cooking spray
Garnish: fresh cilantro sprigs

Combine first 4 ingredients. Combine 2 teaspoons seasoning mixture, beans, tomato, onion, and chopped cilantro. Cover and set aside.

Trim fat from steak. Spread remaining seasoning mixture evenly over surface of steak. Coat grill rack with cooking spray; place over medium-hot coals (350° to 400°). Place steak on rack; grill, covered, 8 minutes on each side. Remove steak from grill. To serve, cut steak diagonally across grain into thin slices. Serve with black bean salsa. Garnish, if desired. Yield: 4 servings.   Carla Hampton Macartney

Stephens Remembered, Recollections & Recipes
Stephens College Denver Area Club
Lakewood, Colorado

Fajitas

A super simple marinade intensifies the steak's flavor. Piled with your favorite Tex-mex toppings, these fajitas are crowd pleasers.

2 pounds lean flank steak
¾ cup beer
½ cup Italian salad dressing
¼ cup Worcestershire sauce
3 tablespoons fresh lime juice
½ teaspoon garlic salt
½ teaspoon pepper
12 (8-inch) flour tortillas
Toppings: pico de gallo, diced chile verde, chopped tomato, chopped onion, guacamole
Garnish: fresh cilantro sprigs

Place steak in a large heavy-duty, zip-top plastic bag. Combine beer and next 5 ingredients; stir well. Pour marinade over steak. Seal bag securely; marinate in refrigerator 3 hours, turning occasionally.

Heat tortillas according to package directions; keep warm.

Remove steak from marinade, reserving marinade. Bring marinade to a boil. Grill steak, covered, over medium-hot coals (350° to 400°) 6 minutes on each side or to desired degree of doneness, basting with reserved marinade. Cut steaks diagonally across grain into thin strips.

Serve steak in warm tortillas; top with pico de gallo, chile verde, chopped tomato, onion, and guacamole. Garnish, if desired. Yield: 6 servings.   H. Joaquin Jackson

The Authorized Texas Ranger Cookbook
Texas Ranger Museum
Hamilton, Texas

Delicious Summer Hamburgers

Eat this juicy hamburger with a knife and fork or douse it with your favorite toppings, and serve it up on a bun.

1 large egg, lightly beaten	1 tablespoon pressed garlic
1 pound ground chuck	1 teaspoon ground red pepper
20 saltine crackers, crushed	½ teaspoon dried thyme
¼ cup chopped sweet onion	1 teaspoon dried parsley
2 (¾-ounce) slices American cheese, torn into small pieces	Dash of Worcestershire sauce
	Vegetable cooking spray

Combine first 10 ingredients in a large bowl; stir well. Shape mixture into four 4½-inch patties.

Coat grill rack with cooking spray; place on grill over medium-hot coals (350° to 400°). Place patties on rack; grill, uncovered, 6 minutes on each side or until done. Yield: 4 servings.   Paul Malopolski

Pepper Lovers Club Cookbook, Volume I
Pepper Lovers Club of Virginia Beach, Virginia

Grilled Veal Chops and Zucchini with Rosemary

The rosemary skewers aren't just for looks. They permeate the meat with extra herb appeal.

1 tablespoon plus 1 teaspoon grated lemon rind
2 tablespoons fresh lemon juice
⅓ cup olive oil
1 tablespoon minced fresh rosemary
½ teaspoon salt
⅛ teaspoon pepper

4 (1¼-inch-thick) boneless veal loin chops
4 (4-inch) woody rosemary branches with leaves
2½ pounds zucchini, sliced diagonally into ½-inch-thick pieces
Vegetable cooking spray

Combine first 6 ingredients in a 13- x 9- x 2-inch baking dish. Stir well; set aside.

Wrap tail end of each chop flush against the loin portion; pierce a hole through the entire length of tail end and loin chop with a metal skewer. Skewer each chop through the pierced hole with a rosemary branch to secure. Place chops in dish with marinade; cover and marinate in refrigerator 3 hours, turning chops occasionally. Add zucchini to marinade the last hour.

Remove chops and zucchini from marinade, discarding marinade. Coat grill rack with cooking spray; place rack over medium-hot coals (350° to 400°). Place chops on rack, and grill 8 to 9 minutes on each side or to desired degree of doneness. Grill zucchini 8 to 10 minutes on each side or until tender. Yield: 4 servings.   Dave Gostanian

In the Serving Tradition
Durham Woman's Club
Durham, Connecticut

Grilled Leg of Lamb Dijon

Earthy pecan shell chips turn on their smoky charm for this leg of lamb's debut.

1 (5- to 6-pound) leg of lamb, boned and butterflied	2 tablespoons minced fresh ginger
4 cloves garlic, crushed	1 tablespoon dried rosemary
2 (8-ounce) jars Dijon mustard	1 tablespoon dried thyme
¼ cup plus 1 tablespoon soy sauce	1 teaspoon salt
¼ cup plus 1 tablespoon olive oil	1 teaspoon ground red pepper
	Pecan shell chips
	Vegetable cooking spray

Trim fat from lamb. Combine garlic and next 8 ingredients in a medium bowl; stir well with a wire whisk.

Pour half of marinade into a 13- x 9- x 2-inch baking dish. Place lamb in dish. Spread remaining half of marinade over lamb. Cover and marinate in refrigerator 8 hours.

Soak pecan shell chips in water to cover 1 hour. Drain well. Wrap chips in heavy-duty aluminum foil, and make several holes in foil.

Light gas grill on one side; place foil-wrapped chips directly on hot coals. Coat grill rack on opposite side with cooking spray. Place rack over cool lava rocks; let grill preheat 10 to 15 minutes or until chips smoke.

Remove lamb from marinade, discarding marinade. Place lamb on rack opposite hot coals. Grill, covered, 40 minutes or until meat thermometer registers 150° (medium-rare) or 160° (medium). Let stand 10 minutes. Slice diagonally across grain into thin slices. Yield: 8 servings. Chris Snyder

Note: If pecan shell chips are hard to find in your area, substitute whole pecans. Just crack them, leaving the nuts in the shell. This is a good way to use stale pecans.

Cooking on the Coast
Mississippi Gulf Coast YMCA
Ocean Springs, Mississippi

Basil Grilled Lamb Chops

Honey and soy sauce paint a backdrop for herby basil in these chops.

8 (5-ounce) lean lamb loin
  chops (1 inch thick)
½ cup minced onion
¼ cup honey
3 tablespoons chopped fresh
  basil
3 tablespoons vegetable oil

1½ tablespoons soy sauce
1 tablespoon minced fresh
  garlic
1 teaspoon salt
1 teaspoon freshly ground
  pepper

Place chops in a large heavy-duty, zip-top plastic bag. Combine onion and remaining 7 ingredients. Pour over chops. Seal bag; marinate in refrigerator 2 hours, turning once.

Remove chops from marinade, reserving marinade. Bring marinade to a boil. Remove from heat, and set aside.

Grill chops, uncovered, over medium-hot coals (350° to 400°) 5 to 6 minutes on each side or to desired degree of doneness, basting frequently with marinade. Yield: 8 servings.   Karen Rockenbach

A Cook's Tour of Libertyville
Main Street Libertyville
Libertyville, Illinois

Tasty Tenderloin of Pork

Perk up this grilled pork with a hint of cinnamon in the marinade, and enjoy the surprise kick that the spice adds.

1 (1-pound) pork tenderloin
½ teaspoon ground cinnamon
2 tablespoons brown sugar
2 tablespoons soy sauce

1 tablespoon cooking sherry
½ teaspoon salt
Vegetable cooking spray

Rub tenderloin with cinnamon; place in a large heavy-duty, zip-top plastic bag. Combine brown sugar and next 3 ingredients; pour marinade over tenderloin. Seal bag; marinate in refrigerator at least 8 hours, turning occasionally.

Coat grill rack with cooking spray; place on grill over medium-low coals (300° to 350°). Place tenderloin on rack, and grill, covered, 25 minutes or until meat thermometer inserted in thickest part registers 160° (medium), turning once. Yield: 4 servings.   Marla Corts

Note: Cooking sherry and other cooking wines are not served as beverages like other wines. That's because they have added salt. If you'd like more sherry flavor, we recommend using dry sherry.

The Collection
Mountain Brook Baptist Church
Birmingham, Alabama

Sabi Babi Grilled Pork

1 **cup salted roasted peanuts**
1 **cup sliced onion**
¼ **cup fresh lemon juice**
¼ **cup soy sauce**
2 **tablespoons ground coriander**
2 **tablespoons brown sugar**
2 **cloves garlic**
1 **teaspoon dried crushed red pepper**
½ **teaspoon pepper**
½ **cup chicken broth**
½ **cup butter or margarine, melted**
1 **(2-pound) boneless pork loin roast, cut into 1-inch cubes**
Vegetable cooking spray

Position knife blade in food processor bowl; add first 9 ingredients. Process until smooth. Transfer mixture to a medium saucepan; bring to a boil. Stir in chicken broth and butter; remove from heat. Let cool 30 minutes.

Place pork cubes in a large shallow dish; pour marinade over pork. Cover and marinate in refrigerator 3 hours.

Thread pork onto eight 12-inch metal skewers, discarding marinade. Coat grill rack with cooking spray; place on grill over medium-hot coals (350° to 400°). Place kabobs on rack, and grill, covered, 14 minutes, turning occasionally. Yield: 8 servings.   Clara Harker

We Like It Here
Mukwonago High School
Mukwonago, Wisconsin

Bourbon-Basted Pork Chops

1 lemon
½ cup soy sauce
3 tablespoons butter or
 margarine
2 tablespoons bourbon
1 tablespoon minced onion
¼ teaspoon hot sauce
⅛ teaspoon salt
⅛ teaspoon pepper
4 (1-inch-thick) rib pork chops,
 trimmed

Cut lemon in half. Squeeze juice from both halves into a small saucepan; add lemon halves. Add soy sauce and next 6 ingredients, stirring to combine. Bring to a boil, reduce heat, and simmer 5 minutes. Reserve half of sauce.

Brush sauce evenly over both sides of pork chops. Grill, covered, over medium-hot coals (350° to 400°) 8 minutes on each side or until done, basting often with sauce. Serve chops with reserved sauce. Yield: 4 servings.

Virginia Fare
The Junior League of Richmond, Virginia

Honey-Garlic Pork Chops

4 (1½-inch-thick) lean boneless
 center-cut loin pork chops
¼ cup lemon juice
¼ cup honey
2 tablespoons soy sauce
1 tablespoon dry sherry
2 cloves garlic, minced

Place pork chops in a large heavy-duty, zip-top plastic bag. Combine lemon juice and remaining 4 ingredients. Pour over chops. Seal bag; marinate in refrigerator 4 to 6 hours, turning occasionally.

Remove chops from marinade, reserving marinade. Bring marinade to a boil. Grill chops, covered, over medium-hot coals (350° to 400°) 9 minutes on each side or until chops are done, basting occasionally with reserved marinade. Yield: 4 servings.   Debra Baranello

A Feast for the Eyes
Cataract Care Center
Johnstown, New York

Hickory Ribs

Inexpensive hickory chips lend smoky appeal to these sweet, tender ribs.

4 to 6 pounds pork spareribs
Hickory chips
Vegetable cooking spray
1 (8-ounce) can tomato sauce
½ cup dry sherry
½ cup honey
2 tablespoons white wine vinegar
2 tablespoons minced onion
1 clove garlic, minced
¼ teaspoon Worcestershire sauce

Place ribs in a large roasting pan. Bake at 350° for 30 minutes.

Soak hickory chips in water to cover at least 30 minutes; drain. Wrap hickory chips in heavy-duty aluminum foil, and make several holes in foil.

Light gas grill on one side; place foil-wrapped chips directly on hot coals. Coat grill rack on opposite side with cooking spray. Place rack over cool lava rocks; let grill preheat 10 to 15 minutes.

Place ribs on rack opposite hot coals; cover and cook 40 minutes.

Combine tomato sauce and remaining 6 ingredients in a small saucepan. Bring to a boil; reduce heat, and simmer over medium heat 6 minutes.

Place ribs on rack over hot coals. Grill, covered, 20 minutes, basting frequently with sauce. Yield: 4 servings.

Cafe Oklahoma
The Junior Service League of Midwest City, Oklahoma

Sunshine Ribs

3 pounds pork spareribs
¼ cup water
½ (6-ounce) can frozen
   pineapple-orange juice
   concentrate, thawed

2 tablespoons vegetable oil
1 tablespoon grated orange
   rind
¼ teaspoon pepper

Place ribs in a large heavy-duty, zip-top plastic bag. Combine water and remaining 4 ingredients; pour mixture over ribs. Seal bag, and marinate in refrigerator 8 hours, turning bag occasionally.

Drain ribs, reserving marinade. Bring to a boil in a saucepan.

Grill ribs, covered, over medium-hot coals (350° to 400°) 1 hour and 20 minutes or until done, turning and basting occasionally with marinade. Yield: 3 servings.

Joy Holen

Years and Years of Goodwill Cooking
Goodwill Circle of New Hope Lutheran Church
Upham, North Dakota

Easy Grilled Ham

1 (4-pound) cooked ham roast
   (about 2 inches thick)
½ cup ginger ale
½ cup orange juice
¼ cup firmly packed brown
   sugar

1 tablespoon vegetable oil
1½ teaspoons white vinegar
1 teaspoon dry mustard
¼ teaspoon ground ginger
⅛ teaspoon ground cloves

Place roast in a large heavy-duty, zip-top plastic bag. Combine ginger ale and remaining 7 ingredients, stirring until sugar dissolves. Pour over roast. Seal bag; marinate in refrigerator 8 hours, turning bag occasionally.

Remove roast from marinade, discarding marinade. Grill, covered, over medium-hot coals (350° to 400°) 10 minutes on each side or until meat thermometer inserted in thickest portion registers 140°. Yield: 10 servings.

Shirley Ruskay

Collard Greens, Watermelons, and "Miss" Charlotte's Pie
Swansboro United Methodist Women
Swansboro, North Carolina

Grilled Brats with Onion-Sauerkraut Relish

For your next tailgate event, cook the brats in beer at home, and finish them off on the grill at the party site.

8 fresh bratwurst (about 2 pounds)
1 (12-ounce) can beer

8 hoagie rolls or French bread rolls
Onion-Sauerkraut Relish

Combine bratwurst and beer in a Dutch oven. Bring almost to a boil; reduce heat, and simmer, uncovered, 10 minutes. Remove bratwurst from beer; drain. Grill bratwurst, uncovered, over medium-hot coals (350° to 400°) 7 to 8 minutes or until done.

Serve on rolls with Onion-Sauerkraut Relish. Yield: 8 servings.

Onion-Sauerkraut Relish

¼ cup vegetable oil
½ cup sugar
2 cups coarsely chopped onion
1 (14.5-ounce) can sauerkraut, well drained

¼ teaspoon salt
¼ cup cider vinegar
¼ cup dry white wine
½ teaspoon caraway seeds

Heat oil in a large skillet over medium heat. Add sugar, and cook stirring constantly, 10 minutes or until mixture turns a light caramel color. Add onion, sauerkraut, and salt; simmer, uncovered, over medium heat 15 minutes, stirring often. (Caramelized sugar will harden when onion and sauerkraut are added, but will dissolve as mixture simmers.) Add vinegar, wine, and caraway seeds; simmer, uncovered, 30 minutes. Store leftovers in refrigerator up to 1 week. Yield: 2½ cups.

The Tailgate Cookbook
National Kidney Foundation of Kansas and Western Missouri
Westwood, Kansas

Grilled Venison with Apricot and Green Peppercorn Glaze

Yes, this recipe really does call for ¼ cup minced garlic in the glaze and 6 more cloves in the marinade. Garlic sweetens as it cooks and, in this recipe, it enhances the piquant peppercorn glaze.

¼ cup olive oil
2 teaspoons chopped fresh marjoram
2 teaspoons chopped fresh rosemary
2 teaspoons chopped fresh thyme
6 cloves garlic, cut in half
1 (1½-pound) boneless venison loin
¼ cup minced garlic
½ cup minced shallot

2 tablespoons olive oil
2 cups Marsala wine
¼ cup balsamic vinegar
¼ cup canned green peppercorns, drained
1 (6-ounce) package dried apricot halves, cut into thin strips
1½ to 2 quarts canned beef broth, undiluted
Salt and pepper to taste

Combine first 5 ingredients in a large shallow dish; stir well. Add venison, turning to coat meat. Cover and marinate in refrigerator 8 to 24 hours, turning once.

Cook ¼ cup garlic and shallot in 2 tablespoons hot oil in a large skillet over medium heat, stirring constantly, until browned. Add wine and next 3 ingredients; bring to a boil. Reduce heat and simmer 2 minutes. Add broth; bring to a boil. Reduce heat, and simmer 45 minutes or until thickened. Add salt and pepper to taste; set aside, and keep warm.

Drain venison, discarding marinade. Grill, covered, over medium-hot coals (350° to 400°) 25 minutes or until meat thermometer inserted in thickest part registers 150° (medium-rare), turning once.

To serve, slice venison across grain into thin slices. Serve with warm glaze. Yield: 4 servings.

West of the Rockies
The Junior Service League of Grand Junction, Colorado

Basil Grilled Chicken

Pats of garlic-basil butter lie lazily on these grilled chicken breasts.

½ cup butter or margarine, softened

2 tablespoons minced fresh basil

1 tablespoon grated Parmesan cheese

¼ teaspoon garlic powder

⅛ teaspoon salt

⅛ teaspoon pepper

¾ teaspoon coarsely ground pepper

4 chicken breast halves, skinned

⅓ cup butter or margarine, melted

2 tablespoons chopped fresh basil

Garnish: fresh basil sprigs

Position knife blade in food processor bowl; add first 6 ingredients. Process until smooth, stopping once to scrape down sides. Place butter mixture in a small serving bowl; cover and chill.

Press coarsely ground pepper evenly onto meaty sides of chicken breast halves. Combine ⅓ cup melted butter and 2 tablespoons chopped basil, and lightly brush on chicken breasts. Grill, covered, over medium-hot coals (350° to 400°) 15 minutes on each side or until chicken is done, basting frequently with remaining melted butter mixture.

Serve chicken with chilled butter mixture. Garnish, if desired. Yield: 4 servings.   Kaye Bruno

The Fabulous Footnotes' Cookbook
Sandy Paustian's Fabulous Footnotes
Jensen Beach, Florida

Lemon Barbecued Chicken

Cooking for more than just two? This recipe can be doubled, even tripled, easily.

2 large chicken breast halves
¾ teaspoon salt
½ teaspoon grated lemon rind
½ teaspoon Worcestershire
    sauce
¼ teaspoon dry mustard

¼ teaspoon dried oregano
¼ cup vegetable oil
¼ cup lemon juice
1 tablespoon chopped green
    onions
Vegetable cooking spray

Place chicken breasts in a large heavy-duty, zip-top plastic bag. Combine salt and next 4 ingredients in a small bowl. Gradually add oil and lemon juice, stirring well. Stir in green onions. Pour over chicken; seal bag. Marinate in refrigerator 3 hours, turning occasionally.

Remove chicken from marinade, reserving marinade. Place marinade in a small saucepan. Bring marinade to a boil; set aside.

Light gas grill on one side; coat grill rack on opposite side with cooking spray. Place rack over cool lava rocks, and let grill preheat 10 to 15 minutes.

Arrange chicken breasts on rack opposite hot coals; cover and grill 45 minutes, basting with reserved marinade, turning once. Yield: 2 servings.   Cathy Wearstler

Friends and Fellowship Cookbook
First Christian Church of Stow, Ohio

Grilled Honey Chicken Breasts

Fragrant rosemary accents the sweet honey marinade for these tender chicken breasts.

½ cup honey
¼ cup plus 2 tablespoons
   butter or margarine, melted
¼ cup fresh lime juice
2 tablespoons Dijon mustard
1 tablespoon chopped fresh
   rosemary

2 cloves garlic, crushed
½ teaspoon dried savory
½ teaspoon salt
¼ teaspoon pepper
6 skinned and boned chicken
   breast halves
Vegetable cooking spray

Combine first 7 ingredients in a large shallow dish. Sprinkle salt and pepper over chicken; add chicken to marinade in dish, turning once. Cover and marinate in refrigerator 2 hours.

Coat grill rack with cooking spray; place on grill over medium-hot coals (350° to 400°). Remove chicken from marinade, discarding marinade. Place chicken on rack; grill, covered, 5 minutes on each side or until done. Yield: 6 servings.   Barbara Sargent

Phi Bete's Best
Phi Beta Psi Sorority, Theta Alpha Gamma Chapter
Bedford, Indiana

Southwestern Grilled Chicken

This chicken tastes subtly southwestern with its avocado and Monterey Jack cheese. If you want to turn up the heat, substitute Monterey Jack cheese with jalapeño peppers for the regular Monterey Jack cheese.

4 skinned and boned chicken breast halves	½ teaspoon dried dillweed
2 tablespoons cider vinegar	½ teaspoon dried basil
2 tablespoons olive oil	1 ripe avocado, peeled and sliced
1 tablespoon Dijon mustard	1 cup (4 ounces) shredded Monterey Jack cheese
¼ teaspoon onion salt	Salsa
½ teaspoon coarsely ground pepper	Lime slices (optional)

Place chicken in a large heavy-duty, zip-top plastic bag; set aside. Combine vinegar and next 6 ingredients in a small bowl; stir well with a wire whisk. Pour marinade mixture over chicken. Seal bag securely, and marinate in refrigerator 30 minutes.

Remove chicken from marinade, discarding marinade. Grill, covered, over medium-hot coals (350° to 400°) 8 minutes on each side or until chicken is done. Place chicken on an ungreased baking sheet. Top chicken evenly with avocado slices and shredded cheese. Broil 5½ inches from heat (with electric oven door partially opened) 1 minute or until cheese melts. Serve chicken topped with salsa. Garnish with lime slices, if desired. Yield: 4 servings.

Food for Thought
The Junior League of Birmingham, Alabama

Cajun Grilled Turkey

2 teaspoons chili powder	½ teaspoon salt
1 teaspoon garlic powder	½ teaspoon pepper
1 teaspoon dry mustard	1 (3-pound) boneless turkey breast
1 teaspoon cumin	Vegetable cooking spray
1 teaspoon dried sage	

Combine first 7 ingredients; set aside.

Rinse turkey breast thoroughly with cold water; pat dry with paper towels. Gently separate skin from breast. Rub half of dry mixture under skin on breast; sprinkle remaining mixture over skin. Insert meat thermometer into thickest part of breast.

Light gas grill on one side. Coat grill rack on opposite side with cooking spray. Place rack over cool lava rocks; let grill preheat 10 to 15 minutes. Place turkey breast on rack opposite hot coals; cover and grill 1½ hours or until meat thermometer registers 170°. Yield: 6 to 8 servings.   Lisa Higby

Cooper's Cookin' It Up!
Cooper Elementary School
Milwaukee, Wisconsin

Grilled Wild Duck Breasts

This duck is so tender and juicy, not greasy like some duck can be.

12 skinned and boned wild duck breast halves	1 teaspoon Worcestershire sauce
2 tablespoons Dijon mustard	12 slices bacon
½ cup dry sherry	¼ teaspoon pepper
½ cup Italian salad dressing	

Rinse duck breasts with cold water; pat dry with paper towels. Brush mustard evenly over both sides of duck breasts; place in a 13- x 9- x 2-inch baking dish.

Combine sherry, salad dressing, and Worcestershire sauce; pour over duck breasts. Cover and marinate in refrigerator 1 hour.

Remove duck breasts from marinade, discarding marinade. Wrap each duck breast with 1 slice of bacon; secure with wooden picks. Sprinkle with pepper.

Grill duck breasts, uncovered, over medium-hot coals (350° to 400°) 10 minutes on each side or until bacon is crisp. Remove wooden picks. Yield: 6 servings.

Charted Courses
Child and Family Agency of Southeastern Connecticut
New London, Connecticut

Grilled Quail

Jalapeño peppers are a simple but not-so-subtle seasoning for this quail. For a tamer flavor, cut off stem ends of the peppers, and remove the seeds with a grapefruit knife.

8 slices bacon	**Mesquite chips**
8 quail, dressed	**Vegetable cooking spray**
8 jalapeño peppers	

Place bacon on a rack in a 13- x 9- x 2-inch baking dish; cover with paper towels. Microwave at HIGH 3 to 4 minutes or until bacon is partially cooked. Drain bacon; set aside.

Rinse quail thoroughly with cold water; pat dry with paper towels. Place a jalapeño pepper into body cavity of each quail; tie ends of legs together with string. Wrap 1 bacon slice around each quail, and secure with wooden picks.

Soak mesquite chips in water 10 minutes; drain. Wrap chips in heavy-duty aluminum foil, and make several holes in foil. Light gas grill on one side; place foil-wrapped chips directly on hot coals. Coat grill rack on opposite side with cooking spray. Place rack over cool lava rocks; let grill preheat 10 to 15 minutes or until chips smoke. Arrange quail on rack opposite hot coals; cover and grill 25 minutes. Yield: 4 servings.   Roberto D. Garza, Jr.

The Authorized Texas Ranger Cookbook
Texas Ranger Museum
Hamilton, Texas

Chicken Salad with Corn and Peppers

Alongside the chicken, we grilled our corn in the husks which imparts a fresh, smoky flavor. Substitute fresh cooked corn if you don't have room on the grill.

6 skinned and boned chicken breast halves
½ cup lime juice
1 tablespoon dried oregano
½ teaspoon salt
⅛ teaspoon pepper
2 tablespoons olive oil
4 ears fresh corn in husks
Vegetable cooking spray
1 large sweet red pepper, chopped

3 green onions, thinly sliced
2 tablespoons lime juice
2 tablespoons olive oil
½ teaspoon salt
⅛ teaspoon pepper
1 teaspoon dried oregano
½ teaspoon ground cumin
1 bunch arugula, separated into leaves

Place chicken in a large heavy-duty, zip-top plastic bag. Combine lime juice and next 3 ingredients; pour over chicken. Seal bag securely; marinate in refrigerator 1 hour. Remove chicken from marinade, discarding marinade; brush chicken with 2 tablespoons oil.

Soak corn in husks in water 15 minutes.

Coat grill rack with cooking spray; place on grill over medium-hot coals (350° to 400°). Place chicken on rack; grill, covered, 7 minutes on each side or until done. Remove and let cool 10 minutes. Cut chicken into thin strips.

Grill corn in husks, covered, over medium-hot coals (350° to 400°) 15 to 20 minutes, turning occasionally. Remove husks, and cut kernels from cob.

Combine corn, red pepper, and green onions in a large bowl. Stir in lime juice and next 5 ingredients, mixing well. Stir in chicken. Serve chicken salad on plates lined with arugula. Yield: 4 servings.

Classic Connecticut Cuisine
Connecticut Easter Seals
Uncasville, Connecticut

Grilled Corn Salad

18 ears fresh corn in husks
1 large sweet red pepper
Vegetable cooking spray
5 green onions, chopped
½ cup plus 1 tablespoon cider
  vinegar

1½ tablespoons honey
¾ teaspoon ground cumin
½ teaspoon salt
¼ teaspoon pepper
⅓ cup vegetable oil

Soak corn in husks in water 15 minutes.

Cut pepper in half lengthwise; remove and discard seeds and membrane, and flatten pepper with palm of hand. Set aside.

Coat food rack with cooking spray, and place on grill over medium-hot coals (350° to 400°). Place sweet pepper, skin side down, on rack; remove corn from water and add corn in husks to grill. Grill, covered, 15 to 20 minutes or until corn is tender and slightly charred, and pepper is charred, turning corn occasionally. Let corn cool. Place pepper in ice water until cool; peel and discard skin.

Remove husks, and cut kernels from cob; place in a large bowl. Chop pepper; add pepper and green onions to corn.

Combine vinegar and next 4 ingredients. Gradually add oil, stirring constantly with a wire whisk. Pour dressing over corn mixture; toss gently. Serve immediately, or chill thoroughly. Yield 8 servings.

Very Virginia: Culinary Traditions with a Twist
The Junior League of Hampton Roads
Newport News, Virginia

Grilled Lettuce with Stilton Cheese

You may have had a wilted lettuce salad before, but this grilled varia-tion adds new meaning to the concept. The flavors are pronounced, so enjoy the salad with a simple entrée so you can savor every bite.

1½ cups olive oil
½ cup balsamic vinegar
1 teaspoon dry mustard
¼ teaspoon salt
¼ teaspoon pepper
1 head romaine lettuce
1 head radicchio
2 heads Belgian endive
1 large sweet red pepper, sliced into 8 rings

1 large green pepper, sliced into 8 rings
1 large yellow pepper, sliced into 8 rings
1 large purple onion, sliced into 8 rings
Vegetable cooking spray
8 ounces Stilton cheese, crumbled

Combine first 5 ingredients in a bowl, stirring well with a wire whisk.

Cut romaine and radicchio into 8 wedges, leaving cores intact. Cut each endive into 4 wedges, leaving cores intact. Dip lettuce wedges, pepper rings, and onion rings into dressing just until moistened.

Coat grill rack with cooking spray; place on grill over medium-hot coals (350° to 400°). Place peppers and onions on rack, and grill 5 minutes on each side or until crisp-tender. Grill lettuces 1 minute on each side or just until wilted.

Arrange romaine, radicchio, and endive on a serving platter. Top with pepper and onion; sprinkle with cheese. Serve immediately. Yield: 8 servings.   Bruce Bartz

Note: Be especially careful when grilling the lettuce—the oil may drip onto the coals and flame up.

True Grits: Tall Tales and Recipes from the New South
The Junior League of Atlanta, Georgia

Grilled Corn Soup with Cilantro and Ancho Chile Cream

This creamy soup embellished with fiery bursts of ancho chile cream and zesty cilantro cream had us asking for seconds.

8 ears fresh corn in husks
Vegetable cooking spray
2 serrano chiles
4 cups canned chicken broth, undiluted
4 medium cloves garlic, minced
2 medium carrots, chopped
2 small onions, chopped
1 large stalk celery, chopped
2 cups whipping cream
½ teaspoon salt
Cilantro Cream
Ancho Chile Cream

Soak corn in husks in water 15 minutes. Remove from water; grill in husks, covered, over medium-hot coals (350° to 400°) 15 to 20 minutes or until tender and slightly charred, turning occasionally. Let cool. Remove husks; cut kernels from cob, and set aside.

Using rubber gloves, seed and mince serrano chiles. Combine chiles, chicken broth, and next 4 ingredients in a large saucepan. Bring to a boil; reduce heat, and simmer, uncovered, 10 minutes. Add corn to vegetable mixture, and simmer 10 minutes or until vegetables are tender. Let cool slightly.

Transfer half of corn mixture to container of an electric blender; process until smooth, stopping once to scrape down sides. Repeat procedure with remaining corn mixture. Return pureed mixture to pan; bring to a boil. Reduce heat; stir in whipping cream and salt. Cook until thoroughly heated. To serve, ladle soup into individual soup bowls, and swirl Cilantro Cream and Ancho Chile Cream evenly into servings. Yield: 6 cups.

Cilantro Cream

5 large spinach leaves
2 cups water
1 cup loosely packed fresh cilantro leaves
3 tablespoons half-and-half
2 tablespoons sour cream

Wash and remove stems from spinach leaves. Bring water to a boil in a small saucepan. Add spinach, and cook 1 minute. Drain and rinse with cold water; drain. Press spinach between paper towels to remove excess moisture.

Place spinach, cilantro, and half-and-half in container of an electric blender; process until smooth, stopping once to scrape down sides. Place puree in a fine wire-mesh strainer over a small bowl; press with back of a spoon against the sides of a strainer to squeeze out liquid. Discard spinach and cilantro in strainer. Add sour cream to mixture in bowl, stirring with a wire whisk until smooth. Yield: ⅓ cup.

Ancho Chile Cream

1 small dried ancho chile pepper	**3 tablespoons half-and-half**
1 cup hot water	**2 tablespoons sour cream**

Using rubber gloves, remove and discard stems and seeds from chile pepper. Wash chile in cold water; drain. Tear chile in half, and place in a small bowl; add hot water. Let stand 20 minutes; drain.

Place chile and half-and-half in container of an electric blender; process until smooth, stopping once to scrape down sides. Place puree in a fine wire-mesh strainer over a small bowl; press with back of a spoon against the sides of a strainer to squeeze out liquid. Discard chile pepper in strainer. Add sour cream to mixture in bowl, stirring well with a wire whisk. Yield: ¼ cup.

Note: Always wear rubber gloves when seeding and chopping peppers. The pepper's oils can burn skin easily.

Dining by Fireflies: Unexpected Pleasures of the New South
The Junior League of Charlotte, North Carolina

Spinach Quesadillas with Grilled Sweet Potato and Four-Pepper Salsa

The colorful salsa can double as a topping for your favorite pork or chicken entrée.

1 (10-ounce) package frozen chopped spinach, thawed
1¾ cups sliced fresh mushrooms
1½ teaspoons butter or margarine, melted
Pinch of ground nutmeg
Pinch of ground red pepper
1 (8-ounce) package cream cheese, softened
10 (10-inch) flour tortillas
2½ cups (10 ounces) shredded Monterey Jack cheese
Grilled Sweet Potato and Four-Pepper Salsa
Sour cream (optional)

Drain spinach, and press between paper towels to remove excess moisture.

Cook spinach and mushrooms in melted butter in a large skillet over medium-high heat, stirring constantly, until mushrooms are tender. Add nutmeg and pepper, stirring well.

Spread cream cheese evenly among 5 tortillas; sprinkle with spinach mixture and shredded cheese. Top with remaining 5 tortillas.

Bake quesadillas, two at a time, at 375° for 7 minutes or until quesadillas are golden. Cut each quesadilla into 4 wedges. Serve with Grilled Sweet Potato and Four-Pepper Salsa and, if desired, sour cream. Yield: 10 servings.

Grilled Sweet Potato and Four-Pepper Salsa

2 large sweet potatoes (about 1½ pounds)
1 large green pepper
1 large sweet yellow pepper
1 large sweet red pepper
1 large jalapeño pepper
Vegetable cooking spray
1 medium-size purple onion, diced
4 cloves garlic, minced
¼ cup chopped fresh cilantro
½ cup extra virgin olive oil
2 tablespoons balsamic vinegar
2 teaspoons red wine vinegar
Salt and pepper to taste

Wash sweet potatoes; bake at 375° for 40 minutes. Allow potatoes to cool to touch. Peel and cut into ½-inch slices. Set aside.

Cut peppers in half lengthwise; remove and discard seeds and membranes.

Coat food rack with cooking spray, place on grill over medium-hot coals (350° to 400°). Place sweet potato slices and peppers on rack, and grill, covered, 5 minutes on each side or until potato is done and peppers are lightly charred.

Chop potato slices and peppers. Add onion and remaining 6 ingredients; stir well. Cover and chill at least 4 hours. Toss before serving. Yield: 4½ cups.

Dining by Fireflies: Unexpected Pleasures of the New South
The Junior League of Charlotte, North Carolina

Sesame Grilled Eggplant

1 medium eggplant (about 1 pound)
½ teaspoon salt
1 tablespoon sesame seeds, toasted
2 cloves garlic, pressed
¼ teaspoon dried crushed red pepper
3 tablespoons rice vinegar
2 tablespoons dark sesame oil
1½ teaspoons lemon juice
Vegetable cooking spray

Cut eggplant diagonally into 6 slices; place on layers of paper towels. Sprinkle salt on both sides of eggplant; let stand 15 minutes. Pat dry with paper towels.

Combine sesame seeds and next 5 ingredients; stir well. Brush both sides of eggplant with sesame mixture; let stand 10 minutes.

Coat grill rack with cooking spray; place on grill over medium-hot coals (350° to 400°). Place eggplant on rack, and grill, uncovered, 5 minutes on each side or until slightly soft, basting with sesame mixture. Yield: 6 servings.

Maine Ingredients
The Junior League of Portland, Maine

Black Lake Potatoes

6 (8-ounce) baking potatoes, unpeeled
3 small onions, thinly sliced
Vegetable cooking spray
¼ cup butter or margarine, melted
½ teaspoon garlic powder
1 teaspoon salt
½ teaspoon pepper

Wash potatoes, and pat dry with paper towels; slice potatoes vertically to within ½ inch of bottom. Place onion slices between potato slices. Cut six 12- x 12-inch pieces of aluminum foil; coat one side of foil with cooking spray. Place a potato in center of each piece of foil.

Combine butter, garlic powder, salt, and pepper. Drizzle over potatoes. Fold ends of foil over potato; crimp to seal securely. Grill, covered, over medium-hot coals (350° to 400°) 1 hour or until done, turning occasionally. Yield: 6 servings. Patricia Uttaro

Literally Delicious
Friends of the Gates Public Library
Rochester, New York

Grilled Vidalia Onions

All you need are sweet onions and salad dressing for a sweet and savory side dish.

4 large Vidalia onions (about 3 pounds), cut into ½-inch-thick slices
1 (8-ounce) bottle zesty Italian salad dressing
Vegetable cooking spray

Place onion slices in a large heavy-duty, zip-top plastic bag. Pour dressing over onion. Seal bag; marinate in refrigerator at least 3 hours, turning occasionally. Remove onion from marinade, discarding marinade. Coat food rack with cooking spray, place on grill over medium-hot coals (350° to 400°). Place onion on rack; grill, covered, 5 minutes on each side or until tender. Yield: 8 servings. Lisa R. Miller

The Collection
Mountain Brook Baptist Church
Birmingham, Alabama

Grilled Summer Vegetables with Balsamic Vinaigrette

Balsamic vinegar lends a tangy-sweet distinction to these grilled vegetables. Made from sweet grapes, it's pungently sweet and has a more full-bodied flavor than other vinegars. Like wine, it's aged in wooden barrels for a distinctive flavor and, as with any fine wine, it's pricier than its counterparts.

⅓ cup balsamic vinegar
½ cup olive oil
1 (.7-ounce) envelope Italian salad dressing mix
2 tablespoons olive oil
1 small eggplant, cut into ¼-inch-thick slices
2 sweet red peppers, quartered
2 small zucchini, cut lengthwise into ¼-inch-thick slices
2 small yellow squash, cut lengthwise into ¼-inch-thick slices
6 large red potatoes, cut into ½-inch-thick slices
Vegetable cooking spray
Garnishes: fresh basil leaves, fresh rosemary sprigs

Combine first 3 ingredients; stir well. Set aside.

Drizzle 2 tablespoons olive oil over vegetables. Coat food rack with cooking spray; place rack on grill over medium-hot coals (350° to 400°). Place vegetables on rack, and grill, covered, 5 to 10 minutes or until done, turning once and basting occasionally with vinegar mixture. Serve with remaining vinegar mixture. Garnish, if desired. Yield: 6 servings.

Appealing Fare
Frost & Jacobs
Cincinnati, Ohio

Grilled "Banana Splits"

Remember those camp cookouts as a kid? Children of all ages will enjoy making—as well as eating—this campfire favorite.

4 firm ripe bananas, unpeeled
¼ cup miniature marshmal-
   lows
¼ cup semisweet chocolate
   mini-morsels

¼ cup chunky peanut butter
   (optional)

Cut a lengthwise slit to, but not through, bottom of each banana. Stuff banana slit with 1 tablespoon each of marshmallows, chocolate morsels, and peanut butter, if desired.

Place each banana, bottom side down, on four squares of aluminum foil folded to resemble a boat. Grill bananas, uncovered, over medium coals (300° to 350°) 5 minutes or until chocolate morsels melt. Yield: 4 servings.   Whitingham Brownie Troop #235

Town Hill Playground Cookbook
Town Hill Playground Committee
Whitingham, Vermont

Quick & Easy Recipes

Genoese Meatballs, page 53

Amaretto Freeze

Kick back and let slushy Amaretto Freeze take you on a dream vacation to the tropics.

½ cup white crème de cacao
¼ cup amaretto
¼ cup Grand Marnier or other orange-flavored liqueur
¼ cup Cointreau or other orange-flavored liqueur
¼ cup Triple Sec or other orange-flavored liqueur
½ gallon vanilla ice cream, softened
Garnish: fresh strawberries

Combine liqueurs; stir well. Place one-third of liqueur mixture and one-third of ice cream in container of an electric blender. Process until smooth. Pour into a 2-quart pitcher. Repeat procedure twice with remaining ingredients. Serve in wine glasses. Garnish, if desired. Serve immediately. Yield: 8 cups.   Lynda Belle

Note: If you're a big connoisseur of orange-flavored liqueur, you'll appreciate the flavor intrigue of using the three types called for in this recipe. If you're partial to one type, use that one for the entire amount.

Add a Pound of Love
Geauga Humane Society
Chardon, Ohio

Black Bean Dip

1 (15-ounce) can black beans, rinsed and drained
½ cup mild salsa
2 tablespoons fresh cilantro
2 tablespoons fresh lime juice
¼ teaspoon ground cumin
Salt and freshly ground pepper to taste

Position knife blade in food processor bowl; add all ingredients. Process until smooth, stopping once to scrape down sides. Serve with tortilla chips. Yield: 1½ cups.

Healthful Recipes from "Friends of Bear"
Bear Necessities Pediatric Cancer Foundation
Cary, Illinois

Marinated Pineapple

Lime juice and orange liqueur tease these sweet pineapple chunks with tanginess. Provide wooden picks to serve the pineapple as appetizers, or spoon the syrupy chunks into small bowls for dessert.

1 cup sugar
½ cup water
½ cup Grand Marnier or other orange-flavored liqueur
½ cup lime juice

1 tablespoon grated orange rind (about 1 medium orange)
2 fresh pineapples, peeled, cored, and cubed

Combine sugar and water in a saucepan. Bring to a boil; cook 1 minute. Add liqueur, lime juice, and orange rind; stir well. Place pineapple in a bowl. Pour sugar mixture over pineapple. Cover and chill at least 1 hour, stirring occasionally. Yield: 24 appetizer servings.

Of Tide & Thyme
The Junior League of Annapolis, Maryland

Cheese Quesadillas

4 cups (16 ounces) shredded Monterey Jack cheese
2 green onions, chopped
4 pickled jalapeño peppers, finely chopped
2 tablespoons minced fresh cilantro

1 teaspoon ground cumin
2 tablespoons butter or margarine, softened
8 (7-inch) flour tortillas

Combine first 5 ingredients; stir well. Set aside.

Spread butter evenly on 1 side of tortillas. Spoon cheese mixture evenly over unbuttered side of 4 tortillas; top with remaining 4 tortillas, buttered side up.

Cook quesadillas, one at a time, in a large skillet over medium-high heat 2 minutes on each side or until lightly browned. To serve, cut tortillas in half. Yield: 8 servings.   Sue Ann Graves

A Place Called Hope
The Junior Auxiliary of Hope, Arkansas

Fish Parmesan

1½ pounds orange roughy
1 clove garlic, minced
½ teaspoon dried oregano
¼ teaspoon salt
⅛ teaspoon pepper

1 (8-ounce) can tomato sauce
½ cup (2 ounces) shredded
 mozzarella cheese
2 tablespoons freshly grated
 Parmesan cheese

Sprinkle fish with garlic, oregano, salt, and pepper. Place in a lightly greased 13- x 9- x 2-inch baking dish. Pour tomato sauce over fillets. Sprinkle with cheeses.

Bake, uncovered, at 425° for 19 minutes or until fish flakes easily when tested with a fork. Yield: 4 servings.

Note: If orange roughy isn't available in your area, substitute another light-colored, delicate-flavored lean fish like cod, grouper, halibut, or sole.

Around Our Table: California Cooks Kosher
The Jewish Family Service of Los Angeles, California

Oven-Baked Salmon Steaks

Fresh salmon never had it so good. Slather an easy-to-make herbed butter over the steaks, and pop them in the oven.

4 (6-ounce) salmon steaks
¼ cup butter or margarine,
 melted
1 teaspoon lemon-pepper
 seasoning

1 teaspoon garlic salt
1 teaspoon paprika
Lemon wedges

Place salmon steaks in an 11- x 7- x 1½-inch baking dish. Combine butter, lemon-pepper seasoning, and garlic salt in a small bowl; stir well. Pour over steaks in dish. Sprinkle with paprika. Bake, uncovered, at 500° for 10 to 12 minutes or until fish flakes easily when tested with a fork. Serve with lemon wedges. Yield: 4 servings.

The Artful Table
Dallas Museum Art League
Dallas, Texas

Grilled Lake Trout

An old camp favorite, this recipe was meant to be cooked over an open-hearth fire, but a grill or oven makes the trout equally tender. Sealing the fish in foil is the trick.

Vegetable cooking spray
4 trout fillets (about 2 pounds)
1 cup dry white wine
½ cup vegetable oil
1 (4-ounce) can mushroom
   stems and pieces, drained
¼ cup chopped onion

2 tablespoons chopped fresh
   parsley
2 tablespoons lemon juice
2 teaspoons salt
¼ teaspoon dried thyme
¼ teaspoon ground bay leaves

Coat four 18- x 18-inch squares of heavy-duty aluminum foil with cooking spray. Place a fillet on each square, bringing up edges of foil.

Combine wine and remaining 8 ingredients; pour evenly over fillets. Close foil around fish, sealing tightly.

Place packets on rack, and grill, covered, over hot coals (400° to 500°) 15 minutes or until fish flakes easily when tested with a fork. Yield: 4 servings.   Deanie Platt

Note: You can also bake these fish packets at 375° for 25 minutes.

A Culinary Tour of Homes
Big Canoe Chapel Women's Guild
Big Canoe, Georgia

Shrimp Marinara with Angel Hair Pasta

Shrimp, garlic, and crushed red pepper jazz up a jar of marinara for a sauce that mimics homemade.

1 pound unpeeled medium-size fresh shrimp	2 cloves garlic, minced
1 (9-ounce) package fresh angel hair pasta	1 (14-ounce) jar marinara sauce
1 tablespoon olive oil	1 tablespoon lime juice
	1 teaspoon dried crushed red pepper

Peel shrimp, and devein, if desired.

Cook pasta according to package directions. Drain and set aside. Heat oil in a large skillet over medium heat. Add garlic; cook 1 minute, stirring constantly. Add shrimp, and cook 3 to 5 minutes or until shrimp turn pink, stirring often. Add marinara sauce, lime juice, and red pepper; cook over medium heat until thoroughly heated. Serve over pasta. Yield: 4 servings.   Bonnie Wall

Angel Food
St. Vincent de Paul School
Salt Lake City, Utah

Whiskey Steaks

Drench these skillet-sautéed steaks in a rich whiskey-inspired cream sauce.

4 (5-ounce) beef tenderloin steaks (1 inch thick)	2 tablespoons olive oil
½ teaspoon salt	½ cup Irish whiskey
2 teaspoons freshly ground pepper	½ cup whipping cream
	2 tablespoons finely chopped fresh parsley

Sprinkle steaks with salt and pepper. Pour olive oil into a large non-stick skillet; place over medium-high heat until hot. Add steaks, and cook 10 to 15 minutes or until a meat thermometer registers 160° (medium) or to desired degree of doneness, turning once. Pour whiskey over steaks. Ignite with a long match. Stir until flames die down. Remove steaks, reserving drippings in skillet. Set steaks aside, and keep warm.

Stir cream and parsley into drippings in skillet. Bring to a boil; reduce heat, and simmer, stirring constantly, 4 minutes or until thickened. Pour over steaks. Serve immediately. Yield: 4 servings.

Global Feast Cookbook
Mystic Seaport Museum Stores
Mystic, Connecticut

Chicken Fried Steak

This is comfort food at its finest, stirred up from pantry staples.

¼ cup plus 2 tablespoons
  all-purpose flour
½ teaspoon salt
¼ teaspoon pepper
2 large eggs, beaten

1 tablespoon water
4 (4-ounce) cube steaks
1½ cups fine, dry breadcrumbs
¼ cup margarine
White Sauce Gravy

Combine flour, salt, and pepper; set aside. Combine eggs and water; set aside. Dredge steaks in flour mixture; dip in egg mixture, and dredge in breadcrumbs.

Melt margarine in a large nonstick skillet over medium-high heat; add cube steaks, and fry 10 minutes, turning once. Top with White Sauce Gravy. Yield: 4 servings.

White Sauce Gravy

1 tablespoon margarine
1 tablespoon all-purpose flour
1 cup milk

¼ teaspoon salt
¼ teaspoon pepper

Melt margarine in a heavy saucepan over low heat; add flour, stirring until smooth. Cook 1 minute, stirring constantly. Gradually add milk; cook over medium heat, stirring constantly, until thickened and bubbly. Stir in salt and pepper. Yield: 1 cup. Liz Fournier

Town Hill Playground Cookbook
Town Hill Playground Committee
Whitingham, Vermont

Sirloin Tips with Garlic Butter

The savory garlic butter makes more than enough for this dish. Roll the extra into logs to slice and top steamed fresh vegetables.

2 cups butter, softened
4 cloves garlic, minced
¼ cup dry white wine
1 tablespoon chopped fresh parsley
¼ teaspoon freshly ground pepper
1 large onion, sliced
1 (8-ounce) package sliced fresh mushrooms
1½ pounds sirloin steak, cut into 1-inch pieces
½ teaspoon salt
¼ teaspoon pepper
2 tablespoons dry sherry
6 cups cooked egg noodles

Combine first 5 ingredients; stir garlic butter well.

Melt 3 tablespoons garlic butter in a large skillet over medium-high heat. Add onion, and cook 3 minutes or until golden. Add mushrooms, and cook, stirring constantly, 4 minutes or until tender. Remove onion mixture from skillet. Set aside.

Sprinkle steak with salt and pepper. Melt 3 tablespoons garlic butter in skillet over medium-high heat; add steak. Cook 5 minutes or to desired degree of doneness, stirring constantly. Return onion mixture to skillet. Stir in sherry. Cook, stirring constantly, until thoroughly heated. Serve over noodles. Yield: 6 servings.   Cathy McGurl

Note: To chill butter in logs, spoon butter mixture onto a sheet of wax paper. Wrap in wax paper, and chill at least 30 minutes or until slightly firm. Roll butter in wax paper, back and forth, to make a log. Chill up to 2 days. You can also freeze butter logs.

What's Cooking at Allied
Allied Services Nurse Retention and Recruitment Committee
Scranton, Pennsylvania

Genoese Meatballs

1 pound ground veal
3 tablespoons fine, dry
　breadcrumbs
1 clove garlic, minced
⅓ cup finely chopped fresh
　parsley
⅓ cup chopped fresh
　mushrooms

2 tablespoons grated Parmesan
　cheese
1 large egg, lightly beaten
½ teaspoon nutmeg
½ teaspoon salt
¼ teaspoon pepper
Vegetable cooking spray

Combine first 10 ingredients in a large bowl, and stir well. Shape meat mixture into 1-inch meatballs, and place on a rack in broiler pan coated with cooking spray. Broil 5½ inches from heat (with electric oven door partially opened) for 16 minutes, turning occasionally. Yield: 4 servings.　　　　　　　　　　　　　　　　　Jane Martin

Savor the Brandywine Valley, A Collection of Recipes
The Junior League of Wilmington, Delaware

Grilled Lamb Chops

4 (6-ounce) lamb rib chops,
　(1½ inches thick)
⅔ cup dry red wine
⅓ cup vegetable oil
⅓ cup lemon juice
1 tablespoon honey

1 tablespoon tarragon wine
　vinegar
2 teaspoons minced fresh
　thyme
1 clove garlic, minced
Vegetable cooking spray

Place chops in a large heavy-duty, zip-top plastic bag. Combine wine and next 6 ingredients; stir well. Pour marinade over chops. Seal bag securely; marinate in refrigerator 8 hours, turning occasionally.

Remove chops from marinade, reserving marinade. Bring marinade to a boil; remove from heat, and set aside.

Coat grill rack with cooking spray; place on grill over medium coals (300° to 350°). Place lamb chops on rack, and grill, covered, 8 to 10 minutes on each side or to desired degree of doneness, basting often with marinade. Yield: 4 servings.　　　　　　　　　　　　Karen Haggard

A Fare to Remember
The Service League of Dublin, Georgia

Roast Pork Tenderloin

A delicate rosemary-kissed orange sauce makes this pork tenderloin memorable.

2 (¾-pound) pork tenderloins
2 tablespoons olive oil
¼ teaspoon salt
¼ teaspoon pepper
½ cup dry red wine, divided

2 fresh rosemary sprigs
1 medium onion, sliced
2 tablespoons butter or
    margarine, melted
½ cup fresh orange juice

Brush pork with oil; sprinkle with salt and pepper. Place pork in a roasting pan. Pour ¼ cup wine over pork. Place rosemary on pork. Bake, uncovered, at 350° for 15 minutes.

Pour remaining ¼ cup wine over pork. Bake 20 additional minutes or until meat thermometer inserted in thickest part of tenderloin registers 160° (medium).

Cook onion in butter in a small saucepan over medium-high heat, stirring constantly, until tender. Add orange juice, and cook 5 minutes, stirring occasionally. Serve tenderloins with onion mixture. Yield: 6 servings.

Celebrating California
Children's Home Society of California
San Diego, California

Pork Tenderloin Fillets

To lap up every drop of the luscious gravy, serve these pork medaillons over rice.

1 (1-pound) pork tenderloin, cut into ¾-inch-thick slices
½ teaspoon salt
½ teaspoon pepper
2 tablespoons butter or margarine, melted
1 medium tomato, peeled and sliced

1 medium onion, sliced
¼ cup dry white wine
¼ cup beef broth
1½ tablespoons all-purpose flour
1 tablespoon sour cream
½ teaspoon salt
¼ teaspoon pepper

Place pork between two sheets of heavy-duty plastic wrap; flatten to ¼-inch thickness, using a meat mallet or rolling pin. Sprinkle pork with ½ teaspoon salt and ½ teaspoon pepper.

Cook pork in butter in a large skillet over medium-high heat until browned on both sides. Add tomato and onion; cover, reduce heat to medium-low, and cook 20 minutes or until pork is done, stirring occasionally. Remove pork from skillet. Set aside, and keep warm.

Combine wine and remaining 5 ingredients, stirring until smooth; add to tomato mixture in skillet. Cook, stirring constantly, over medium heat until gravy is thickened and bubbly. Serve with pork. Yield: 4 servings.

Nelly Gutierrez

Canticle of Cookery
St. Irenaeus Church Music Ministry
Cypress, California

Oriental Chops and Rice

4 (1¼-inch) bone-in pork loin
  chops
¾ teaspoon salt, divided
½ teaspoon pepper
½ teaspoon ground ginger,
  divided
1 tablespoon vegetable oil

1 cup long-grain rice, uncooked
2 cups water
2 tablespoons soy sauce
½ cup sliced green onions
½ cup chopped celery
½ cup chopped green pepper

Sprinkle chops with ¼ teaspoon salt, pepper, and ¼ teaspoon ginger. Heat oil in a large skillet; add chops, and brown in oil. Add rice, water, remaining ½ teaspoon salt, soy sauce, and remaining ¼ teaspoon ginger; stir well. Cover, reduce heat, and simmer 20 minutes. Add green onions, celery, and green pepper; cover and simmer 10 additional minutes. Yield: 4 servings.   Joan Perceful

A Century of Cooking
Eden Chapel United Methodist Church
Perkins, Oklahoma

Ham Slices in Orange Sauce

Here's a kid pleaser that'll even delight the cook–this ham is on the table in less than 20 minutes.

2 (8-ounce) ham slices
  (½ inch thick)
10 whole cloves
¾ cup orange juice

½ cup firmly packed brown
  sugar
1 tablespoon cornstarch
⅛ teaspoon ground ginger

Place ham slices in an 11- x 7- x 1½-inch baking dish. Insert cloves into ham slices. Combine orange juice and remaining 3 ingredients; pour over ham. Microwave, uncovered, at HIGH 4 minutes. Baste ham with sauce; microwave at HIGH 4 additional minutes. Cover and let stand 2 minutes. Yield: 4 servings.   Sherry Fairchild

Signature Edition
The Junior Woman's Club of Green Bay, Wisconsin

Sausage and Cheese Turnovers

Pop open a can of refrigerated biscuits, and you've got a quick dough to encase seasoned sausage and cheese for a speedy dinner or filling snack.

½ pound mild Italian sausage
¼ teaspoon dried Italian seasoning
1 (4-ounce) can mushroom stems and pieces, drained
1 cup (4 ounces) shredded mozzarella cheese

1 (10-ounce) can refrigerated flaky biscuits
1 large egg, beaten
1 tablespoon grated Parmesan cheese

Remove and discard casing from sausage. Brown sausage in a large skillet, stirring until it crumbles. Drain and place in a medium bowl. Stir in Italian seasoning, mushrooms, and mozzarella cheese; set aside.

Roll each biscuit into a 5-inch circle. Spoon meat mixture evenly onto each circle. Moisten edges with beaten egg. Fold in half; press edges together with a fork to seal.

Brush turnovers with beaten egg; sprinkle with Parmesan cheese. Place on a lightly greased baking sheet. Bake at 350° for 10 minutes or until golden. Yield: 10 turnovers.

Seasoned with Love
Mahoning County Foster Parent Association
Youngstown, Ohio

Chicken with Dried Tomatoes

A creamy wine sauce flecked with smoky dried tomatoes dresses this chicken entrée for company.

½ cup dried tomatoes (packed without oil)
1 cup hot water
8 skinned and boned chicken breast halves
1 teaspoon salt
½ teaspoon freshly ground pepper

¼ cup plus 2 tablespoons unsalted butter, melted
2 large shallots, minced
1⅓ cups whipping cream
1 cup dry white wine
¼ teaspoon dried marjoram

Place dried tomato and hot water in a small bowl; let stand 10 minutes. Drain and coarsely chop tomato; set aside.

Slice each chicken breast diagonally into 5 strips; sprinkle with salt and pepper. Cook chicken strips in butter in a large skillet over medium heat 9 minutes or until done, turning occasionally. Remove chicken from skillet; set aside, and keep warm.

Add shallot to skillet, and cook, stirring constantly, 2 minutes or until tender. Add chopped tomato, whipping cream, wine, and marjoram. Bring to a boil; reduce heat, and cook, uncovered, 15 minutes or until sauce is slightly thickened. Return chicken to skillet; cook, uncovered, 3 minutes or until thoroughly heated. Yield: 8 servings.

Sterling Performances
Guilds of the Orange County Performing Arts Center
Costa Mesa, California

Amish Chicken Casserole

Chunks of chicken fill this noodle casserole–a potluck pleaser.

8 ounces medium egg noodles,
    uncooked
½ cup butter or margarine
⅓ cup all-purpose flour
2 cups chicken broth
1 cup milk
2 teaspoons salt

½ teaspoon pepper
2 cups chopped cooked
    chicken
1 (4-ounce) can sliced
    mushrooms, drained
⅓ cup grated Parmesan cheese

Cook noodles according to package directions; drain and set aside.

Melt butter in a medium saucepan over low heat; gradually add flour, stirring until smooth. Cook 1 minute, stirring constantly. Gradually add chicken broth and milk; cook over medium heat, stirring constantly, until mixture is slightly thickened and bubbly. Stir in salt and pepper; set aside.

Combine noodles, chicken, and mushrooms; stir in sauce. Spoon mixture into a lightly greased 13- x 9- x 2-inch baking dish; sprinkle with cheese. Bake, uncovered, at 350° for 20 minutes or until thoroughly heated. Yield: 6 servings.   Georgianne Bowman

Lawtons Progressors, 50 Years and Still Cookin'
Lawtons Progressors 4-H Club
North Collins, New York

Julie's Rotini with Artichokes

Three colors of rotini or corkscrew pasta compose a backdrop for this artichoke-tomato sauce.

1½ cups tricolored rotini,
   uncooked
2 cloves garlic, minced
2 tablespoons olive oil
1 (14½-ounce) can stewed
   tomatoes, chopped
¾ cup marinated artichoke
   hearts, drained and sliced

½ cup ripe olives, sliced
½ teaspoon salt
¼ teaspoon freshly ground
   pepper
Grated Romano cheese

Cook pasta according to package directions; drain well. Set aside, and keep warm.

Cook garlic in oil in a large skillet over medium-high heat 30 seconds, stirring constantly. Add tomatoes and next 4 ingredients; bring to a boil. Reduce heat, and simmer, uncovered, 7 minutes. Stir in pasta; cook 2 minutes or until thoroughly heated. Sprinkle with Romano cheese. Serve immediately. Yield: 5 servings.

Another Taste of Aloha
The Junior League of Honolulu, Hawaii

Eggplant Parmigiana Express

Plump eggplant slices are baked to a crispy finish and blanketed under tomato sauce and cheese.

½ cup fine, dry breadcrumbs
¾ cup grated Parmesan cheese
¼ cup mayonnaise
1 (1½-pound) eggplant, cut into
   ½-inch slices

1 (26-ounce) jar spaghetti sauce
4 (1½-ounce) slices mozzarella
   cheese

Combine breadcrumbs and Parmesan cheese. Thinly spread mayonnaise on each side of eggplant slices; dip both sides of eggplant in crumb mixture. Reserve remaining crumb mixture. Place eggplant on an ungreased baking sheet, and bake at 425° for 15 minutes or until tender and lightly browned.

Place eggplant slices in a lightly greased 13- x 9- x 2-inch baking dish. Pour half of spaghetti sauce over slices; top with mozzarella cheese. Pour remaining spaghetti sauce over cheese; top with reserved crumb mixture. Bake at 375° for 15 minutes or until cheese melts. Yield: 6 servings.   Margie Hollinger

Angel Food
St. Vincent de Paul School
Salt Lake City, Utah

Broccoli Bake

Dotted with bits of smoky bacon, cheesy Broccoli Bake is a fresh alternative to the typical broccoli-rice casserole.

1½ pounds fresh broccoli	4 slices bacon, cooked and
5 large eggs, lightly beaten	crumbled
1 cup cottage cheese	½ cup (2 ounces) shredded
2 tablespoons all-purpose flour	Cheddar cheese
½ teaspoon salt	

Remove and discard broccoli leaves and tough ends of stalks; cut into flowerets. Arrange broccoli in a steamer basket over boiling water. Cover and steam 3 minutes or until crisp-tender.

Place broccoli in a lightly greased 11- x 7- x 1½-inch baking dish. Combine eggs and next 4 ingredients, stirring well; pour over broccoli. Bake at 350° for 20 minutes. Sprinkle evenly with Cheddar cheese. Bake 5 additional minutes. Let stand 5 minutes before serving. Yield: 6 servings.   Nancy Rumbaugh

Lake Murray Presbyterian Preschool Cookbook
Lake Murray Presbyterian Preschool Parents Organization
Chapin, South Carolina

Indian Peas

1 medium onion, chopped
3 tablespoons butter or
  margarine, melted
1 (10-ounce) package frozen
  English peas
3 tablespoons chopped fresh
  cilantro

2 tablespoons minced fresh
  ginger
1 tablespoon ground cumin
¼ teaspoon salt

Cook onion in butter in a large skillet over medium-high heat, stirring constantly, until tender. Add peas and remaining ingredients. Cover and cook over medium heat 4 to 5 minutes or until peas are tender, stirring often. Yield: 4 servings.   Kym Kohli

Cooking with Class
Park Maitland School
Maitland, Florida

Pineapple Casserole

We couldn't decide whether we liked this best as a sweet and crunchy side dish or with a scoop of ice cream for a warm dessert. You decide.

1 (8-ounce) can pineapple
  chunks, undrained
1 (8-ounce) can crushed
  pineapple, undrained
¼ cup plus 2 tablespoons
  all-purpose flour
⅓ cup sugar

2 cups (8 ounces) shredded
  Cheddar cheese
1½ cups round buttery cracker
  crumbs (about 35 crackers)
½ cup butter or margarine,
  melted

Combine first 5 ingredients, stirring well. Spoon mixture into a greased 13- x 9- x 2-inch pan. Combine cracker crumbs and butter, stirring well. Sprinkle mixture evenly over casserole. Bake, uncovered, at 350° for 30 minutes. Yield: 8 servings.   Judy Johnson

Carolinas Heritage
47th National Square Dance Convention
Charlotte, North Carolina

Rosemary Roasted Potatoes

Less work than mashed potatoes and more flavorful than plain rice, these crisp roasted potatoes will become a favorite dinner partner.

2 pounds round red potatoes, unpeeled and quartered	1 tablespoon olive oil
2 cloves garlic, minced	2 teaspoons chopped fresh rosemary
¼ teaspoon salt	⅛ teaspoon pepper
½ teaspoon dried thyme	

Combine all ingredients in a large bowl or large heavy-duty, zip-top plastic bag. Stir mixture in bowl or seal bag, and shake well to coat. Arrange potato in a well-greased 13- x 9- x 2-inch baking dish. Bake, uncovered, at 450° for 40 minutes or until potato is tender. Yield: 4 servings.   Loretta and Gerald Lambert

Not by Bread Alone
Catholic Committee on Scouting and Camp Fire
for the Diocese of Lake Charles, Louisiana

Chinese Egg Drop Soup

Here's a quick version of the trademark soup many Chinese restaurants serve.

3 cups chicken broth	¼ cup coarsely chopped fresh snow pea pods
2 large eggs, beaten	
1 cup sliced fresh mushrooms	1 tablespoon soy sauce
¼ cup diced water chestnuts	½ cup bean sprouts (optional)

Bring chicken broth to a boil in a large saucepan. Gradually add eggs, stirring well.

Stir in mushrooms and remaining ingredients, including bean sprouts, if desired; reduce heat to low, and cook until thoroughly heated. Yield: 3½ cups.   Iola Sugg

Sampler Cookbook
Clarence Log Cabin Quilters
Clarence, New York

Beaten Biscuits via Food Processor

Trade in your rolling pin for a food processor, and forget hours of endless rolling for the perfect beaten biscuit. These compact biscuits with flaky layers split naturally to form perfect pockets for their traditional partner, country ham.

2 cups all-purpose flour
1 teaspoon salt
½ cup cold butter, cut into
　 small pieces

⅓ cup ice water

Position knife blade in food processor bowl; add flour and salt. Process 5 seconds; add butter, and process 10 seconds or until mixture is crumbly.

Pour water through food chute with processor running; process until mixture forms a ball. Turn dough out onto a lightly floured surface. Roll dough into a ⅛-inch-thick rectangle. Fold dough in half lengthwise; cut with a 1-inch biscuit cutter. Place on an ungreased baking sheet. Prick top of each biscuit with a fork three times. Bake at 400° for 20 minutes or until lightly browned. Yield: 28 biscuits.

Emory Seasons, Entertaining Atlanta Style
Emory University Woman's Club
Atlanta, Georgia

Prosciutto-Parmesan Pull-Apart Loaf

Salty prosciutto and butter dot every bite-size piece of this bread.

1 (16-ounce) loaf unsliced
　 Italian bread
¾ cup butter or margarine,
　 softened
½ cup coarsely chopped
　 prosciutto (about 2 ounces)

⅓ cup grated Parmesan cheese
2 teaspoons dried basil
½ teaspoon freshly ground
　 pepper

Slice bread cutting to, but not through, bottom in a crisscross fashion, making a diamond pattern.

Combine butter and remaining 4 ingredients, stirring well. Spread butter mixture between bread slices. Place on an ungreased baking sheet. Bake at 450° for 5 minutes or until thoroughly heated. Yield: 8 servings. Sue Dankovich

From Our Kitchens with Love
St. Mark Orthodox Church
Rochester Hills, Michigan

Crescent Cheese Soufflé

Refrigerated crescent rolls make a quick and flaky crust for this cheesy breakfast casserole with sausage filling.

1 (8-ounce) can refrigerated crescent dinner rolls
6 large eggs, lightly beaten
½ cup milk
2 cups (8 ounces) shredded Cheddar cheese

¾ cup ground mild pork sausage, cooked and drained
¼ teaspoon salt
⅛ teaspoon pepper

Unroll crescent rolls, and place in an ungreased 11- x 7- x 1½-inch baking dish. Press 1 inch up sides to form a crust; seal perforations. Set aside.

Combine eggs and remaining 5 ingredients; pour evenly over dough. Bake at 350° for 40 minutes or until set. Serve immediately. Yield: 8 servings. Lorraine Roe

Heavenly Recipes
Rosebud WELCA, Lemmon Rural Lutheran Parish
Lemmon, South Dakota

Apple Pizzas

Shape these novel breakfast pizzas from refrigerated biscuits. Piled with melted cheese, apples, and a sprinkling of cinnamon sugar, these quick bites take only minutes to make.

2 tablespoons all-purpose flour
½ cup firmly packed brown
   sugar
1 teaspoon ground cinnamon
1 (17.3-ounce) can refrigerated
   biscuits

1 cup (4 ounces) shredded
   Cheddar cheese
2 small cooking apples, peeled,
   cored, and sliced
¼ cup butter or margarine

Combine first 3 ingredients in a small bowl; stir well.

Roll biscuits into 4-inch circles, and place on a lightly greased baking sheet. Sprinkle shredded cheese evenly over circles, leaving ¼-inch borders. Arrange apple slices over cheese. Sprinkle cinnamon mixture over apples, and dot with butter. Bake at 350° for 18 to 20 minutes. Yield: 8 pizzas.   Kim Love

Seasonings
The 20th Century Club Juniors of Park Ridge, Illinois

Rhode Island Jonnycakes

1 cup cornmeal
1 teaspoon salt
1 teaspoon sugar

1 to 1½ cups boiling water
1 cup shortening, melted
Maple syrup

Combine first 3 ingredients in a medium bowl; stir well. Gradually add boiling water, stirring until smooth and very thick.

Heat shortening in a 10-inch cast-iron skillet over medium-high heat until hot. Drop batter by one-fourth cupfuls into hot shortening in skillet. Fry 3 minutes on each side or until jonnycakes are crisp and golden; drain on paper towels. Serve immediately with maple syrup. Yield: 6 jonnycakes.   Governor Bruce Sundlun

Gaspee Days Cookbook
Gaspee Days Committee
Warwick, Rhode Island

Gingerbread

Hot from the oven, this moist cake demands a dollop of whipped cream and a fork. And if there's any left over, enjoy a glass of milk with this spiced snack cake.

½ cup shortening	1 teaspoon ground cinnamon
½ cup sugar	1 teaspoon ground allspice
2 large eggs	1 teaspoon ground ginger
½ cup molasses	1 cup hot water
1½ cups all-purpose flour	Whipped cream
1 teaspoon baking soda	

Beat shortening at medium speed of an electric mixer until light and fluffy; gradually add sugar, beating well. Add eggs and molasses, mixing well.

Combine flour and next 4 ingredients; add to shortening mixture alternately with water, beginning and ending with flour mixture. Mix after each addition. Pour batter into a greased and floured 8-inch square pan.

Bake at 350° for 30 minutes or until a wooden pick inserted in center of cake comes out clean. Serve cake dolloped with whipped cream. Yield: 9 servings.   Laura Peavy Graham

Stephens Remembered, Recollections & Recipes
Stephens College Denver Area Club
Lakewood, Colorado

Sinful Seven-Layer Cookies

Rich with chocolate chips, butterscotch morsels, and toasted coconut, these bar cookies are sinfully delicious.

½ cup butter or margarine
1 cup graham cracker crumbs
1 cup (6 ounces) semisweet
  chocolate morsels
1 cup (6 ounces) butterscotch
  morsels

1 cup flaked coconut
1 (14-ounce) can sweetened
  condensed milk
1 cup chopped pecans

Place butter in a 13- x 9- x 2-inch baking dish. Preheat dish in oven at 350° for 5 minutes or until butter melts. Layer graham cracker crumbs and next 3 ingredients over butter. Pour condensed milk over coconut; top with pecans. Bake at 350° for 30 minutes. Cool on a wire rack; cut into squares. Yield: 15 cookies.   Tammy Armstrong

Cooking Around the Authority
Charlotte-Mecklenburg Hospital Authority
Charlotte, North Carolina

Brickle Bars

A box of cake mix is the quick secret behind these chewy Brickle Bars.

1 (18.25-ounce) package yellow
  cake mix without pudding
⅓ cup butter or margarine,
  melted
1 large egg, lightly beaten

1 (7.5-ounce) package almond
  brickle chips
1 (14-ounce) can sweetened
  condensed milk
½ cup chopped pecans

Combine first 3 ingredients in a large bowl, stirring well. Press mixture into bottom of a 13- x 9- x 2-inch pan. Combine brickle chips, condensed milk, and pecans; spread over crust in pan. Bake at 350° for 25 minutes. Remove from oven, and let cool completely before cutting into bars. Yield: 2 dozen.   Colleen Moudry

St. Aloysius Rosary Society Cookbook
St. Aloysius Rosary Society
Carlmar, Iowa

Fast Fudge Pots de Crème

1 (3.4-ounce) package
  chocolate-flavored pudding
  mix

2 cups milk
1 cup (6 ounces) semisweet
  chocolate morsels

Combine pudding mix and milk in a saucepan; stir well. Cook, stirring constantly, over medium heat until mixture comes to a boil; remove from heat. Add chocolate morsels, stirring until chocolate melts.

Spoon mixture evenly into eight 4-ounce pots de crème cups or soufflé cups. Serve warm or chilled. Yield: 8 servings.   Arlene James

The Chancellor's Table
Friends of the Chancellor's Residence at
The University of Missouri-Rolla
Rolla, Missouri

Easy Cherry Cobbler

You can assemble this cobbler in minutes, let it cook while you enjoy dinner, and it'll be ready just in time for dessert. Crown it with a scoop of ice cream to melt on top.

¼ cup butter or margarine
¾ cup all-purpose flour
1 teaspoon baking powder
¼ teaspoon salt
½ cup sugar

½ cup milk
¼ teaspoon almond extract
1 (16-ounce) can pitted tart red
  cherries, undrained

Place butter in an 8-inch square baking dish. Preheat dish in oven at 350° for 5 minutes or until butter melts.

Combine flour and next 3 ingredients in a medium bowl; add milk and almond extract, stirring until smooth. Pour batter over melted butter. (Do not stir.) Pour cherries over batter.

Bake at 350° for 40 minutes or until lightly browned. Serve warm. Yield: 6 servings.   Judy Webb

A Taste of the Past and Present
First Baptist and Pastor's Sunday School Class
Philadelphia, Tennessee

Toffee Ice Cream Pie and Sauce

A buttery sauce drizzled over frozen ice cream pie with brickle chips doubles the toffee flavor.

1⅓ cups vanilla wafer crumbs	½ cup evaporated milk
¼ cup butter or margarine, melted	2 tablespoons butter or margarine
1 quart vanilla ice cream, softened	2 tablespoons light corn syrup
½ cup almond brickle chips	Dash of salt
⅔ cup sugar	½ cup almond brickle chips

Combine wafer crumbs and melted butter; press firmly in bottom and up sides of a 9-inch pieplate. Bake at 375° for 8 minutes. Cool completely.

Combine softened ice cream and ½ cup brickle chips; spoon into prepared crust. Cover and freeze until firm.

Combine sugar and next 4 ingredients in a small saucepan; bring to a boil over low heat, stirring constantly. Cook 1 minute. Remove from heat, and stir in ½ cup brickle chips. Let sauce cool, stirring occasionally. Serve with pie. Yield: one 9-inch pie.   Peggy Powell

Food for the Spirit
St. Thomas Aquinas Home & School Association
Hammond, Louisiana

Appetizers & Beverages

Chicken Satay with Spicy Peanut Sauce, page 83

Butterscotch Dip for Fruit

Dunk an apple wedge into this creamy dip, and you'll think you're eating a caramel apple.

½ cup butter or margarine
1 cup firmly packed light
  brown sugar
1 (14-ounce) ounce can
  sweetened condensed milk

1 teaspoon coconut extract
1 teaspoon almond extract
½ teaspoon rum extract

Combine butter and brown sugar in a 3-quart saucepan; cook over medium-low heat 10 minutes, stirring occasionally. Add sweetened condensed milk; cook over medium-low heat 6 minutes or until thickened and bubbly. Remove from heat, and stir in flavorings. Serve warm with sliced apple. Yield: 2¼ cups.   Pat Oglesbee

Note: This creamy dip forms small crystals after cooling. Reheat it over low heat just before serving to dissolve crystals.

Food for the Spirit
St. Thomas Aquinas Home & School Association
Hammond, Louisiana

Blue Ribbon Dip

8 ounces blue cheese,
  crumbled
2 cloves garlic, chopped
2 tablespoons red wine vinegar
1 tablespoon lemon juice

½ cup olive oil
½ cup finely chopped purple
  onion
½ cup minced fresh parsley
¼ teaspoon pepper

Position knife blade in food processor bowl; add first four ingredients. Process until smooth, stopping once to scrape down sides. Gradually pour olive oil through food chute with processor running, blending just until mixture is smooth. Stir in onion, parsley, and pepper. Serve dip with baguette slices or assorted fresh vegetables. Yield: 2 cups.

Gold'n Delicious
The Junior League of Spokane, Washington

Hot Seafood Dip

You'll find a lump of crabmeat or a shapely little shrimp in every bite of this sinfully rich appetizer. If small shrimp are unavailable, substitute medium-size shrimp and cut them in half.

1¼ pounds unpeeled small fresh shrimp
2 tablespoons butter or margarine
2 cups mayonnaise
1 cup freshly grated Parmesan cheese
½ cup chopped green onions
3 jalapeño peppers, seeded and chopped

2 tablespoons lemon juice
2 or 3 drops of hot sauce
1 pound fresh lump crabmeat, drained
2 (14-ounce) cans artichoke hearts, drained and finely chopped
½ teaspoon salt
⅓ cup sliced almonds

Peel shrimp, and devein, if desired.

Cook shrimp in butter in a medium skillet over medium-high heat 2 minutes, stirring constantly. Drain and set aside. Combine mayonnaise and next 5 ingredients in a large bowl. Add shrimp, crabmeat, artichoke hearts, and salt; stir well. Spoon mixture into a greased 13- x 9- x 2-inch baking dish. Sprinkle with almonds.

Bake at 375° for 25 minutes or until mixture is thoroughly heated. Serve with melba toast rounds. Yield: 9 cups.   Cathy Seymour

Cane River's Louisiana Living
The Service League of Natchitoches, Louisiana

Garlic-Herb Cheese Spread

Sage leaves, chive sprigs, or violets make an easy but elegant garnish for this buttery-rich spread.

½ cup fresh parsley
1 tablespoon fresh thyme
   leaves
1 tablespoon fresh basil
1 tablespoon fresh tarragon
1 clove garlic
2 (8-ounce) packages cream
   cheese
½ cup butter or margarine,
   softened
1 teaspoon Worcestershire
   sauce
½ teaspoon red wine vinegar

3 cups (12 ounces) shredded
   sharp Cheddar cheese
⅓ cup sour cream
¼ cup butter or margarine,
   softened
¼ cup milk
3 tablespoons fresh sage leaves
1 tablespoon chopped fresh
   chives
1 teaspoon Dijon mustard
Garnishes: fresh herbs, fresh
   edible flowers

Line a 1½-quart soufflé dish with plastic wrap, leaving a 1-inch over-hang around edges. Set aside.

Position knife blade in food processor bowl; add first 5 ingredients, and process until finely chopped, stopping once to scrape down sides. Add cream cheese and next 3 ingredients; process until blended, stopping once to scrape down sides.

Spoon cream cheese mixture into prepared dish, spreading evenly; set aside.

Combine Cheddar cheese and next 3 ingredients in processor; process until smooth, stopping once to scrape down sides. Add sage, chives, and mustard; process until combined, stopping once to scrape down sides. Spoon mixture over cream cheese layer, spreading evenly. Cover and chill at least 8 hours.

Unmold onto a serving platter. Garnish, if desired. Serve with assorted crackers. Yield: 5 cups.   Mary Jane McBeath

Historically Delicious–An Almanac Cookbook
Tri-Cities Historical Society
Grand Haven, Michigan

Crowd-Pleasin' Chutney Spread

2 (8-ounce) packages
   Neufchâtel cheese, softened
3 tablespoons curry powder
1 teaspoon salt
1 (8-ounce) jar mango-ginger
   chutney

1 bunch green onions, sliced
   (about 1 cup)
10 slices bacon, cooked and
   crumbled
¼ cup finely chopped toasted
   almonds

Combine first 3 ingredients; stir well. Spread cheese mixture in bottom of 10-inch quiche dish. Spread chutney over cheese mixture. Sprinkle with green onions, bacon, and almonds. Serve with assorted crackers. Yield: 2½ cups.
                        Becky Hamlin

Note: If you like a smooth spread, process the chutney in your food processor. If chutney isn't available, you can substitute ginger preserves.

Savor the Brandywine Valley, A Collection of Recipes
The Junior League of Wilmington, Delaware

Chili Cheese Balls

We recommend a glass of robust red wine with these spunky little appetizers that are a twist on the standby party cheese ball.

3 cups (12 ounces) shredded
   Monterey Jack cheese
1 cup (4 ounces) shredded
   fontina cheese
1 (3-ounce) package cream
   cheese, softened
3 to 4 tablespoons prepared
   mustard

1 teaspoon Worcestershire
   sauce
½ teaspoon garlic powder
1 tablespoon plus 1 teaspoon
   chili powder

Combine first 6 ingredients in a medium bowl; mix well. Shape into 1-inch balls. Sprinkle chili powder in a large bowl; add cheese balls, and toss gently to coat. Cover and chill. Yield: 3½ dozen.

What's Cooking at Cathedral Plaza
Cathedral Plaza
Denver, Colorado

Marinated Mozzarella

Tie some raffia to a jar of this inspired mozzarella, and you've got a delicious, not to mention beautiful, gift for any cheese lover.

1 pound mozzarella cheese, cut into 1-inch cubes
1 (7-ounce) jar roasted red peppers, drained and cut into thin strips
2 cloves garlic, cut in half lengthwise

1¼ cups olive oil
1 tablespoon plus 1 teaspoon dried Italian seasoning
1 teaspoon dried crushed red pepper
Fresh rosemary or thyme sprigs (optional)

Combine cheese, pepper strips, and garlic in a 1-quart jar, and set aside.

Combine olive oil, Italian seasoning, and crushed red pepper. Pour over cheese mixture. Add fresh rosemary or thyme sprigs, if desired. Cover tightly, and shake vigorously. Chill at least 4 hours. Drain and serve with assorted crackers. Store in refrigerator up to 2 weeks. Yield: 4 cups.
                                                                    Debbie Martin

Dining with Duke Cookbook
Badger Association of the Blind
Milwaukee, Wisconsin

Excellent Asparagus Canapés

18 fresh asparagus spears
1 large egg, beaten
1 (8-ounce) package cream cheese, softened
8 ounces Roquefort cheese

1 tablespoon mayonnaise
1 (16-ounce) loaf sliced white bread
¼ cup butter or margarine, melted

Snap off tough ends of asparagus. Remove scales with a vegetable peeler, if desired. Set aside.

Combine egg and next 3 ingredients in a medium bowl, and stir mixture well.

Trim crusts from bread. Spread cheese mixture evenly over bread slices. Place 1 asparagus spear on each slice; roll up bread, jellyroll fashion, around asparagus. Place seam side down on ungreased baking sheets, and brush with butter.

Bake at 350° for 15 to 20 minutes or until golden. Serve immediately. Yield: 18 appetizers.   Marlene Genovese

Note: We don't recommend substituting canned asparagus for fresh in this recipe. Look for fresh asparagus with long, slender stalks that are especially tender.

Appetizers from A to Z
Christ Child Society
Phoenix, Arizona

Fried Cheese with Italian Sauce

Now you can make this restaurant favorite at home. The freezing time helps keep the cheese from leaking out of its golden fried shell.

2 (8-ounce) packages part-skim mozzarella cheese, cut into 1-inch cubes
3 large eggs, lightly beaten
½ cup all-purpose flour
¾ cup Italian-seasoned breadcrumbs
1 clove garlic, minced
1 teaspoon vegetable oil

1 (28-ounce) can whole tomatoes, undrained and chopped
1 teaspoon dried oregano
½ teaspoon sugar
¼ teaspoon salt
¼ teaspoon dried basil
Vegetable oil

Dip cheese in beaten egg. Dredge in flour. Dip coated cheese in beaten egg again; dredge in breadcrumbs, pressing firmly so that crumbs adhere. Place cheese cubes on a wax paper-lined baking sheet, and freeze at least 1 hour.

Cook garlic in 1 teaspoon oil in a large skillet over medium-high heat, stirring constantly, until tender. Add tomatoes and next 4 ingredients. Bring to a boil, reduce heat, and simmer, uncovered, 45 minutes or until thickened, stirring occasionally. Set aside, and keep warm.

Pour oil to depth of 1½ inches into a Dutch oven; heat to 375°. Fry cheese cubes until golden. Drain on paper towels. Serve immediately with tomato sauce. Yield: 20 appetizers.   Mary Hules

Sharing Our Feast
Holy Apostles Episcopal Church
Memphis, Tennessee

Dried Tomato and Herb Cheese Strudel

Flaky phyllo wraps tomato-kissed cheese in these strudels that can be prepared and stored in an airtight container up to 2 days.

8 ounces goat cheese, softened
1 (8-ounce) package cream cheese, softened
¼ cup plus 2 tablespoons oil-packed dried tomatoes, drained and finely chopped
2 tablespoons minced fresh parsley

2 tablespoons minced fresh oregano
½ teaspoon freshly ground pepper
12 sheets frozen phyllo pastry, thawed in refrigerator
⅓ cup olive oil

Combine first 6 ingredients in a bowl, mixing well.

Place 1 sheet of phyllo pastry on a damp towel, keeping remaining phyllo covered with a slightly damp towel. Lightly brush phyllo with olive oil. Layer 2 additional sheets of phyllo over first sheet, brushing each sheet lightly with olive oil. Fold stack in half lengthwise; brush top with oil. Spoon ½ cup cheese mixture down long side of phyllo, shaping into a 1-inch log, leaving 1-inch borders. Fold each short end over filling. Starting at long side, carefully roll up phyllo, jellyroll fashion, into a log. Carefully place roll, seam side down, on a greased baking sheet. Make 14 diagonal slits, about ¼ inch deep, down the length of the strudel, using a sharp knife. Repeat procedure 3 times with remaining phyllo, oil, and cheese mixture.

Bake at 375° for 15 minutes or until golden. Let cool completely. To serve, slice strudels through diagonal slits. Yield: 5 dozen appetizers.

Entertaining in Kingwood
Kingwood Women's Club
Kingwood, Texas

Baked Jalapeños

Boiling the peppers tames the heat of the jalapeños in this recipe. Even the most sensitive taste buds will love these stuffed peppers after the 10-minute boiling time. For hot pepper lovers, boil only 5 minutes.

25 medium jalapeño peppers
1 (8-ounce) package cream cheese, softened
3 cups (12 ounces) shredded Cheddar cheese
1½ teaspoons Worcestershire sauce
4 slices bacon, cooked and crumbled

Cut jalapeño peppers in half lengthwise; remove seeds.

Cook peppers in boiling water 5 to 10 minutes. Drain well.

Combine cream cheese, Cheddar cheese, and Worcestershire sauce; stir well. Place 1 heaping teaspoon cheese mixture in each pepper half; sprinkle with bacon. Place on a baking sheet. Bake at 400° for 5 minutes or until cheese is melted. Yield: 50 appetizers.

Saint Louis Days, Saint Louis Nights
The Junior League of St. Louis, Missouri

Crostini al Pomodoro

8 plum tomatoes, diced
1 teaspoon salt
2 cloves garlic, minced
2 tablespoons chopped fresh basil
2 tablespoons chopped fresh flat-leaf parsley
⅛ teaspoon freshly ground pepper
¼ cup olive oil
24 (¼-inch-thick) slices Italian bread, toasted

Combine tomato and salt, and stir well. Place mixture in a wire-mesh strainer; drain 30 minutes. Combine tomato mixture, garlic, and next 4 ingredients in a medium bowl; stir well with a wire whisk. Serve tomato mixture with toasted bread slices. Yield: 8 appetizer servings.

Elizabeth Mueller

The Educated Palate: The Hamlin School Cookbook
The Hamlin School
San Francisco, California

Oyster Overture

Shucked oysters are key to this symphony. Opening them is as easy as inserting a screwdriver or oyster knife into the hinge, and twisting.

½ cup fine, dry breadcrumbs
¼ cup grated Parmesan cheese
¼ cup chopped fresh parsley
3 tablespoons finely chopped shallot
1 tablespoon chopped fresh basil
1 clove garlic, minced
¼ cup olive oil
½ cup butter, melted
⅛ teaspoon salt
⅛ teaspoon pepper
⅛ teaspoon dried crushed red pepper
3 dozen fresh oysters (in the shell)

Combine all ingredients except oysters; stir well, and set aside.

Scrub oyster shells with a stiff brush under cold running water; open shells, discarding tops. Arrange shell bottoms (containing oysters) in a 15- x 10- x 1-inch jellyroll pan. Spread breadcrumb mixture evenly over tops of oysters. Cover with aluminum foil, and bake at 300° for 15 minutes. Uncover and broil 3½ inches from heat (with electric oven door partially opened) 4 minutes or until edges of oysters begin to curl. Serve immediately. Yield: 3 dozen.

A Culinary Concerto
Brick Hospital Association
Brick, New Jersey

Braised Shrimp with Garlic Rémoulade

1 pound unpeeled medium-size fresh shrimp
½ cup dry white wine
1 cup water
1 clove garlic, minced
1 sprig fresh thyme
1 teaspoon salt
1 tablespoon black peppercorns
1 cup mayonnaise
½ cup sour cream
2 green onions, chopped
3 cloves garlic, minced
1 tablespoon chopped fresh parsley
1 tablespoon lemon juice
Salt and ground white pepper to taste

Peel shrimp, and devein, if desired; set aside. Combine wine and next 5 ingredients in a large saucepan. Bring to a boil; add shrimp, and cook 3 to 5 minutes or until shrimp turn pink. Drain well; rinse with cold water. Chill.

Combine mayonnaise and next 5 ingredients; stir until blended. Add salt and white pepper to taste. Serve shrimp with sauce. Yield: 6 appetizer servings.

Ten Years of Taste, An Adventure in Food and Wine
Adaptive Aquatics Center
Bakersfield, California

Mongolian Meat Sticks

Honor the influence of the Orient. Soy sauce, fresh ginger, and sesame oil give this appetizer its Asian accent.

2½ **pounds flank steak**	2 **tablespoons soy sauce**
½ **cup hoisin sauce**	½ **teaspoon sugar**
2 **tablespoons peanut oil**	½ **teaspoon pepper**
2 **tablespoons sesame oil**	½ **teaspoon grated fresh ginger**
2 **tablespoons dry sherry**	1 **clove garlic, crushed**

Slice steak diagonally across grain into ⅛-inch-thick strips. Place in a large heavy-duty, zip-top plastic bag. Set aside.

Combine hoisin sauce and remaining 8 ingredients; stir well. Pour marinade over steak; seal bag securely. Marinate in refrigerator 8 hours, turning occasionally.

Thread steak onto 32 (6-inch) wooden skewers, discarding marinade. Broil 3 inches from heat (with electric oven door partially opened) 2 to 3 minutes on each side or to desired degree of doneness. Yield: 32 appetizers.   Mary Ann Harding

Note: Unlike metal skewers, wooden skewers can burn under the broiler. Make sure you soak wooden skewers in water at least 10 minutes before threading food on them to prevent any flare-ups.

A Slice of Orange: Favorite VOLS Recipes
University of Tennessee College of Human Ecology/
Women's Athletics Department
Knoxville, Tennessee

Egg Rolls with Sweet-and-Sour Sauce

Golden fried egg rolls stuffed with cabbage, water chestnuts, and pork take a dip in a tangy sauce, beating Chinese takeout every time.

1½ cups ketchup
⅔ cup firmly packed brown
    sugar
⅔ cup sugar
1 tablespoon fresh lemon juice
1 teaspoon ground ginger
½ teaspoon ground cinnamon
2 cups finely shredded cabbage
1 cup thinly sliced celery
1 medium onion, chopped
1 clove garlic, minced
½ teaspoon ground ginger

1 tablespoon vegetable oil
½ pound ground pork, cooked
    and drained
½ cup diced water chestnuts
½ teaspoon salt
2 tablespoons soy sauce
1 tablespoon cornstarch
1 teaspoon all-purpose flour
1 teaspoon water
1 (1-pound) package egg roll
    wrappers
Vegetable oil

Combine first 6 ingredients in a medium saucepan. Bring to a boil over low heat. Simmer 45 minutes, stirring occasionally. Set aside, and let cool.

Cook cabbage and next 4 ingredients in 1 tablespoon hot oil in a large skillet over medium-high heat, stirring constantly, until vegetables are crisp-tender. Add pork, water chestnuts, and salt.

Combine soy sauce and cornstarch, stirring well. Stir into vegetable mixture, and cook 1 minute, stirring constantly. Remove from heat, and let cool.

Combine flour and water; stir well, and set aside.

Mound ⅓ cup cooled filling in center of 1 egg roll wrapper. Fold top corner of wrapper over filling; then fold left and right corners over filling. Lightly brush exposed corner of wrapper with flour mixture. Tightly roll the filled end of the wrapper toward the exposed corner; gently press the corner to seal securely. Repeat with remaining filling and egg roll wrappers.

Pour oil to depth of 1½ inches into a Dutch oven; heat to 375°. Place 2 egg rolls in hot oil, and fry 45 seconds on each side or until golden; drain on paper towels. Repeat with remaining egg rolls. Serve with reserved sauce. Yield: 9 egg rolls. Susie Skjoldal

Heavenly Recipes
Rosebud WELCA, Lemmon Rural Lutheran Parish
Lemmon, South Dakota

Chicken Satay with Spicy Peanut Sauce

1¼ pounds skinned and boned
  chicken breast halves
2 tablespoons lemon juice
¼ cup sherry
¼ cup soy sauce
2 tablespoons sesame oil

2 teaspoons minced garlic
2 teaspoons minced fresh
  ginger
Dash of hot sauce
Spicy Peanut Sauce

Cut chicken into 3- x ½-inch strips. Combine lemon juice and next 6 ingredients in a heavy-duty, zip-top plastic bag. Add chicken, and seal bag securely. Marinate in refrigerator 1½ hours, turning once.

Remove chicken from marinade, discarding marinade. Thread chicken onto 8-inch wooden skewers. Place skewers on greased baking sheets, and bake at 375° for 10 minutes or until done. Serve with warm Spicy Peanut Sauce. Yield: 24 appetizers.

Spicy Peanut Sauce

1 tablespoon vegetable oil
2 teaspoons sesame oil
½ cup purple onion, finely
  chopped
1 teaspoon minced garlic
1 teaspoon minced fresh ginger
1 tablespoon brown sugar
1 tablespoon red wine vinegar

½ cup hot water
½ cup creamy peanut butter
3 tablespoons soy sauce
3 tablespoons ketchup
1 tablespoon lemon juice
½ teaspoon ground coriander
Dash of hot sauce

Heat oils in a small saucepan over medium-high heat. Add onion, garlic, and ginger; cook until tender, stirring often. Add brown sugar and vinegar; cook over medium heat, stirring until sugar dissolves. Remove from heat; add hot water and remaining ingredients, stirring until peanut butter melts. Yield: 2 cups. Carol Ceresa

Fanconi Anemia Family Cookbook
Fanconi Anemia Research Fund
Eugene, Oregon

Refreshing Mint Tea

Cool off the summer's sultry heat with a tall glass of lemon mint tea.

7 lemons
12 fresh mint sprigs
2 family-size tea bags

8 cups boiling water
2 cups sugar
8 cups water

   Peel 3 lemons with a vegetable peeler, leaving inner white pith on fruit. Set lemons aside. Combine lemon rind, mint sprigs, tea bags, and boiling water in a large saucepan. Cover and steep 12 minutes.
   Remove and discard lemon rind, mint sprigs, and tea bags, squeezing tea bags gently; stir in sugar. Squeeze juice from all 7 lemons; stir into tea. Pour mixture through a wire-mesh strainer into a large pitcher; stir in water. Cover and chill thoroughly. Yield: 1 gallon.

   Note: To prevent your tea from dilution, make ice cubes out of tea instead of water. You can even add a sprig of mint to each section of the ice cube tray for added flavor before pouring the tea.

Texas Tapestry
The Junior Woman's Club of Houston, Texas

Yogurt Smoothie

Kids of all ages will enjoy this smooth, fruity drink.

1 ripe banana, peeled and cut
   into pieces
1 (8-ounce) carton vanilla
   low-fat yogurt

1 cup orange juice
2 tablespoons sugar

   Combine all ingredients in container of an electric blender. Process 2 minutes or until smooth, stopping once to scrape down sides. Yield: 2½ cups.
                                              Brent and Kelsey Ricks

Amazing Graces: Meals and Memories from the Parsonage
Texas Conference United Methodist Minister's Spouses Association
Palestine, Texas

Cranberry Christmas Punch

The vibrant red color of this fizzy cranberry punch makes it perfect for a holiday gathering.

1 (3-ounce) package cherry-flavored gelatin
1 cup boiling water
1 (6-ounce) can frozen orange juice concentrate

1 (32-ounce) bottle cranberry juice, chilled
3 cups cold water
1 (12-ounce) can ginger ale, chilled

Dissolve gelatin in boiling water. Add orange juice concentrate, stirring until it melts. Stir in cranberry juice and water. Gently pour cherry mixture into a punch bowl. Gently stir in ginger ale. Serve immediately. Yield: 11 cups.   Betty Pearson

Generations
Twilight Optimist Club of Conway, Arkansas

White Wine Sangría Cooler

Slices of brightly colored oranges, lemons, and limes sparkle in this white wine version of the traditional Spanish drink.

2 oranges
2 lemons
2 limes
4 cups dry white wine
2 tablespoons brandy (optional)

2 tablespoons honey
1 (3-inch) stick cinnamon
1 cup seedless green grapes
1 quart ginger ale

Cut 1 orange, 1 lemon, and 1 lime in half, reserving one-half of each fruit. Slice remaining half of each fruit into thin slices for garnish; cover and chill fruit slices.

Squeeze juice from reserved fruit halves and remaining orange, lemon, and lime into pitcher. Add wine and next 4 ingredients. Cover and chill at least one hour. Just before serving, stir in ginger ale. Add reserved fruit slices; serve over ice. Yield: 10 cups.   Dorothy Wood

Appetizers from A to Z
Christ Child Society
Phoenix, Arizona

Mediterranean Coffee

If you like black coffee, you'll love this full-bodied brew. For a sweeter taste, add ½ cup of sugar to the slow cooker.

4 (3-inch) sticks cinnamon
1½ teaspoons whole cloves
8 cups strongly brewed coffee
¼ cup chocolate syrup
⅓ cup sugar

½ teaspoon anise extract
Whipped cream
Garnish: orange or lemon rind
    curls

Place cinnamon and cloves on a 4-inch square of cheesecloth; tie with string, and set aside.

Combine coffee, syrup, sugar, and anise in a 4-quart slow cooker. Add cheesecloth bag. Cover and cook on LOW 2 to 3 hours.

Pour into mugs; top each with a dollop of whipped cream. Garnish, if desired. Yield: 10 cups.   Joan Keller

Quilters Guild of Indianapolis Cookbook
Quilters Guild of Indianapolis, Indiana

Hot Apple Cider Nog

3 cups milk
1 cup apple cider or apple juice
½ cup sugar
2 large eggs, beaten
¼ teaspoon ground cinnamon

⅛ teaspoon ground nutmeg
½ cup whipping cream,
    whipped
Ground nutmeg

Combine first 6 ingredients in a medium saucepan; stir well. Cook over medium heat, stirring constantly, until mixture reaches 160°. (Do not boil.) Pour mixture into mugs; top each with whipped cream, and sprinkle with additional nutmeg. Yield: 5 cups.

En Pointe: Culinary Delights from Pittsburgh Ballet Theatre
Pittsburgh Ballet Theatre School
Pittsburgh, Pennsylvania

Breads

Out-of-This-World Pecan Waffles, page 90

Orange Glazed Cranberry-Pumpkin Bread

Lightly drizzled with a sweet orange glaze, this moist loaf bread features fall's harvest of tart cranberries, pumpkin, and walnuts.

3½ cups all-purpose flour
1 teaspoon baking powder
2 teaspoons baking soda
¾ teaspoon salt
1⅔ cups sugar
2 teaspoons pumpkin pie spice
1 (16-ounce) can whole-berry
   cranberry sauce

1 (15-ounce) can pumpkin
4 large eggs, lightly beaten
⅔ cup vegetable oil
¾ cup chopped walnuts
Orange Glaze

Combine first 6 ingredients in a large bowl; make a well in center of mixture.

Combine cranberry sauce and next 3 ingredients; add to dry ingredients, stirring just until blended. Stir in walnuts. Pour batter into two greased 9- x 5- x 3-inch loafpans.

Bake at 350° for 1 hour or until a wooden pick inserted in center comes out clean. Cool in pans on wire racks 10 minutes; remove from pans, and let cool completely on wire racks. Drizzle with Orange Glaze. Yield: 2 loaves.

Orange Glaze

1 cup sifted powdered sugar
¼ cup frozen orange juice
   concentrate, thawed

⅛ teaspoon ground allspice

Combine all ingredients in a small bowl, and stir until smooth. Yield: ½ cup.

Martha Jane Serbeck

Weymouth Township's Heritage of Recipes
Weymouth Township Civic Association
Dorothy, New Jersey

Green Tomato Bread

Pluck your homegrown tomatoes before they ripen for a unique sweet bread that'll send you back to that vine again and again.

3 cups all-purpose flour	2 large eggs, lightly beaten
¼ teaspoon baking powder	1 cup vegetable oil
1 teaspoon baking soda	1 teaspoon vanilla extract
1 teaspoon salt	2 cups finely chopped green
2 cups sugar	tomato (about 2 medium)
1 tablespoon ground cinnamon	1½ cups chopped pecans

Combine first 6 ingredients in a large bowl; make a well in center of mixture. Combine eggs, oil, and vanilla; stir well. Add to dry ingredients, stirring just until moistened. Fold in tomato and pecans.

Spoon batter into two greased and floured 8½- x 4½- x 3-inch loaf-pans. Bake at 350° for 1 hour or until a wooden pick inserted in center of bread comes out clean. Cool in pans on a wire rack 10 minutes. Remove from pans, and let cool completely on wire rack. Yield: 2 loaves.

Mary Solomon

Carolinas Heritage
47th National Square Dance Convention
Charlotte, North Carolina

Blueberry 'n' Cheese Coffee Cake

This so-easy coffee cake showcases fresh juicy blueberries, chunks of cream cheese, and a lemon-sugar topping. We gave this moist cake our highest rating.

½ cup butter or margarine,
   softened
1¼ cups sugar
2 large eggs
2 cups all-purpose flour
1 teaspoon baking powder
1 teaspoon salt
¾ cup milk
¼ cup water

2 cups fresh blueberries
1 (8-ounce) package cream
   cheese, softened and cubed
½ cup all-purpose flour
½ cup sugar
2 tablespoons grated lemon
   rind
2 tablespoons butter or
   margarine, softened

Beat ½ cup butter at medium speed of an electric mixer until creamy; gradually add 1¼ cups sugar, beating well. Add eggs one at a time, beating until blended after each addition.

Combine 2 cups flour, baking powder, and salt; stir well. Combine milk and water; stir well. Add flour mixture to butter mixture alternately with milk mixture, beginning and ending with flour mixture. Mix at low speed after each addition until mixture is blended. Gently stir in blueberries and cream cheese. Pour batter into a greased 9-inch square pan.

Combine ½ cup flour and remaining 3 ingredients; stir well with a fork. Sprinkle mixture over batter. Bake at 375° for 50 to 55 minutes or until golden. Serve warm, or let cool completely on a wire rack. Yield: 16 servings.

Donna Pope

Historically Delicious–An Almanac Cookbook
Tri-Cities Historical Society
Grand Haven, Michigan

Out-of-This-World Pecan Waffles

2½ cups all-purpose flour
1 tablespoon plus 1 teaspoon
   baking powder
¾ teaspoon salt
1½ tablespoons sugar

2 large eggs, beaten
2¼ cups milk
¾ cup vegetable oil
½ cup ground pecans

Combine first 4 ingredients in a large bowl. Combine eggs, milk, and oil; add to flour mixture, stirring just until moistened. Stir in pecans.

Bake in a preheated, oiled waffle iron until golden. Yield: 22 (4-inch) waffles. Cheryl and John Barron Harris

Note: In our Test Kitchens we found that finely chopped pecans worked nicely as a replacement for ground pecans.

The Authorized Texas Ranger Cookbook
Texas Ranger Museum
Hamilton, Texas

The Finnish Pear Pancake

This pancake resembles a betty, a baked pudding, instead of a flapjack. The pancake features fresh pears in a cinnamon syrup.

1½ cups milk
5 large eggs
2 cups all-purpose flour
¼ cup sugar
½ teaspoon salt
4 pears, peeled, cored and thinly sliced
2 tablespoons lemon juice

1 cup butter or margarine, melted
1 cup firmly packed brown sugar
2 tablespoons ground cinnamon
Whipped cream
Ground cinnamon

Combine milk and eggs in a large mixing bowl; beat at medium speed of an electric mixer until blended. Combine flour, ¼ cup sugar, and salt. Add flour mixture to milk mixture; beat until smooth. Set aside.

Toss pears with lemon juice; arrange, spoke fashion, in two buttered 9-inch deep-dish pieplates.

Combine butter, brown sugar, and 2 tablespoons cinnamon; pour evenly over pears. Pour reserved batter evenly over sugar mixture. Bake at 400° for 25 to 30 minutes or until set and browned. Serve warm with whipped cream and cinnamon. Yield: two 9-inch pancakes.

Maine Course Cookbook
YMCA
Bar Harbor, Maine

Hot Cheesy Biscuits

Sharp Cheddar cheese gives these free-form biscuits extra appeal.

2 cups all-purpose flour
2 teaspoons baking powder
½ teaspoon salt
½ teaspoon ground red pepper
1 cup (4 ounces) shredded
  sharp Cheddar cheese
¼ cup shortening
1 cup buttermilk

Combine first 4 ingredients in a bowl; cut in cheese and shortening with pastry blender until mixture is crumbly. Add buttermilk, stirring just until dry ingredients are moistened.

Drop by heaping tablespoonfuls onto greased baking sheets. Bake at 450° for 9 minutes or until golden. Yield: 2 dozen.   Chad Bailey

Evening Shade, Volume II
Evening Shade School Foundation
Evening Shade, Arkansas

Herbed Roquefort Biscuits

1 (3.5-ounce) package
  Roquefort cheese, crumbled
2 tablespoons minced green
  onion tops
1 teaspoon dried basil
½ teaspoon dried thyme
2 cups all-purpose flour
1 tablespoon baking powder
¼ teaspoon baking soda
½ teaspoon salt
¼ cup plus 2 tablespoons
  unsalted butter, cut into
  pieces
¾ cup buttermilk

Combine first 4 ingredients in a small bowl.

Combine flour, baking powder, soda, and salt in a medium bowl; cut in cheese mixture and butter with pastry blender until mixture is crumbly. Add buttermilk, stirring just until dry ingredients are moistened.

Turn dough out onto a lightly floured surface; knead 4 or 5 times. Roll dough to ½-inch thickness; cut with a 1½-inch biscuit cutter. Place on lightly greased baking sheets. Bake at 450° for 8 minutes or until golden. Yield: 40 biscuits.   Willard Helander

A Cook's Tour of Libertyville
Main Street Libertyville
Libertyville, Illinois

Banana-Chocolate Chip Muffins

Almost like a cupcake, these banana-nut muffins laced with mini chocolate chips are just as good at snack time as breakfast.

⅓ cup butter or margarine, softened
1 cup sugar
1 cup mashed ripe banana
1 large egg
1½ cups all-purpose flour
1 teaspoon baking powder
½ teaspoon baking soda
½ teaspoon salt
½ cup buttermilk
½ teaspoon vanilla extract
½ cup (3 ounces) semisweet chocolate mini-morsels
3 tablespoons chopped almonds
2 tablespoons sugar

Beat butter at medium speed of an electric mixer until creamy; gradually add 1 cup sugar, beating well. Add banana and egg, beating well.

Combine flour and next 3 ingredients; add to butter mixture alternately with buttermilk, beginning and ending with flour mixture. Mix at low speed after each addition until blended. Stir in vanilla and chocolate morsels.

Spoon batter into greased muffin pans, filling three-fourths full. Sprinkle almonds and 2 tablespoons sugar evenly over batter. Bake at 375° for 20 minutes. Remove from pans immediately, and cool on wire racks. Yield: 16 muffins.   Vicki Volden

Seasonings
20th Century Club Juniors of Park Ridge, Illinois

Quivey's Grove Raspberry Muffins

2¼ cups all-purpose flour
1 teaspoon baking soda
¼ teaspoon salt
½ cup plus 2 tablespoons sugar
¼ teaspoon ground allspice
1 large egg, beaten

1 cup buttermilk
¼ cup butter or margarine, melted
1 cup fresh raspberries
1 tablespoon sugar

Combine first 5 ingredients in a large bowl; make a well in center of mixture. Combine egg, buttermilk, and butter; add to dry ingredients, stirring just until moistened. Stir in raspberries.

Spoon batter into greased muffin pans, filling three-fourths full. Sprinkle 1 tablespoon sugar over batter. Bake at 425° for 18 minutes. Remove from pans immediately. Yield: 1 dozen.   Laurie Jones

The Guild Cookbook, Volume IV
The Valparaiso University Guild
Valparaiso, Indiana

Palmer's Pecan Popovers

Palmer's puffy popovers are light and airy on the inside and crispy on the outside. The only thing that makes them better is slathering on the honey butter.

¼ cup plus 2 tablespoons
   butter, softened
¼ cup plus 2 tablespoons
   honey
¾ teaspoon grated lemon rind

1 cup all-purpose flour
½ teaspoon salt
1 cup milk
2 large eggs, lightly beaten
¼ cup finely chopped pecans

Combine first 3 ingredients; stir well, and chill. Combine flour and next 3 ingredients; beat with a wire whisk just until smooth. Stir in pecans. Pour batter evenly into six 6-ounce greased custard cups. Bake at 425° for 30 minutes or until golden. Serve immediately with chilled butter. Yield: 6 popovers.   Terry Palmer

Sun Valley Celebrity & Local Heroes Cookbook
Advocates for Survivors of Domestic Violence
Hailey, Idaho

Yam Cornbread

2 cups yellow cornmeal
2 cups all-purpose flour
2½ tablespoons baking powder
2 teaspoons salt
½ cup sugar

4 large eggs, lightly beaten
¾ cup milk
⅓ cup vegetable oil
2⅔ cups cooked, mashed yams

Combine first 5 ingredients; make a well in center of mixture.

Combine eggs, milk, and oil; add to dry ingredients, stirring just until moistened. Stir in yams.

Spoon batter into two greased 8-inch square pans. Bake at 425° for 25 to 30 minutes or until golden. Cut into squares, and serve warm with butter. Yield: 12 servings.   Tina Burke

A Place Called Hope
The Junior Auxiliary of Hope, Arkansas

Old Virginia Spoonbread

Soufflélike spoonbread bakes up light and fluffy and is irresistible with butter melting over a serving.

4 cups milk
1 cup white cornmeal
1½ teaspoons salt

3 tablespoons butter or
   margarine
4 large eggs, well beaten

Place milk in top of a double boiler, bring water to a boil. Heat milk until tiny bubbles begin to appear around edges of pan. Gradually add cornmeal, stirring constantly with a wire whisk. Add salt and butter. Cook, stirring constantly, 10 to 12 minutes or until butter melts and mixture is very thick.

Gradually stir about one-fourth of hot mixture into eggs; add to remaining hot mixture, stirring constantly. Spoon mixture into a lightly greased 2-quart baking dish or soufflé dish. Bake at 425° for 40 to 45 minutes or until golden. Serve with additional butter. Yield: 10 servings.   DiAnn Wheeler

Saints Alive!
Ladies' Guild of St. Barnabas Anglican Church
Atlanta, Georgia

Jalapeño Fritters

Stirring jalapeños into a piquant batter and deep-frying transforms them into a spicy hush puppy.

1 cup all-purpose flour
½ cup yellow cornmeal
1 teaspoon salt
1 teaspoon ground turmeric
1 teaspoon ground coriander
1 teaspoon ground cumin
1 teaspoon chili powder
2½ cups chopped fresh
   mushrooms

1½ cups chopped onion
½ cup seeded, chopped
   jalapeño peppers (about 5
   large)
¾ cup sour cream
Vegetable oil
Sour cream

Combine first 7 ingredients in a large bowl. Add mushrooms, onion, and jalapeño pepper; stir well. Add ¾ cup sour cream; stir until dry ingredients are moistened.

Pour oil to depth of 2 inches into a large Dutch oven; heat to 375°. Carefully drop batter by heaping tablespoonfuls into hot oil, cooking 5 to 6 fritters at a time. Cook about 3 to 4 minutes or until golden, turning once. Drain well on paper towels. Serve warm with additional sour cream. Yield: 3 dozen.   Paul Malopolski

Note: Use rubber gloves when seeding jalapeño peppers to keep hands from blistering.

Pepper Lovers Club Cookbook, Volume I
Pepper Lovers Club of Virginia Beach, Virginia

Best-Ever White Bread

Nothing says homemade more than the warm aroma of freshly baked bread. And these golden loaves welcome you to the table.

1 package active dry yeast
¼ cup warm water (105° to 115°)
6 cups all-purpose flour, divided

2 cups warm milk (105° to 115°)
1 tablespoon sugar
1 tablespoon shortening
2 teaspoons salt

Combine yeast and water in a 1-cup liquid measuring cup; let stand 5 minutes.

Place 3 cups flour in a large mixing bowl. Add yeast mixture, milk, and remaining 3 ingredients; beat at medium speed of an electric mixer until well blended. Gradually stir in enough of remaining 3 cups flour to make a soft dough.

Turn dough out onto a well-floured surface, and knead until smooth and elastic (about 10 minutes). Place in a well-greased bowl, turning to grease top.

Cover and let rise in a warm place (85°), free from drafts, 1 hour or until doubled in bulk.

Punch dough down; cover and let rise in a warm place, free from drafts, 30 minutes or until almost doubled in bulk.

Punch dough down; turn out onto a lightly floured surface, and knead lightly 4 or 5 times. Divide dough in half. Roll 1 portion of dough into a 14- x 7-inch rectangle. Roll up dough, starting at short side, pressing firmly to eliminate air pockets; pinch ends to seal. Place dough, seam side down, in a well-greased 9- x 5- x 3-inch loafpan. Repeat procedure with remaining portion of dough.

Cover and let rise in a warm place, free from drafts, 30 minutes or until doubled in bulk.

Bake at 375° for 35 minutes or until loaves sound hollow when tapped. Remove bread from pans immediately; let cool on wire racks. Yield: 2 loaves.

Sandy Douglas

Rainbow of Recipes, Volume I
The Dream Factory of Louisville, Kentucky

Onion Rye Bread

Hearty rye, mellow onion, and pungent caraway seeds make a memorable taste trio in this crusty loaf. Served warm with dinner or as a sandwich stacked with your favorite meats, cheeses, and tomato slices, this bread is a winner—a state fair blue ribbon winner.

3 cups all-purpose flour, divided
1½ cups rye flour, divided
1 package active dry yeast
2 tablespoons sugar
2 teaspoons salt
1 cup warm milk (120° to 130°)
½ cup warm water (120° to 130°)
2 tablespoons vegetable oil
¾ cup finely chopped onion
2 tablespoons caraway seeds
1 large egg, beaten
1 tablespoon whipping cream
2 teaspoons water

Combine 1½ cups all-purpose flour, ½ cup rye flour, yeast, sugar, and salt in a large bowl. Combine milk, water, and oil; add to flour mixture, stirring 1 minute or until mixture is smooth. Stir in chopped onion and caraway seeds. Gradually stir in remaining 1 cup rye flour and enough of remaining 1½ cups all-purpose flour to make a soft dough.

Turn dough out onto a floured surface, and knead until smooth and elastic (about 10 minutes). Place in a well-greased bowl, turning to grease top. Cover and let rise in a warm place (85°), free from drafts, 1 hour or until doubled in bulk.

Punch dough down; turn out onto a lightly floured surface, and knead lightly 4 or 5 times. Roll dough into a 14- x 7-inch rectangle. Roll up dough, starting at short side, pressing firmly to eliminate air pockets; pinch ends to seal. Place dough, seam side down, in a well-greased 9- x 5- x 3-inch loafpan.

Combine egg, whipping cream, and 2 teaspoons water in a small bowl. Brush loaf with egg mixture. Cover and let rise in a warm place, free from drafts, 15 minutes or until doubled in bulk.

Bake at 375° for 35 minutes or until loaf sounds hollow when tapped. Remove bread from pan immediately; let cool on a wire rack. Yield: 1 loaf.

Kim von Keller

Ribbon Winning Recipes
South Carolina State Fair
Columbia, South Carolina

Greek Stuffed Bread

1 (10-ounce) package frozen chopped spinach, thawed
2 packages active dry yeast
2 teaspoons sugar
2⅔ cups warm water (105° to 115°)
6½ cups bread flour
2 teaspoons salt
¾ cup mayonnaise
2 tablespoons dried oregano
1 tablespoon lemon juice
2 teaspoons dried thyme
1 teaspoon dried basil
1 clove garlic, pressed
¾ pound crumbled feta cheese
1½ cups (6 ounces) shredded mozzarella cheese
½ cup seeded, chopped tomato
1 medium-size purple onion, sliced
20 kalamata olives, pitted and chopped
1 large egg, lightly beaten

Cook spinach according to package directions. Drain well, and press between paper towels to remove excess moisture. Set aside.

Combine yeast, sugar, and water in a 4-cup liquid measuring cup; let stand 5 minutes.

Combine yeast mixture, 3¼ cups flour, and salt in a large mixing bowl; beat at medium speed of an electric mixer until well blended. Gradually stir in enough of remaining 3¼ cups flour to make a soft dough. Turn dough out onto a well-floured surface, and knead until smooth and elastic (about 8 minutes). Place in a well-greased bowl, turning to grease top. Cover and let rise in a warm place (85°), free from drafts, 1 hour or until doubled in bulk.

Punch dough down; cover and let rest 10 minutes. Turn dough out onto a well-floured surface, and knead 4 or 5 times. Roll dough into a 20-inch circle.

Combine mayonnaise and next 5 ingredients. Spread mayonnaise mixture over dough to within ½ inch of edge. Layer cheeses, tomato, onion, olives, and spinach over mayonnaise mixture. Fold each side of dough over filling, overlapping edges 1 inch. Pinch seams to seal. (Loaf will be square in shape.)

Carefully place loaf, seam side down, on a greased baking sheet; reshape into a round loaf. Brush with egg. Cut 4 (3-inch-long) slits in top of loaf. Bake at 400° for 35 minutes or until browned. (Loaf will be hard, but will soften as it cools.) Serve warm. Yield: 8 servings.

Sun Valley Celebrity & Local Heroes Cookbook
Advocates for Survivors of Domestic Violence
Hailey, Idaho

Squash Rolls

Pureed summer squash tenderizes these dinner rolls. Your family will love them.

1¾ cups chopped yellow squash	3 cups all-purpose flour, divided
1 cup water	¼ cup sugar
1 package active dry yeast	¼ cup shortening
½ cup warm water (105° to 115°)	1 teaspoon salt
½ cup warm milk (105° to 115°)	½ teaspoon ground nutmeg
	¼ teaspoon ground mace

Combine squash and 1 cup water in a medium saucepan; bring to a boil. Reduce heat, and simmer, uncovered, 20 to 25 minutes or until squash is very tender. Drain.

Position knife blade in food processor bowl; add squash. Process until smooth, stopping once to scrape down sides. Set aside.

Combine yeast and ½ cup water in a 1-cup liquid measuring cup; let stand 5 minutes.

Combine squash, yeast mixture, milk, 2 cups flour, sugar, and remaining 4 ingredients in a large mixing bowl; beat at medium speed of an electric mixer until well blended. Gradually stir in enough of remaining 1 cup flour to make a soft dough. (Dough will be sticky.)

Turn dough out onto a well-floured surface, and knead until smooth and elastic (about 5 minutes). Place in a well-greased bowl, turning to grease top.

Cover and let rise in a warm place (85°), free from drafts, 1 hour or until doubled in bulk.

Punch dough down, and divide into 18 portions. (Dough will be sticky.) Shape each portion into a ball, and place 2 inches apart on lightly greased baking sheets.

Cover and let rise in a warm place, free from drafts, 40 minutes or until doubled in bulk. Bake at 400° for 12 to 15 minutes or until golden. Yield: 1½ dozen.   Lillian Proctor

More Country Living
Waterloo Area Historical Society
Stockbridge, Michigan

Orange Sticky Buns

1 package active dry yeast
¼ cup warm water (105° to 115°)
1 cup warm milk (105° to 115°)
½ cup butter or margarine, softened
4½ to 5 cups all-purpose flour, divided
1 cup quick-cooking oats, uncooked
⅓ cup firmly packed brown sugar
2 large eggs

1 teaspoon salt
⅔ cup firmly packed brown sugar
1 cup chopped pecans, divided
1 tablespoon grated orange rind
1 teaspoon ground cinnamon
¼ cup butter or margarine, melted
¼ cup light corn syrup
2 tablespoons butter or margarine, melted and divided

Combine yeast and water in a 1-cup liquid measuring cup; let stand 5 minutes.

Combine milk and ½ cup butter in a large mixing bowl, stirring until butter melts. Add yeast mixture, 1 cup flour, oats, and next 3 ingredients; beat at medium speed of an electric mixer until well blended. Gradually stir in enough of remaining flour to make a soft dough. (Dough will be sticky.) Turn dough out onto a lightly floured surface; knead until smooth and elastic (about 5 minutes). Place in a well-greased bowl, turning to grease top. Cover and let rise in a warm place (85°), free from drafts, 1 hour or until doubled in bulk.

Combine ⅔ cup brown sugar, ½ cup pecans, orange rind, and cinnamon; stir well. Set aside.

Combine remaining ½ cup pecans, ¼ cup butter, and syrup. Divide mixture evenly between two 8- or 9-inch cakepans. Set aside.

Punch dough down. Divide dough in half. Roll 1 portion into a 16- x 12-inch rectangle. Spread 1 tablespoon melted butter over dough. Sprinkle half of reserved pecan mixture over dough. Roll up dough, starting at short side, pressing firmly to eliminate air pockets; pinch seams to seal. Slice roll into 8 (1½-inch) slices. Place slices, cut side down, in one prepared cakepan. Repeat procedure.

Cover and let rise in a warm place, free from drafts, 40 minutes or until doubled in bulk. Bake at 350° for 35 minutes. Remove from pans immediately. Yield: 16 buns.   Mary I. Martin

Recipes from the Heart II
South Suburban Humane Society Auxiliary
Park Forest, Illinois

Praline Rolls

A buttery brown sugar-nut topping invites you to savor these sweet spiral rolls.

¼ cup warm water (105° to 115°)
⅓ cup milk
⅓ cup butter or margarine
2¾ cups all-purpose flour, divided
2 teaspoons baking powder
½ teaspoon salt

2 tablespoons sugar
1 package active dry yeast
1 large egg
⅓ cup butter or margarine
¾ cup firmly packed brown sugar
1 cup chopped walnuts, divided

Combine water, milk, and ⅓ cup butter in a saucepan; heat until butter melts, stirring occasionally. Cool to 120° to 130°.

Combine 2 cups flour, baking powder, salt, 2 tablespoons sugar, and yeast in a large mixing bowl. Gradually add liquid mixture to flour mixture, beating at high speed of an electric mixer. Add egg, and beat 2 additional minutes at medium speed. Gradually stir in enough of remaining ¾ cup flour to make a soft dough.

Turn dough out onto a floured surface, and knead 4 or 5 times. Roll dough into a 15- x 10-inch rectangle.

Combine ⅓ cup butter and brown sugar in a small bowl; beat at medium speed until creamy. Spread half of sugar mixture over dough; sprinkle with ½ cup walnuts. Roll up dough, starting at long side, pressing firmly to eliminate air pockets. Cut into 1-inch slices. Place slices on a greased baking sheet; flatten each slice to ½ inch. Spread remaining sugar mixture evenly over tops of flattened slices, and sprinkle with remaining ½ cup walnuts.

Cover and let rise in a warm place (85°), free from drafts, 1 hour or until doubled in bulk.

Bake at 425° for 10 to 12 minutes or until golden. Serve immediately. Yield: 15 rolls.

Joanne E. Gatz

The Guild Cookbook, Volume IV
The Valparaiso University Guild
Valparaiso, Indiana

Cakes

Nut Graham Picnic Cake, page 114

Fall Apple-Dapple Streusel Cake

Fall's inviting flavors–tart apples, aromatic cinnamon, and chopped pecans–star in this streusel-laced sheet cake.

1 cup butter or margarine, softened
¾ cup sugar
¾ cup firmly packed brown sugar
2 large eggs
2½ cups all-purpose flour
1¼ teaspoons baking powder
1 teaspoon baking soda
½ teaspoon salt
1 teaspoon ground cinnamon
1 cup buttermilk
2 cups shredded unpeeled cooking apple

⅓ cup raisins
½ cup all-purpose flour
⅓ cup sugar
⅓ cup firmly packed brown sugar
⅓ cup quick-cooking oats, uncooked
⅓ cup chopped pecans
3 tablespoons butter or margarine, softened
2 tablespoons sesame seeds
½ cup sifted powdered sugar
⅓ cup orange juice

Beat 1 cup butter at medium speed of an electric mixer until creamy; gradually add ¾ cup sugar and ¾ cup brown sugar, beating well. Add eggs, one at a time, beating after each addition.

Combine 2½ cups flour and next 4 ingredients; stir well. Add to butter mixture alternately with buttermilk, beginning and ending with flour mixture. Mix at low speed after each addition until blended. Stir in apple and raisins. Pour half of batter into a lightly greased 13- x 9- x 2-inch pan.

Combine ½ cup flour and next 6 ingredients in a small bowl; stir well. Sprinkle half of streusel mixture over batter in pan. Top with remaining batter, and sprinkle with remaining streusel mixture.

Bake at 350° for 40 to 45 minutes or until a wooden pick inserted in center comes out clean. Let cool slightly on a wire rack.

Combine powdered sugar and orange juice; pour over warm cake. Cut into squares. Yield: 20 servings.

Shared Recipes Among Friends
The Junior Auxiliary of Russellville, Arkansas

Cinnamon Chocolate Cake

2 cups all-purpose flour
2 cups sugar
1 teaspoon ground cinnamon
1 cup water
½ cup butter or margarine
½ cup shortening
¼ cup cocoa
½ cup buttermilk
2 large eggs

1 teaspoon baking soda
1 teaspoon vanilla extract
½ cup butter or margarine
¼ cup plus 2 tablespoons milk
¼ cup cocoa
1 (16-ounce) package powdered
  sugar, sifted
½ cup chopped pecans
  (optional)

Combine flour, 2 cups sugar, and cinnamon in a large bowl; stir well.

Combine water, ½ cup butter, shortening, and ¼ cup cocoa in a medium saucepan; bring to a boil, stirring until butter melts. Gradually add chocolate mixture to flour mixture. Beat at medium speed of an electric mixer until smooth. Combine buttermilk, eggs, soda, and vanilla; beat well. Add to chocolate mixture; beat well (batter will be thin).

Pour batter into a greased and floured 15- x 10- x 1-inch jellyroll pan. Bake at 400° for 20 minutes or until a wooden pick inserted in center comes out clean. Place pan on a wire rack.

Combine ½ cup butter, milk, and ¼ cup cocoa in a medium saucepan; bring to a boil, stirring often. Add powdered sugar, stirring until smooth. Stir in pecans, if desired. Let stand 15 minutes. Pour over cake, spreading to edges. Let cool completely on wire rack. Yield: 24 servings.

Nancy Sullivan

Paws and Refresh
Virginia Living Museum
Newport News, Virginia

Orange-Walnut Cake

½ cup shortening
1 cup sugar
2 large eggs
2 cups all-purpose flour
1 teaspoon baking soda
1 teaspoon salt
1 (6-ounce) can frozen orange
  juice concentrate, thawed,
  undiluted, and divided

½ cup milk
1 cup raisins
½ cup chopped walnuts,
  divided
⅓ cup sugar
1 teaspoon ground cinnamon

Beat shortening at medium speed of an electric mixer until fluffy; gradually add 1 cup sugar, beating well. Add eggs, one at a time, beating after each addition.

Combine flour, baking soda, and salt; add to shortening mixture alternately with ½ cup orange juice concentrate and milk, beginning and ending with flour mixture. Mix at low speed after each addition until blended. Stir in raisins and ¼ cup walnuts. Pour into a greased 13- x 9- x 2-inch pan. Bake at 350° for 25 to 30 minutes or until a wooden pick inserted in center comes out clean.

Brush remaining orange juice concentrate over cake. Combine remaining ¼ cup walnuts, ⅓ cup sugar, and cinnamon; sprinkle mixture evenly over cake. Cool in pan on a wire rack. Cut into squares. Yield: 15 servings.

Fran Hegener

Palette Pleasers
St. Luke Simpson United Methodist Women
Lake Charles, Louisiana

Pineapple Sheet Cake

Topped with a velvety smooth cream cheese frosting and toasted pecans, this cake is sure to be a crowd-pleaser.

2 cups all-purpose flour
2 cups sugar
2 teaspoons baking soda
½ teaspoon salt
1 (20-ounce) can crushed
   pineapple in heavy syrup,
   undrained
2 large eggs, lightly beaten
1 cup chopped pecans
½ teaspoon vanilla extract

1 (8-ounce) package cream
   cheese, softened
½ cup butter or margarine,
   softened
1 teaspoon vanilla extract
1 (16-ounce) package powdered
   sugar, sifted
½ cup chopped toasted pecans

Combine first 4 ingredients in a large bowl; stir well. Combine pineapple and eggs; add to flour mixture, stirring well. Stir in 1 cup pecans and ½ teaspoon vanilla. Pour mixture into a greased 15- x 10- x 1-inch jellyroll pan. Bake 350° for 30 minutes. Let cool completely in pan on a wire rack.

Beat cream cheese and butter at medium speed of an electric mixer until creamy; add 1 teaspoon vanilla, beating well. Gradually add powdered sugar, beating until mixture is smooth. Spread cream cheese mixture over cake; sprinkle evenly with ½ cup pecans. Cut into squares. Yield: 30 servings.   Judy Rome

Des Schmecht Goot
St. Peter Christian Mothers
Collyer, Kansas

Almond Cake with Raspberry Puree

Float each thin, rich slice of Almond Cake atop a ruby-red pool of tart Raspberry Puree for an impressive dessert.

1 (8-ounce) can almond paste
½ cup unsalted butter, softened
¾ cup sugar
3 large eggs
¼ cup all-purpose flour

¼ teaspoon baking powder
1 tablespoon kirsch
¼ teaspoon almond extract
Powdered sugar
2 cups fresh raspberries
2 tablespoons sugar

Heavily grease and lightly flour an 8-inch round cakepan. Set aside.

Beat almond paste and butter at medium speed of an electric mixer until creamy; gradually add ¾ cup sugar, beating well. Add eggs, one at a time, beating after each addition.

Combine flour and baking powder; add to butter mixture. Mix at low speed just until blended. Stir in kirsch and almond extract. Pour batter into prepared pan.

Bake at 350° for 30 minutes or until a wooden pick inserted in center comes out clean. Cool completely in pan on a wire rack.

Invert cake onto a serving platter. Sprinkle with powdered sugar.

Place raspberries and 2 tablespoons sugar in container of an electric blender; process until smooth. Place puree in a wire-mesh strainer over a bowl; press with back of a spoon against sides of the strainer. Discard pulp and seeds remaining in strainer. Serve puree with Almond Cake. Yield: one 8-inch cake.   Lucretia Edwards

The Richmond Museum of History Cookbook
Richmond Museum of History
Richmond, California

Old-Fashioned Pineapple Upside-Down Cake

Buttery caramelized pineapple rings crown this classic cake when you invert the pan.

⅔ cup firmly packed brown sugar
¼ cup butter or margarine
1 (15¼-ounce) can pineapple slices, undrained
6 to 8 pecan halves
1 cup all-purpose flour
¾ cup sugar
1½ teaspoons baking powder
½ teaspoon salt
½ cup milk
¼ cup shortening
2 large eggs
Garnish: whipped cream

Melt brown sugar and butter in a 10-inch cast-iron skillet over low heat. Remove from heat.

Drain pineapple, reserving 2 tablespoons juice. Set juice aside. Place 1 slice in center of skillet. Arrange remaining slices in a single layer around middle slice in skillet. Place a pecan half in center of each pineapple slice.

Combine flour and next 3 ingredients in a large mixing bowl; add milk and shortening. Beat at high speed of an electric mixer 2 minutes until fluffy. Add reserved pineapple juice and eggs; beat mixture 2 additional minutes.

Pour batter over pineapple in skillet. Bake at 350° for 30 to 35 minutes or until golden and cake springs back when lightly touched. Let stand 5 minutes. Invert cake onto a serving plate. Garnish, if desired. Yield: one 10-inch cake.

Joanne Almond

Happy Memories and Thankful Hearts:
Traditions Kept and Blessings Shared
St. Christina's Catholic Church
Parker, South Dakota

Old-Fashioned Coconut Cake

1½ cups sugar
1 cup vegetable oil
3 large eggs
2 cups all-purpose flour
2 teaspoons baking powder
½ teaspoon baking soda
½ teaspoon salt
1 cup buttermilk

½ cup butter or margarine
1 cup sugar
1 cup evaporated milk
3 large eggs, separated
1 teaspoon vanilla extract
2 cups flaked coconut, divided
1 cup light corn syrup
½ cup sugar

Beat 1½ cups sugar and oil at medium speed of an electric mixer until blended. Add 3 eggs, one at a time, beating after each addition.

Combine flour, baking powder, soda, and salt; add to sugar mixture alternately with buttermilk, beginning and ending with flour mixture. Mix at low speed after each addition until blended. Pour batter into three greased and floured 8-inch round cakepans.

Bake at 350° for 20 to 25 minutes or until a wooden pick inserted in center comes out clean. Cool in pans on wire racks 10 minutes; remove from pans, and let cool completely on wire racks. Cover and set aside.

Melt butter in a small heavy saucepan; add 1 cup sugar, milk, and 3 egg yolks. Cook over medium heat, stirring constantly, until mixture thickens and comes to a boil. Boil 1 minute, stirring constantly. Remove from heat; add vanilla, and stir well. Cool completely. Stir in 1½ cups coconut. Spread coconut mixture between layers. Set aside.

Combine syrup and ½ cup sugar in a small heavy saucepan. Cook over medium heat, stirring constantly, until clear. Cook, without stirring, until candy thermometer registers 232°.

While syrup cooks, beat 3 egg whites until soft peaks form; continue to beat, adding hot syrup in a heavy stream. Continue beating just until stiff peaks form and frosting is thick enough to spread. Immediately spread frosting on top and sides of cake. Sprinkle remaining ½ cup coconut on top of cake. Cover and chill thoroughly. Yield: one 3-layer cake. Muriel Gresham

Note: As with many cakes with filling, we recommend chilling this family favorite overnight to let the filling and cake "set up."

Simply Irresistible
The Junior Auxiliary of Conway, Arkansas

Italian Cream Cheese Cake

1 cup butter or margarine,
   softened
2 cups sugar
5 large eggs, separated
2 cups all-purpose flour
1 teaspoon baking soda
¼ teaspoon salt

1 cup buttermilk
1 teaspoon vanilla extract
1 cup chopped pecans
1 cup flaked coconut
Italian Cream Cheese Cake
   Frosting

Beat butter at medium speed of an electric mixer until creamy; gradually add sugar, beating well. Add egg yolks, one at a time, beating after each addition.

Combine flour, baking soda, and salt; add to butter mixture alternately with buttermilk, beginning and ending with flour mixture. Mix at low speed after each addition until blended. Stir in vanilla. Add pecans and coconut; stir well.

Beat egg whites at high speed until stiff peaks form. Gently fold into batter. Spoon batter into two greased and floured 9-inch round cakepans. Bake at 350° for 30 to 35 minutes or until a wooden pick inserted in center comes out clean. Cool in pans on wire racks 10 minutes; remove from pans, and let cool completely on wire racks.

Spread Italian Cream Cheese Cake Frosting between layers and on top and sides of cake. Cover and store in refrigerator. Yield: one 2-layer cake.

Italian Cream Cheese Cake Frosting

1 (8-ounce) package cream
   cheese, softened
½ cup butter or margarine,
   softened

1 (16-ounce) package powdered
   sugar, sifted
1 cup chopped pecans, toasted
1 teaspoon vanilla extract

Beat cream cheese and butter at medium speed until creamy; gradually add sugar, beating until smooth. Stir in pecans and vanilla. Yield: 3½ cups.   Earl R. Pearson and Gwenette Pearson

The Authorized Texas Ranger Cookbook
Texas Ranger Museum
Hamilton, Texas

Sweet Potato Surprise Cake

You'll be delighted with the delicate taste of sweet potato in the layers of this cake.

2 cups sugar
1½ cups vegetable oil
4 large eggs, separated
¼ cup hot water
2½ cups sifted cake flour
1 teaspoon ground cinnamon
1 teaspoon ground nutmeg

¼ teaspoon salt
1½ cups peeled, grated sweet
    potato
1 cup chopped pecans
1 teaspoon vanilla extract
Frosting

Beat sugar and oil at medium speed of an electric mixer until smooth. Add egg yolks, beating well. Add hot water; beat well. Combine flour and next 3 ingredients; stir well. Add to sugar mixture, and beat well. Stir in sweet potato, pecans, and vanilla; set aside.

Beat egg whites at high speed until stiff peaks form. Gently fold into batter. Spoon batter into three greased and floured 9-inch round cakepans.

Bake at 350° for 25 to 30 minutes or until a wooden pick inserted in center comes out clean. Cool in pans on wire racks 10 minutes; remove from pans, and let cool completely on wire racks. Spoon Frosting between layers and on top of cake. Yield: one 3-layer cake.

Frosting

1 (12-ounce) can evaporated
   milk
1 cup sugar
3 egg yolks

½ cup butter or margarine
1 teaspoon vanilla extract
1⅓ cups flaked coconut

Combine first 4 ingredients in a heavy saucepan; bring to a boil over medium heat, stirring constantly. Cook 12 minutes, stirring constantly. Remove from heat; add vanilla and coconut. Stir until frosting cools. (Frosting will be thin.) Yield: 2½ cups.

BMC on Our Menu
Baptist Medical Center Auxiliary of Volunteers
Columbia, South Carolina

"Treasure Island" Chocolate Cake

Cream cheese, coconut, and chocolate morsels comprise the hidden treasure in this chocolate-mocha cake.

2 cups sugar	1 cup buttermilk
1 cup vegetable oil	1 teaspoon vanilla extract
2 large eggs	**Filling**
3 cups all-purpose flour	3 tablespoons hot water
2 teaspoons baking powder	2 tablespoons butter or
2 teaspoons baking soda	margarine, melted
1 teaspoon salt	1 cup sifted powdered sugar
¾ cup cocoa	2 tablespoons cocoa
1 cup strongly brewed coffee	2 teaspoons vanilla extract

Combine first 3 ingredients in a large mixing bowl; beat at medium speed of an electric mixer until blended. Combine flour and next 4 ingredients; add to egg mixture alternately with coffee and buttermilk, beginning and ending with flour mixture. Mix at low speed after each addition until blended. Stir in 1 teaspoon vanilla.

Pour two-thirds of batter into a greased and floured 12-cup Bundt pan or 10-inch tube pan. Spoon Filling evenly over batter in pan; top with remaining batter. Bake at 350° for 1 hour. Cool in pan on a wire rack 10 to 15 minutes; remove from pan, and let cool completely on wire rack. Combine hot water and butter; add powdered sugar and 2 tablespoons cocoa, and blend until smooth. Stir in 2 teaspoons vanilla. Spoon glaze over cake. Yield: one 10-inch cake.

Filling

¼ cup sugar	1 teaspoon vanilla extract
1 (8-ounce) package cream	1 cup (6 ounces) semisweet
cheese, softened	chocolate morsels
1 large egg	½ cup flaked coconut

Combine first 4 ingredients in a medium bowl, and beat until smooth. Add chocolate morsels and coconut, stirring mixture well. Yield: 2½ cups.

Rachel M. Glick

Read'em and Eat
Middleton Public Library
Middleton, Wisconsin

Nut Graham Picnic Cake

1 cup butter or margarine, softened
1 cup firmly packed brown sugar
½ cup sugar
3 large eggs
2 cups all-purpose flour
1 teaspoon baking powder
1 teaspoon baking soda
1 teaspoon salt
½ teaspoon ground cinnamon
1 cup graham cracker crumbs
1 cup orange juice
1 cup chopped pecans
1 tablespoon grated orange rind
Glaze
½ cup chopped pecans, toasted

Beat butter at medium speed of an electric mixer until creamy; gradually add sugars, beating well. Add eggs, one at a time, beating after each addition.

Combine flour and next 5 ingredients; add to butter mixture alternately with orange juice, beginning and ending with flour mixture. Mix at low speed after each addition until blended. Stir in 1 cup pecans and orange rind. Pour batter into a greased and floured 10-inch tube pan.

Bake at 350° for 50 to 55 minutes or until a wooden pick inserted in center comes out clean. (Cake will not rise to top of pan.) Cool in pan on a wire rack 15 minutes; remove from pan, and let cool completely on wire rack. Drizzle with Glaze, and sprinkle with ½ cup pecans. Yield: one 10-inch cake.

Glaze

1 tablespoon milk
1 tablespoon plus 1 teaspoon brown sugar
2 teaspoons butter or margarine
½ cup sifted powdered sugar

Combine first 3 ingredients in a small saucepan, and cook over low heat until sugar and butter melt, stirring occasionally. Remove from heat, and add powdered sugar; stir until mixture is smooth. Yield: ⅓ cup.

Sharon Reames

A Century of Cooking
Eden Chapel United Methodist Church
Perkins, Oklahoma

Glazed Orange-Rum Cake

1 **cup butter or margarine, softened**	⅛ **teaspoon salt**
2 **cups sugar**	¾ **cup milk**
5 **large eggs**	½ **teaspoon light rum**
3 **cups sifted cake flour**	2 **tablespoons grated orange rind**
1 **tablespoon baking powder**	**Glaze**

Beat butter at medium speed of an electric mixer until creamy; gradually add sugar, beating well. Add eggs, one at a time, beating well after each addition. Combine flour, baking powder, and salt; add to butter mixture alternately with milk, beginning and ending with flour mixture. Stir in rum and orange rind. Spoon batter into a greased and floured 10-inch tube pan.

Bake at 350° for 50 minutes or until a wooden pick inserted in center comes out clean. Cool in pan on a wire rack 2 minutes. Pour Glaze evenly over cake in pan while cake is still hot. Cool cake completely before removing from pan. Yield: 16 servings.

Glaze

¼ **cup butter or margarine**	⅓ **cup orange juice**
⅔ **cup sugar**	2 **tablespoons light rum**

Combine first 3 ingredients in a small saucepan; cook over medium heat 3 minutes or until sugar dissolves. Remove from heat, and stir in rum. Yield: 1 cup.   Sara Stine

Sharing Our Feast
Holy Apostles Episcopal Church
Memphis, Tennessee

Chocolate-Raspberry Pound Cake

1 cup seedless raspberry
  preserves, divided
⅔ cup butter or margarine,
  softened
1½ cups sugar
2 large eggs
2 cups all-purpose flour

¾ cup cocoa
1½ teaspoons baking soda
1 teaspoon salt
2 cups sour cream
1 teaspoon vanilla extract
Sifted powdered sugar

Place preserves in a microwave-safe bowl. Microwave at HIGH 1 minute or until preserves melt, stirring after 30 seconds. Let cool.

Beat butter at medium speed of an electric mixer 2 minutes or until creamy. Gradually add 1½ cups sugar, beating 5 to 7 minutes. Add eggs, one at a time, beating just until yellow disappears.

Combine flour, cocoa, soda, and salt; add to butter mixture alternately with sour cream, beginning and ending with flour mixture. Mix at low speed just until blended after each addition. Stir in ¾ cup preserves and vanilla. Pour batter into a greased and floured 12-cup Bundt pan. Bake at 350° for 1 hour or until a wooden pick inserted in center comes out clean. Cool in pan on a wire rack 10 minutes. Remove from pan; place on wire rack. Brush remaining preserves over cake. Let cool completely. Sprinkle with powdered sugar. Yield: one 10-inch cake.

Jeanne Knobbe

Old Favorites from New Friends
Stillwater Newcomers Club
Stillwater, Oklahoma

Ginger Pound Cake

⅔ cup butter or margarine,
  softened
1 cup sugar
3 large eggs
2¼ cups all-purpose flour
1 teaspoon baking powder

1 teaspoon salt
½ cup milk
2 tablespoons grated fresh
  ginger
½ teaspoon vanilla extract

Beat butter at medium speed of an electric mixer 2 minutes or until creamy; gradually add sugar, beating 5 to 7 minutes. Add eggs, one at a time, beating just until yellow disappears.

Combine flour, baking powder, and salt; add to butter mixture alternately with milk, beginning and ending with flour mixture. Mix at low speed just until blended after each addition. Stir in ginger and vanilla. Pour batter into a greased 9- x 5- x 3-inch loafpan. Bake at 325° for 1 hour and 10 minutes or until a wooden pick inserted in center comes out clean. Cool in pan on a wire rack 10 minutes; remove from pan, and let cool completely on wire rack. Yield: one 9-inch loaf.

Food for the Journey
St. Francis Xavier College Church Choir
St. Louis, Missouri

Chocolate Chip Cupcakes

These cupcakes remind us of a chewy chocolate chip cookie.

½ cup butter or margarine, softened
¼ cup plus 2 tablespoons sugar
¾ cup plus 2 tablespoons firmly packed brown sugar, divided
1 large egg
1 teaspoon vanilla extract, divided

1 cup plus 2 tablespoons all-purpose flour
½ teaspoon baking soda
½ teaspoon salt
1 large egg
⅛ teaspoon salt
1 cup (6 ounces) semisweet chocolate morsels
½ cup chopped pecans

Beat butter at medium speed of an electric mixer until creamy; gradually add sugar and ¼ cup plus 2 tablespoons brown sugar, beating well. Add 1 egg and ½ teaspoon vanilla; beat well.

Combine flour, soda, and ½ teaspoon salt; add to sugar mixture, beating well. Drop by rounded tablespoonfuls into paper-lined muffin pans. Bake at 375° for 12 minutes. Remove from oven. Set aside.

Combine remaining ½ cup brown sugar, 1 egg, and ⅛ teaspoon salt. Beat at medium speed until thickened (about 2 minutes). Stir in chocolate morsels, pecans, and ½ teaspoon vanilla. Spoon evenly over each cupcake. Bake 12 additional minutes. Remove immediately to a wire rack; cool completely. Yield: 16 cupcakes.   Lucille Johnson

The Collection
Mountain Brook Baptist Church
Birmingham, Alabama

Chocolate Roulage

Fluffy whipped cream, dark chocolate cake, and fudgy frosting swirl in this impressive dessert.

6 large eggs, separated
½ teaspoon cream of tartar
1 cup sugar, divided
¼ teaspoon salt
1 teaspoon vanilla extract
¼ cup all-purpose flour

¼ cup cocoa
2 tablespoons powdered sugar
2 tablespoons cocoa, divided
1 cup whipping cream,
   whipped
Frosting (optional)

Grease bottom and sides of a 15- x 10- x 1-inch jellyroll pan; line pan with wax paper, and grease wax paper. Set pan aside.

Beat egg whites, cream of tartar, and ½ cup sugar at high speed of an electric mixer until stiff peaks form; set aside.

Beat egg yolks, salt, and vanilla in a large mixing bowl until thick and pale. Stir in remaining ½ cup sugar, flour, and ¼ cup cocoa. (Mixture will be very thick.) Fold one-third of egg white mixture into yolk mixture. Carefully fold remaining egg white mixture into chocolate mixture. Spread batter evenly in prepared pan. Bake at 325° for 20 minutes.

Sift powdered sugar in a 15- x 10-inch rectangle on a towel. Loosen cake from sides of pan; turn cake out onto towel; peel off wax paper. Dust top of cake with 1 tablespoon cocoa. Starting at narrow end, roll up cake and towel together. Place cake roll, seam side down, on a wire rack; let cool 30 minutes. Unroll cake, and remove towel. Spread cake with whipped cream. Carefully reroll cake without towel. Place on a serving plate, seam side down. Dust cake with remaining 1 tablespoon cocoa or frost with Frosting, if desired. Yield: 12 servings.

Frosting

1 cup (6 ounces) semisweet
   chocolate morsels, melted

1 cup sour cream

Combine chocolate morsels and sour cream; beat at medium speed of an electric mixer until creamy. Yield: 2 cups.   Sandy Wheeler

Briarwood Recipes to Crown Your Table
Women's Ministries of Briarwood Presbyterian Church
Birmingham, Alabama

Chocolate-Amaretto Cheesecake

Dollops of whipped cream adorn this sinfully rich chocolate cheesecake that's laced with amaretto and topped with a semisweet chocolate topping.

1¼ cups chocolate wafer crumbs
¼ cup butter or margarine, melted
2 tablespoons sugar
2 (8-ounce) packages cream cheese, softened
½ cup sugar
2 large eggs
1 cup (6 ounces) semisweet chocolate morsels, melted

⅔ cup sour cream
⅓ cup amaretto
1 teaspoon vanilla extract
½ teaspoon almond extract
½ cup (3 ounces) semisweet chocolate morsels
1 tablespoon butter or margarine
Garnishes: whipped cream, toasted sliced almonds

Grease bottom of an 8-inch springform pan; set aside.

Combine first 3 ingredients in a medium bowl; stir well. Press mixture on bottom and 1 inch up sides of prepared pan. Chill.

Beat cream cheese at high speed of an electric mixer until creamy. Gradually add ½ cup sugar, beating well. Add eggs, one at a time, beating after each addition. Add melted chocolate and next 4 ingredients; beat until smooth. Pour into prepared crust.

Bake at 300° for 1 hour. Turn oven off; partially open oven door, and let cheesecake cool in oven 1 hour. Remove cheesecake from oven, and let cool to room temperature in pan on a wire rack; cover and chill at least 8 hours. Carefully remove sides of springform pan.

Combine ½ cup chocolate morsels and 1 tablespoon butter in a small saucepan. Cook over low heat, stirring constantly, until chocolate melts. Let cool slightly. Spread over cheesecake. Garnish, if desired. Yield: 10 servings.   Christine A. Ouellette

A Cook's Tour of Libertyville
Main Street Libertyville
Libertyville, Illinois

Cheesecake Supreme

This creamy cheesecake deserves its name! Topped with tantalizing strawberries and pineapple, it received our highest rating.

1 cup all-purpose flour
¼ cup sugar
1 teaspoon grated lemon rind
⅓ cup butter or margarine
1 egg yolk, lightly beaten
½ teaspoon vanilla extract, divided
5 (8-ounce) packages cream cheese, softened
1¾ cups sugar
4 large eggs

2 egg yolks
3 tablespoons all-purpose flour
¾ teaspoon grated lemon rind
¼ teaspoon salt
¼ cup whipping cream
1 cup halved fresh strawberries
1 (8-ounce) can sliced pineapple, drained and cut in half
Strawberry Glaze

Combine first 3 ingredients in a bowl; stir well. Cut in butter with pastry blender until mixture is crumbly. Add 1 egg yolk and ¼ teaspoon vanilla; stir with a fork until dry ingredients are moistened.

Press crust mixture on bottom and 1 inch up sides of a 10-inch springform pan. Bake at 400° for 8 minutes or until crust is golden; let cool.

Beat cream cheese at medium speed of a heavy-duty electric mixer until creamy. Gradually add 1¾ cups sugar, beating well. Add eggs and egg yolks, one at a time, beating after each addition. Combine 3 tablespoons flour, ¾ teaspoon lemon rind, and salt. Add to cream cheese mixture; beat until smooth. Stir in whipping cream and ¼ teaspoon vanilla. Pour mixture into prepared crust.

Bake at 325° for 55 minutes or until cheesecake is almost set. Turn oven off, and partially open oven door; leave cheesecake in oven 30 minutes. Let cool to room temperature in pan on a wire rack.

Arrange strawberry halves over top of cheesecake. Place pineapple around strawberry halves. Pour Strawberry Glaze over cake. Cover and chill 8 hours. To serve, carefully remove sides of springform pan. Yield: 12 servings.

Strawberry Glaze

1½ cups fresh strawberries, mashed
1 cup water

¾ cup sugar
1½ tablespoons cornstarch

Combine mashed berries and water in a small saucepan over medium heat. Bring to a boil; reduce heat, and simmer 2 minutes, stirring occasionally. Pour mixture through a wire-mesh strainer into a bowl, discarding seeds and pulp. Return liquid to saucepan.

Combine sugar and cornstarch, stirring well. Stir cornstarch mixture into hot berry liquid. Bring to a boil, and cook 1 minute, stirring constantly. Cool completely. Yield: 1½ cups.   Marilyn Ramunno

Seasoned with Love
Mahoning County Foster Parent Association
Youngstown, Ohio

Turner's Portrait of a Perfect Plum Torte

More like a cobbler, this torte oozes with plump plums and their juices that bubble up through the cake-like crust. Topped with whipped cream or ice cream is the only way to serve it.

½ cup unsalted butter,
   softened
1 cup sugar
2 large eggs
1 cup unbleached flour
1 teaspoon baking powder

⅛ teaspoon salt
10 large plums, pitted and
   halved
1½ teaspoons sugar
¼ teaspoon ground cinnamon
1½ teaspoons lemon juice

Beat butter at medium speed of an electric mixer until creamy; gradually add 1 cup sugar, beating well. Add eggs, one at a time, beating after each addition.

Combine flour, baking powder, and salt; add to butter mixture, beating well. Spread batter in a greased 9-inch springform pan. Place plums, cut side down, on top of batter.

Combine 1½ teaspoons sugar and cinnamon; sprinkle over plums. Drizzle lemon juice over plums. Bake, uncovered, at 350° for 1 hour and 15 minutes or until a wooden pick inserted in center comes out clean. Carefully remove sides of springform pan. Serve torte warm. Yield: 8 servings.   Midge Margolis

Cuisine for Connoisseurs: Food Among the Fine Arts
Boca Raton Museum of Art
Boca Raton, Florida

Walnut Torte

Sliced strawberries stand in grand ovation in the whipped cream atop this cook's masterpiece.

6 large eggs, separated
¾ cup sugar, divided
¼ cup all-purpose flour
⅓ cup fine, dry breadcrumbs
1¼ cups ground walnuts,
 divided

2 cups whipping cream
2 tablespoons powdered sugar
1 teaspoon vanilla extract
1 cup sliced fresh strawberries

Combine egg yolks and ½ cup sugar in a large mixing bowl; beat at high speed of an electric mixer 3 minutes or until thick and pale. Add flour, breadcrumbs, and ⅔ cup ground walnuts; beat at low speed until combined. Set aside.

Beat egg whites at high speed until foamy. Gradually add ¼ cup sugar, 1 tablespoon at a time, beating until stiff peaks form and sugar dissolves (2 to 4 minutes). Gently fold beaten whites into egg yolk mixture. Spread batter evenly into two greased 9-inch round cakepans. Bake at 325° for 21 minutes or until a wooden pick inserted in center comes out clean. Cool in pans on wire racks 10 minutes; remove from pans, and let cool completely on wire racks.

Beat whipping cream until foamy; gradually add powdered sugar and vanilla, beating until soft peaks form. Spread whipped cream mixture between layers and on top and sides of cake. Gently press remaining ground walnuts onto sides of cake. Arrange strawberries on top. Yield: one 9-inch torte.

Elia Straccia Snay

The Lincoln Park Historical Society Cooks!
Lincoln Park Historical Society
Lincoln Park, Michigan

Cookies & Candies

Rocky Road Fudge Bars, page 132

Japanese Almond Cookies

Unlike the typically dense Japanese almond cookie, these gems are light and airy–almost like meringue.

1½ cups blanched whole or
    slivered almonds
2 egg whites

Dash of salt
⅔ cup sugar
54 blanched whole almonds

Spread 1½ cups almonds on a large baking sheet. Bake at 350° for 10 minutes or until lightly toasted. Let cool.

Position knife blade in food processor bowl; add toasted almonds, and process until finely ground.

Beat egg whites and salt in a mixing bowl at high speed of an electric mixer until foamy. Gradually add sugar, 2 tablespoons at a time, beating until stiff peaks form and sugar dissolves (2 to 4 minutes). Gently fold in ground almonds.

Drop mixture by heaping teaspoonfuls 1 inch apart onto lightly greased cookie sheets. Top each with 1 whole almond. Bake at 350° for 7 minutes or just until lightly browned. Remove to wire racks immediately, and let cool completely. Yield: 4½ dozen.

Note: The almonds on top identify these cookies at a glance, but they're just as yummy without them.

Appealing Fare
Frost & Jacobs
Cincinnati, Ohio

Oatmeal-Molasses Cookies

Just like Grandma used to make–soft and chewy with just the right amount of sweetness and a little bit of coconut.

2 cups sugar
1 cup vegetable oil
⅓ cup molasses
2 large eggs
2 cups all-purpose flour
1 teaspoon baking powder
1 teaspoon baking soda

1 teaspoon salt
1 teaspoon ground cinnamon
2 cups quick-cooking oats,
    uncooked
1 cup raisins
1 cup flaked coconut

Combine first 4 ingredients in a large mixing bowl. Beat at medium speed of an electric mixer until smooth.

Combine flour and next 4 ingredients; stir well. Add to sugar mixture, mixing well. Stir in oats, raisins, and coconut.

Drop dough by heaping teaspoonfuls onto lightly greased cookie sheets. Bake at 350° for 10 minutes. Cool slightly on cookie sheets; remove cookies to wire racks, and let cool completely. Yield: about 6 dozen.

Marge Foster

Dundee Presbyterian Church Cook Book
Dundee Presbyterian Church
Omaha, Nebraska

Pumpkin Chippers

White chocolate chunks, butterscotch chips, and chopped walnuts make these pumpkin cookies something to write home about.

2 **cups all-purpose flour**
1 **cup (6 ounces) butterscotch morsels**
1 **teaspoon baking soda**
¾ **cup butter or margarine, softened**
⅔ **cup sugar**
⅔ **cup firmly packed brown sugar**

1 **large egg**
½ **cup canned pumpkin**
1 **cup quick-cooking oats, uncooked**
1 **(6-ounce) premium white chocolate baking bar, chopped**
⅔ **cup chopped walnuts**

Position knife blade in food processor bowl; add flour and butterscotch morsels. Process 30 seconds or until morsels are finely ground.

Combine flour mixture and baking soda; stir well, and set aside.

Beat butter at medium speed of an electric mixer until creamy. Gradually add sugars, beating well. Add egg and pumpkin; beat well. Stir in oats, white chocolate, and walnuts.

Drop by heaping teaspoonfuls onto lightly greased cookie sheets. Bake at 350° for 12 minutes or until golden. Remove to wire racks immediately, and let cool completely. Yield: 6 dozen.

Gardener's Delight
The Ohio Association of Garden Clubs
Grove City, Ohio

Teatime Gingersnaps

Reminiscent of those afternoon tea parties, these crisp delights with the perfect amount of spice are a cup of tea's gracious partner.

¾ cup shortening
1 cup sugar
1 large egg
¼ cup molasses
2 cups all-purpose flour
2 teaspoons baking soda

¼ teaspoon salt
1 teaspoon ground ginger
1 teaspoon ground cinnamon
1 teaspoon ground cloves
Sugar

Beat shortening at medium speed of an electric mixer until fluffy. Gradually add 1 cup sugar, beating well. Add egg; beat well. Add molasses; beat until smooth.

Combine flour and next 5 ingredients; add to shortening mixture, beating well.

Shape dough into 1-inch balls; roll balls in sugar. Place 2 inches apart on lightly greased cookie sheets. Bake at 375° for 10 minutes. Remove cookies to wire racks, and let cool completely. Yield: 4 dozen.

Cafe Oklahoma
The Junior Service League of Midwest City, Oklahoma

Honey Roasted Peanut Crisps

These buttery cookies are chock-full of honey roasted peanuts.

½ cup butter or margarine, softened
½ cup shortening
1 cup firmly packed brown sugar
1 large egg

1 teaspoon vanilla extract
2 cups all-purpose flour
½ teaspoon baking powder
¼ teaspoon salt
2 cups honey roasted peanuts
Sugar

Beat butter and shortening at medium speed of an electric mixer until creamy; gradually add 1 cup brown sugar, beating well. Add egg and vanilla; beat well. Combine flour, baking powder, and salt; gradually add to butter mixture, beating well. Stir in peanuts.

Shape dough into 1¼-inch balls. Place 2 inches apart on ungreased cookie sheets. Dip a flat-bottomed glass in sugar, and flatten each ball to ¼-inch thickness. Bake at 375° for 8 minutes or until edges are golden. Cool slightly on cookie sheets; remove to wire racks, and let cool completely. Yield: 4 dozen.   Lazell Hudson

Note: For a softer cookie, drop dough by rounded tablespoonfuls onto ungreased cookie sheets, and bake at 375° for 7 to 8 minutes or until edges are golden.

Cookin' with the Pride of Cove
Copperas Cove Band Boosters Club
Fort Hood, Texas

Magic Peanut Butter Middles

Creamy peanut butter awaits in each bite of these chewy chocolate cookies.

½ cup butter or margarine, softened
¼ cup creamy peanut butter
½ cup sugar
½ cup firmly packed brown sugar
1 large egg

1 teaspoon vanilla extract
1½ cups all-purpose flour
½ teaspoon baking soda
½ cup cocoa
¾ cup creamy peanut butter
¾ cup sifted powdered sugar
Sugar

Beat butter and ¼ cup peanut butter at medium speed of an electric mixer until creamy; gradually add ½ cup sugar and brown sugar, beating well. Add egg and vanilla; beat well. Combine flour, baking soda, and cocoa; gradually add to butter mixture, beating well. Set aside.

Combine ¾ cup peanut butter and powdered sugar, beating until blended. Shape mixture into 30 (1-inch) balls with floured hands.

Shape about 1 tablespoon chocolate mixture around each peanut butter ball. Place 2 inches apart on ungreased cookie sheets. Dip a flat-bottomed glass in sugar, and flatten each ball into a 1½-inch circle. Bake at 300° for 10 to 12 minutes (cookies will be soft). Cool slightly on cookie sheets; remove to wire racks, and let cool completely. Yield: 2½ dozen.   Cathy Rhodehamel

Family Favorites
Allen County Extension Homemakers
Fort Wayne, Indiana

Rosemary Shortbread Cookies

Temptingly flavored with fragrant rosemary, these unusual cookies surprised us with their mass appeal. We recommend serving these wonderfully tender-crisp cookies with a hot cup of your favorite tea or atop a cool scoop of sherbet.

1½ cups all-purpose flour
½ cup butter or margarine,
    chilled
¼ cup sifted powdered sugar

2 tablespoons minced fresh
   rosemary
2 tablespoons sugar

Position knife blade in food processor bowl; add first 4 ingredients. Process until mixture forms a ball.

Roll dough to ¼-inch thickness on a lightly floured surface. Cut with a 2-inch cookie cutter; place on lightly greased cookie sheets. Bake at 325° for 18 to 20 minutes or until edges are lightly browned. Sprinkle with sugar. Remove to wire racks, and let cool completely. Yield: 1½ dozen.

Queen Anne Goes to the Kitchen
Episcopal Church Women of St. Paul's Parish
Centreville, Maryland

Peppercorn Cookies

You won't be able to eat just one of these seductively addictive dark shortbread cookies. Black and red pepper provide lustful spice appeal to the predominant chocolate presence.

¾ cup butter or margarine,
    softened
1 cup sugar
1 large egg
1½ teaspoons vanilla extract
1½ cups all-purpose flour

¾ cup cocoa
¾ teaspoon ground cinnamon
¼ teaspoon salt
⅛ teaspoon black pepper
⅛ teaspoon ground red pepper
Powdered sugar

Beat butter at medium speed of an electric mixer until creamy; gradually add 1 cup sugar, beating well. Add egg and vanilla; beat well. Combine flour and next 5 ingredients; gradually add to butter mixture, beating well.

Shape cookie dough into a 12-inch roll on a lightly floured surface. Wrap roll in wax paper, and chill at least 2 hours or until firm.

Slice dough into ¼-inch-thick slices, and place on greased cookie sheets. Bake at 375° for 8 minutes. Transfer cookies to wire racks, and let cool completely. Sift powdered sugar over tops of cookies. Yield: 4 dozen.   Sally Chalmers

Favorite Recipes
P.E.O. Chapter BC
Hendersonville, North Carolina

Cranberry Nut Swirls

½ cup butter or margarine, softened	3 tablespoons brown sugar
¾ cup sugar	2 tablespoons milk
1 large egg	½ cup finely ground fresh cranberries
1 teaspoon vanilla extract	
1½ cups all-purpose flour	½ cup finely chopped walnuts
¼ teaspoon baking powder	1 tablespoon grated orange rind
¼ teaspoon salt	

Beat butter at medium speed of an electric mixer until creamy. Gradually add ¾ cup sugar, beating well. Add egg and vanilla; beat well. Combine flour, baking powder, and salt; gradually add to butter mixture, beating well. Shape dough into a ball; cover and chill at least 2 hours.

Roll dough into a 10-inch square on floured wax paper. Combine brown sugar and milk; spread evenly over dough to within ½ inch of edges. Combine cranberries, walnuts, and orange rind; spread evenly over brown sugar mixture. Roll up dough, peeling wax paper from dough while rolling. Pinch seam to seal. (Leave ends open.) Wrap roll in wax paper, and freeze until firm.

Unwrap roll, and cut into ¼-inch-thick slices; place 2 inches apart on lightly greased cookie sheets. Bake at 375° for 12 minutes or until edges are lightly browned. Remove to wire racks, and let cool completely. Yield: 2½ dozen.   Vera Lundgren

Gove County Gleanings: Recipes, Facts, and Photos
Harvested from Gove County, Kansas
Gove Community Improvement Association
Gove, Kansas

Lake Tahoe Chocolate Cookies

These cookies are shaped into three logs before slicing and baking. So dark and rich in chocolate and pecans, these cookies will disappear quickly from the cookie jar.

4 (1-ounce) squares unsweetened chocolate, finely chopped
12 (1-ounce) squares semisweet chocolate, finely chopped
¼ cup unsalted butter, softened
2 cups sugar
4 large eggs

1 teaspoon vanilla extract
1 tablespoon dark rum
½ cup all-purpose flour
½ teaspoon baking powder
½ teaspoon baking soda
⅛ teaspoon salt
2 cups (12 ounces) semisweet chocolate morsels
2 cups chopped pecans

Place chocolate in top of a double boiler; bring water to a boil. Reduce heat to low; cook until chocolate melts, stirring occasionally. Set aside.

Beat butter at medium speed of an electric mixer until creamy; gradually add sugar, beating well. Add eggs, one at a time, beating after each addition. Stir in vanilla and rum.

Combine flour and next 3 ingredients; add to butter mixture. Stir in melted chocolate, chocolate morsels, and pecans, stirring well. Cover and chill 30 minutes.

Shape dough into 3 (11-inch) logs, and wrap in wax paper. Chill at least 8 hours.

Unwrap dough; cut each log into 28 slices, and place slices 2 inches apart on ungreased cookie sheets. Bake at 350° for 10 minutes. Cool completely on cookie sheets. Yield: 7 dozen. Marge Card

Note: We used an electric knife for clean slices.

A Continual Feast
St. Mary's Guild of St. Clement's Episcopal Church
Berkeley, California

Raspberry Sandwich Cookies

Ruby-red raspberry preserves peep through the center of these almond sandwich cookies.

½ cup butter or margarine,
   softened
1 cup sugar, divided
2 large eggs, separated
1½ cups all-purpose flour
¼ teaspoon salt

½ cup ground blanched
   almonds
1 (10-ounce) jar raspberry
   preserves
½ cup semisweet chocolate
   morsels, melted

Beat butter at medium speed of an electric mixer until creamy; gradually add ½ cup sugar, beating well. Add egg yolks, one at a time, beating after each addition.

Combine flour and salt; add to butter mixture, beating well. Shape dough into a ball; cover and chill at least 2 hours.

Divide dough in half; work with 1 portion of dough at a time, keeping remaining dough chilled. Roll dough to ¼-inch thickness on a heavily floured surface; cut with a 2½-inch doughnut cutter, discarding centers. Repeat rolling procedure with other half of dough; cut with a 2½-inch round cookie cutter.

Combine remaining ½ cup sugar and ground almonds; stir well. Beat egg whites until foamy; brush 1 side of all cookie cutouts with egg white, and coat with almond mixture. Place cutouts, coated side up, on ungreased baking sheets. Bake at 375° for 10 minutes; remove to wire racks, and let cool completely.

Spread whole cookies with a thin layer of raspberry preserves; top with cutout cookies. Drizzle tops with melted chocolate. Yield: 1 dozen sandwich cookies.

The Very Special Raspberry Cookbook
Carrie Tingley Hospital Foundation
Albuquerque, New Mexico

Rocky Road Fudge Bars

Ooh so ooey gooey–rich chocolate brownies studded with pecans are topped with a dreamy layer of swirled cream cheese, marshmallows, and chocolate. You may need a fork for these!

½ cup butter or margarine, softened
1 cup sugar
1 (1-ounce) square unsweetened chocolate, melted
2 large eggs
1 cup all-purpose flour
1 teaspoon baking powder
1 teaspoon vanilla extract
1¼ cups chopped pecans, divided
1 (8-ounce) package cream cheese, softened and divided
¼ cup butter or margarine, softened

½ cup sugar
1 large egg, beaten
2 tablespoons all-purpose flour
½ teaspoon vanilla extract
1 cup (6 ounces) semisweet chocolate morsels
2 cups miniature marshmallows
1 (1-ounce) square unsweetened chocolate
¼ cup milk
¼ cup butter or margarine
1 (16-ounce) package powdered sugar, sifted
¼ teaspoon vanilla extract

Beat ½ cup butter at medium speed of an electric mixer until creamy; gradually add 1 cup sugar, beating at medium speed until light and fluffy. Add melted chocolate and 2 eggs, one at a time, beating well after each addition. Combine 1 cup flour and baking powder; stir well. Add flour mixture to creamed mixture. Stir in 1 teaspoon vanilla and 1 cup chopped pecans. Spread batter in a greased 13- x 9- x 2-inch pan. Set aside.

Combine 6 ounces cream cheese and ¼ cup butter; beat at medium speed until smooth. Gradually add ½ cup sugar, beating until creamy. Add 1 egg, 2 tablespoons flour, and ½ teaspoon vanilla; mix well. Stir in remaining ¼ cup pecans.

Spread cream cheese mixture over chocolate layer in pan (do not mix layers together). Sprinkle chocolate morsels evenly over cream cheese layer. Bake at 350° for 35 minutes. Remove from oven; sprinkle evenly with marshmallows. Bake 2 additional minutes. Remove from oven, and set aside.

Combine 1 square chocolate, milk, ¼ cup butter, and remaining 2 ounces cream cheese in top of a double boiler; bring water to a boil. Reduce heat to low; cook until chocolate, butter, and cream cheese melt, stirring occasionally. Remove from heat; stir in powdered sugar and ¼ teaspoon vanilla. Beat at medium speed until smooth. Pour chocolate mixture over marshmallows. Swirl together with a knife. Let cool completely in pan on a wire rack. Cover and chill thoroughly. Cut into bars. Yield: 1 dozen.   Janet Followell

First Family Favorites
First Baptist Church of Orlando, Florida

Chewy Oatmeal Spice Bars

Imagine a soft oatmeal cookie that takes mere minutes to make–here's your sweet fantasy.

1 cup butter or margarine, softened	1 tablespoon ground cinnamon
½ cup sugar	1 teaspoon ground nutmeg
1½ cups firmly packed brown sugar	½ teaspoon ground ginger
2 large eggs	2 teaspoons vanilla extract
1 cup all-purpose flour	2 cups quick-cooking oats, uncooked
1 teaspoon baking soda	1 (3.5-ounce) can flaked coconut
½ teaspoon salt	1 cup raisins

Beat butter at medium speed of an electric mixer until creamy; gradually add ½ cup sugar and 1½ cups brown sugar, beating well. Add eggs, one at a time, beating well after each addition.

Combine flour and next 5 ingredients; add to butter mixture, beating well. Stir in vanilla and remaining ingredients. Spoon batter into a greased 13- x 9- x 2-inch pan. Bake at 350° for 35 to 40 minutes or until a wooden pick inserted in center comes out clean. Let cool slightly before cutting into bars. Yield: 2 dozen.

The Tailgate Cookbook
National Kidney Foundation of Kansas and Western Missouri
Westwood, Kansas

Brownies, Hawaiian Style

Two Hawaiian favorites, macadamia nuts and coconut, make these brownies stand out from the usual fare.

4 (1-ounce) squares
   unsweetened chocolate
½ cup butter or margarine
4 large eggs
1 cup sugar
2 teaspoons vanilla extract
1 cup all-purpose flour

1 cup macadamia nuts,
   chopped
2 cups (12 ounces) semisweet
   chocolate morsels
1 (7-ounce) can shredded
   coconut

Melt unsweetened chocolate and butter in a heavy saucepan over low heat. Let cool.

Beat eggs at medium speed of an electric mixer until foamy; gradually add sugar, vanilla, and melted chocolate mixture, mixing well. Add flour, beating well. Stir in half each of chopped nuts, chocolate morsels, and coconut. Spoon batter into a greased 13- x 9- x 2-inch pan. Sprinkle remaining nuts, chocolate morsels, and coconut over top of batter.

Bake at 350° for 25 minutes. Let cool completely in pan on a wire rack. Cut into squares. Yield: 4 dozen.

Another Taste of Aloha
The Junior League of Honolulu, Hawaii

Candied Grapefruit Peel

Candied citrus is a traditional favorite during the holidays, and the tartness of grapefruit with the snowy sugar coating makes this version irresistible.

1½ cups (¼-inch-wide)
   grapefruit rind strips
   (about 2 grapefruit)
1½ cups sugar
¾ cup water

¼ teaspoon salt
1 (3-ounce) package lemon-
   flavored gelatin
Sugar

Place grapefruit rind strips in water to cover in a medium saucepan. Bring to a boil; reduce heat to medium, and cook grapefruit rind strips 20 minutes. Drain well. Repeat boiling procedure twice. Combine 1½ cups sugar, ¾ cup water, salt, and grapefruit rind strips in saucepan; bring to a boil, reduce heat, and simmer, uncovered, 20 minutes. Gradually add gelatin, stirring until dissolved. Drain grapefruit rind strips, discarding syrup. Arrange strips in a single layer on wire racks; let stand 20 minutes.

Roll strips, a few at a time, in sugar. Arrange in a single layer on wire racks; let dry 4 to 5 hours. Store in an airtight container. Yield: about ½ pound.   Pat Harrison

Watt's Cooking
Oasis Southern Company Services
Atlanta, Georgia

White Chocolate Fudge

Renowned Ghirardelli white chocolate and cream cheese create a creamy fudge.

6 ounces premium white chocolate, chopped	**3 cups sifted powdered sugar**
½ (8-ounce) package cream cheese, softened	**½ teaspoon vanilla extract**
	1 cup chopped pecans
	25 pecan halves

Place white chocolate in top of a double boiler; bring water to a boil. Reduce heat to low; cook until white chocolate melts, stirring occasionally. Remove from heat.

Beat cream cheese at high speed of an electric mixer until creamy. Gradually add sugar; beat at medium speed until smooth. Stir in chocolate and vanilla; beat well. Stir in chopped pecans.

Press mixture into a lightly buttered 8-inch square pan. Cover and chill. Cut into 25 squares. Gently press a pecan half on each square of fudge. Store in an airtight container in the refrigerator. Yield: about 1½ pounds.   Ann Loftin

To Serve with Love
Christian Women's Fellowship of the First Christian Church
Duncan, Oklahoma

Double Almond Crunch

A thin layer of chocolate and almonds tops this almond brittle.

1 cup butter
1⅓ cups sugar
1 tablespoon light corn syrup
3 tablespoons water
1 cup coarsely chopped
  almonds

3 (4-ounce) bars milk
  chocolate
1 cup finely chopped almonds,
  divided

Combine first 4 ingredients in a 3-quart saucepan. Cook over low heat, stirring gently, until sugar dissolves. Cover and cook over medium heat 2 to 3 minutes to wash down sugar crystals from sides of pan. Uncover and cook to hard crack stage (300°). Remove from heat, and stir in coarsely chopped almonds. Pour mixture into an ungreased 13- x 9- x 2-inch pan, quickly spreading to edges of pan. Let cool.

Place chocolate in top of a double boiler; bring water to a boil. Reduce heat to low; cook until chocolate melts, stirring occasionally. Remove from heat.

Run a sharp knife around edge of candy in pan. Spread half of melted chocolate over top of candy; sprinkle with ½ cup finely chopped almonds. Chill 30 minutes. Carefully invert candy onto a wax paper-lined baking sheet. Spread remaining melted chocolate over uncoated side of candy. Sprinkle with remaining ½ cup almonds. Chill 30 minutes. Break candy into pieces. Store in an airtight container. Yield: 2½ pounds.

Janie John

The Richmond Museum of History Cookbook
Richmond Museum of History
Richmond, California

Desserts

Fresh Blueberries Grand Marnier, page 140

Caramel Baked Apples

A warm caramel sauce bathes these brown sugar-baked apples.

½ cup firmly packed brown sugar	½ teaspoon ground cinnamon
¼ cup raisins	6 cooking apples
¼ cup chopped dates	1 cup water
¼ cup chopped walnuts	Caramel Sauce
3 tablespoons butter or margarine, softened	

Combine first 6 ingredients in a medium bowl; stir well, and set aside.

Core apples, cutting to, but not through, bottom; peel top third of each apple. Spoon raisin mixture into cavities of apples. Place apples in an 11- x 7- x 1½-inch baking dish; pour water around apples.

Cover and bake at 350° for 30 minutes. Uncover and bake 50 additional minutes or until apples are tender, basting frequently.

Place apples on a serving platter, using a slotted spoon. Spoon warm Caramel Sauce over apples. Yield: 6 servings.

Caramel Sauce

1 cup sugar	½ cup whipping cream
⅓ cup water	½ cup water
⅛ teaspoon cream of tartar	

Combine sugar, ⅓ cup water, and cream of tartar in a medium saucepan. Cook over medium heat, stirring constantly, until sugar melts and turns light brown. Remove from heat.

Combine whipping cream and ½ cup water in a small saucepan. Cook over medium heat, stirring constantly, until hot (160°). Gradually add whipping cream mixture to syrup, stirring until smooth. Bring sauce to a boil over medium heat, stirring constantly. Remove from heat. Yield: 1¼ cups.   Donna Ianire

What's Cooking in Delaware
American Red Cross in Delaware
Wilmington, Delaware

Crêpes à la Orange

A buttery cream cheese filling is nestled in warm crêpes and served under a mandarin orange sauce.

1   cup all-purpose flour
2   tablespoons butter or
      margarine, melted
1   cup milk
4   large eggs
½   teaspoon salt
Vegetable cooking spray
2   tablespoons cornstarch
1   (11-ounce) can mandarin
      oranges

1   cup orange juice
¼   cup brandy
¼   cup butter or margarine,
      melted
1   (8-ounce) package cream
      cheese, softened
1   cup sifted powdered sugar
½   cup marshmallow cream
¼   teaspoon almond extract
½   cup chopped almonds

Combine first 3 ingredients, beating with a wire whisk until smooth. Add eggs, and beat well; stir in salt. Chill batter at least 2 hours.

Coat bottom of a 6-inch crêpe pan or heavy skillet with cooking spray; place over medium heat until hot.

Pour 2 tablespoons batter into pan; quickly tilt pan in all directions so batter covers bottom of pan. Cook 1 minute or until crêpe can be shaken loose from pan. Turn crêpe over, and cook about 30 seconds. Place crêpe on a towel to cool. Repeat with remaining batter. Stack crêpes between sheets of wax paper to prevent sticking.

Place cornstarch in a small saucepan. Set aside.

Drain mandarin oranges, reserving ¼ cup liquid, and set oranges aside. Combine mandarin orange juice, 1 cup orange juice, and brandy; gradually stir into cornstarch. Cook over medium heat, stirring constantly, until mixture thickens and boils. Boil 1 minute, stirring constantly. Remove from heat; add reserved mandarin oranges. Set aside, and keep warm.

Beat ¼ cup melted butter and cream cheese at medium speed of an electric mixer until creamy; gradually add powdered sugar, beating well. Add marshmallow cream, beating well. Stir in almond extract and almonds.

Spoon filling down center of spotty side of each crêpe; fold sides over. Spoon warm orange sauce over crêpes. Yield: 8 servings.

Classic Connecticut Cuisine
Connecticut Easter Seals
Uncasville, Connecticut

Fresh Blueberries Grand Marnier

¾ cup sugar
2 tablespoons cornstarch
⅛ teaspoon salt
2 cups milk
4 egg yolks, lightly beaten
3 tablespoons Grand Marnier
  or other orange-flavored
  liqueur

2 tablespoons butter or
  margarine
1½ teaspoons vanilla extract
1 cup whipping cream,
  whipped
4 cups fresh blueberries

Combine first 3 ingredients in a saucepan, stirring well. Gradually stir milk into mixture. Cook over medium heat, stirring constantly, until mixture thickens and boils. Boil 1 minute, stirring constantly.

Gradually stir about one-fourth of hot mixture into yolks; add to remaining hot mixture, stirring constantly. Cook over low heat 2 minutes, stirring constantly. Remove from heat; add liqueur, butter, and vanilla, stirring until butter melts. Let cool completely; fold in whipped cream. Cover and chill thoroughly.

To serve, spoon ½ cup blueberries into each of eight stemmed dessert glasses. Top each with ½ cup whipped cream mixture. Yield: 8 servings.   Hickory Stick Farm

Lakes Region Cuisine: A Centennial Celebration 1893-1993
Lakes Region General Hospital Auxiliary
Laconia, New Hampshire

Glazed Cranberry Citrus Compote

1 cup fresh or frozen
  cranberries, thawed
¼ cup sugar
1 tablespoon grated fresh
  ginger
1 tablespoon grated orange
  rind

3 oranges, peeled, sectioned,
  and seeded
2 grapefruit, peeled, sectioned,
  and seeded
1 kiwifruit, peeled and thinly
  sliced

Combine cranberries, sugar, and ginger in a small saucepan. Cover and cook 2 minutes over medium heat. Cook, stirring constantly, 1 to 2 additional minutes or until cranberry skins pop. Remove from heat.

Combine orange rind, orange sections, and grapefruit sections. Stir in cranberry mixture. Spoon fruit mixture evenly into individual dessert cups. Place sliced kiwifruit evenly over fruit mixture. Cover and chill thoroughly. Yield: 6 servings. Janet Simmons

A Culinary Tour of Homes
Big Canoe Chapel Women's Guild
Big Canoe, Georgia

Herbed Figs in White Wine

Figs, a Mediterranean mainstay, are herbed and honeyed for an Old World treat.

1 pound dried figs
2 cups dry white wine
2 teaspoons dried thyme
¼ cup honey

½ cup whipping cream,
  whipped
¼ cup chopped fresh mint

Prick each fig several times with a fork. Combine figs, wine, and thyme in a medium bowl. Cover and let stand at room temperature 48 hours. Add honey, stirring well. To serve, spoon fig mixture into individual dessert dishes. Dollop evenly with whipped cream, and sprinkle with chopped mint. Yield: 9 servings. Nan Rhodes

A Celebration of Food
Sisterhood Temple Beth David
Westwood, Massachusetts

Cocoa-Amaretto Mousse

Amaretto, chocolate, and coconut tango in this easy yet elegant dessert spooned into parfait glasses.

1 envelope unflavored gelatin	3 tablespoons cocoa
¼ cup cold water	2 cups whipping cream
1 (15-ounce) can cream of coconut	Garnishes: whipped cream, chocolate curls
¼ cup amaretto	

Sprinkle gelatin over cold water in a small saucepan; let stand 1 minute. Cook over low heat, stirring constantly, 2 minutes or until gelatin dissolves.

Combine cream of coconut, liqueur, and cocoa in a medium bowl. Add gelatin mixture, stirring well to combine. Cover and chill for 10 minutes.

Beat whipping cream at medium speed of an electric mixer until soft peaks form. Gently fold whipped cream into chocolate mixture. Spoon chocolate mixture evenly into eight dessert dishes. Cover and chill at least 1 hour or until chocolate mixture is set. Garnish, if desired. Yield: 8 servings.   Phyllis Robertson

Plain & Fancy Favorites
Montgomery Woman's Club
Cincinnati, Ohio

Brown Sugar Pudding

This pudding makes a rich sauce in the bottom with a cookie-like crust on top, much like a pudding cake.

½ cup butter or margarine, softened	Pinch of salt
1½ cups firmly packed brown sugar, divided	1 teaspoon ground nutmeg
	1 teaspoon ground cinnamon
1½ cups all-purpose flour	1 cup milk
2 teaspoons baking powder	½ cup raisins
	1½ cups water

Beat butter at medium speed of an electric mixer until creamy; gradually add ½ cup brown sugar, beating well.

Combine flour and next 4 ingredients; add to butter mixture alternately with milk, beginning and ending with flour mixture. Mix at low speed after each addition until blended. Stir in raisins. Pour batter into a greased 2-quart soufflé dish.

Combine remaining 1 cup brown sugar and water in a medium saucepan. Bring to a boil over medium-high heat. Pour sugar mixture over batter in dish. Bake at 375° for 40 minutes or until edges are golden and pull away from sides of dish. Let stand 10 minutes before serving. Yield: 6 servings.

Perfect Endings, The Art of Desserts
Friends of the Arts of the Tampa Museum of Art
Tampa, Florida

Fudge Pudding

Rich, fudgy pudding waits beneath a crunchy crust and beckons for a dollop of whipped cream or scoop of ice cream.

1 cup all-purpose flour	1 teaspoon vanilla extract
2 teaspoons baking powder	¾ cup chopped pecans
½ teaspoon salt	¾ cup firmly packed brown
¾ cup sugar	sugar
2 tablespoons cocoa	¼ cup cocoa
½ cup milk	1¼ cups boiling water
2 tablespoons butter or	Whipped cream or vanilla
margarine, melted	ice cream

Combine first 5 ingredients in a bowl. Add milk, butter, and vanilla, stirring well. Stir in pecans. Pour into a lightly greased 11- x 7- x 1½-inch baking dish.

Combine brown sugar and ¼ cup cocoa; sprinkle over batter. Carefully pour boiling water over top (do not stir).

Bake at 350° for 35 minutes. Serve warm with whipped cream or ice cream. Yield: 6 servings. Evelyn Jensen

Happy Memories and Thankful Hearts:
Traditions Kept and Blessings Shared
St. Christina's Catholic Church
Parker, South Dakota

New Orleans Bread Pudding with Lemon Sauce and Chantilly Cream

This bread pudding, stately in a warm pool of homemade Lemon Sauce, is generously drizzled with Chantilly Cream laced with Grand Marnier.

3 large eggs
1¼ cups sugar
¼ cup unsalted butter, melted
1½ teaspoons vanilla extract
1¼ teaspoons ground nutmeg
1¼ teaspoons ground
   cinnamon
2 cups milk

½ cup coarsely chopped
   pecans, toasted
½ cup raisins
5 cups day-old French bread
   cubes
Lemon Sauce
Chantilly Cream

Beat eggs in a large mixing bowl at high speed of an electric mixer 3 minutes; gradually add sugar, beating well. Add butter and next 3 ingredients, beating well. Gradually add milk, beating until blended. Stir in pecans and raisins.

Place French bread cubes in a greased 9- x 5- x 3-inch loafpan. Pour milk mixture over bread cubes, tossing gently to coat. Cover and chill mixture 45 minutes, pressing bread into liquid occasionally. Bake at 350° for 40 to 45 minutes or until pudding is very firm and lightly browned.

To serve, spoon 1½ tablespoons warm Lemon Sauce in center of each dessert plate; top each with about ½ cup bread pudding. Drizzle ¼ cup Chantilly Cream over bread pudding. Yield: 8 servings.

Lemon Sauce

1 large lemon, halved
¼ cup sugar
¾ cup water, divided

2 teaspoons cornstarch
1 teaspoon vanilla extract

Squeeze juice from lemon; place juice and lemon rind halves in a 1-quart saucepan. Add sugar and ½ cup water to saucepan. Bring mixture to a boil.

Combine cornstarch and remaining ¼ cup water; add to lemon mixture, stirring constantly. Stir in vanilla, and cook 1 minute over medium-high heat, stirring constantly. Remove and discard lemon rind. Yield: ¾ cup.

Chantilly Cream

1 cup whipping cream
1 teaspoon Grand Marnier or
  other orange-flavored liqueur
1 teaspoon brandy
1 teaspoon vanilla extract
¼ cup sugar
2 tablespoons sour cream

Combine first 4 ingredients in a large mixing bowl; beat at medium speed of an electric mixer 1 minute. Add sugar and sour cream; beat until soft peaks form. Yield: 2 cups.

Palette Pleasers
St. Luke Simpson United Methodist Women
Lake Charles, Louisiana

Raspberry Trifle

1 (5.1-ounce) package vanilla
  instant pudding mix
2 cups whipping cream
2 tablespoons sugar
1 teaspoon vanilla extract
1½ cups seedless raspberry jam
1 (1-pound) angel food cake,
  torn into bite-size pieces
½ cup slivered almonds,
  toasted
1½ cups fresh raspberries
Garnishes: toasted sliced
  almonds, fresh raspberries

Prepare pudding mix according to package directions. Beat whipping cream until foamy; gradually add sugar and vanilla, beating until soft peaks form. Fold half of whipped cream into pudding, reserving remaining half of whipped cream.

Cook raspberry jam in a small saucepan over low heat until jam melts. Place half of cake pieces in a 2½-quart trifle bowl; pour half of melted jam over cake. Layer ¼ cup almonds, ¾ cup raspberries, and half the pudding mixture over cake. Repeat layers; top with reserved whipped cream. Cover and chill at least 3 hours. Garnish, if desired. Yield: 15 servings.

Recipes & Reminiscences from the Oil Patch
West Kern Oil Museum
Taft, California

Chocolate-Raspberry Meringue

Free-form chocolate meringues create billowy layers for whipped cream and fresh raspberries.

4 egg whites
Dash of salt
1½ cups sugar
¼ cup cocoa
½ cup ground blanched
  almonds or hazelnuts

1 teaspoon vanilla extract
1 cup whipping cream,
  whipped
2 cups fresh raspberries

Beat egg whites and salt at high speed of an electric mixer until foamy. Gradually add sugar, 1 tablespoon at a time, beating until stiff peaks form and sugar dissolves (2 to 4 minutes).

Sift cocoa over egg white, and gently fold in just until blended. Gently fold in nuts and vanilla.

Spoon mixture into two 8-inch circles on a large parchment paper-lined baking sheet. Bake at 350° for 45 minutes. Let cool. Carefully remove from parchment paper to wire racks, and let cool completely.

Place 1 meringue on a serving platter. Top with half of whipped cream and 1 cup raspberries. Place remaining meringue over raspberries; top with remaining whipped cream and raspberries. Cover and chill 3 hours. Yield: 12 servings.

Note: Blanched nuts mean without skins.

Charted Courses
Child and Family Agency of Southeastern Connecticut
New London, Connecticut

Lemon Schaum Tortes

A takeoff of the classic Austrian dessert, each individual meringue tart makes a pocket for the lemony filling and sweetened whipped cream.

4 egg whites	**Lemon Filling**
½ teaspoon cream of tartar	1 cup whipping cream
¼ teaspoon salt	3 tablespoons sugar
1 cup sugar	Garnish: lemon curls

Combine first 3 ingredients in a large mixing bowl; beat at high speed of an electric mixer until foamy. Gradually add 1 cup sugar, 1 tablespoon at a time, beating until stiff peaks form and sugar dissolves (2 to 4 minutes).

Drop one-eighth of mixture onto a parchment paper-lined baking sheet; spread into a 3-inch circle. Make an indentation in center with back of a spoon. Repeat procedure with remaining mixture.

Bake at 225° for 1 hour; turn oven off, and partially open oven door. Let cool in oven 1 hour. Carefully remove meringues from parchment paper.

Just before serving, spoon Lemon Filling into each meringue.

Beat whipping cream and 3 tablespoons sugar at high speed of an electric mixer until soft peaks form. Spoon evenly over Lemon Filling. Garnish, if desired. Yield: 8 servings.

Lemon Filling

4 egg yolks	¼ cup fresh lemon juice
½ cup sugar	

Combine all ingredients in a medium saucepan. Cook over medium heat, stirring constantly, 4 minutes or until mixture is thickened. Let cool. Yield: ⅔ cup.

Entertaining Recipes II
Madison Zonta Club
Middleton, Wisconsin

Strawberry Meringue Shortcakes

The meringue adds a variation on the theme of the popular American shortcake. It's a delicious way to showcase strawberries.

6 cups ripe strawberries,
   halved lengthwise
¼ cup sugar
¼ cup shortening
1 cup sugar, divided
2 large eggs, separated
1 cup sifted cake flour

1½ teaspoons baking powder
¼ teaspoon salt
½ cup milk
½ teaspoon vanilla extract
½ cup whipping cream,
   whipped

Combine strawberries and ¼ cup sugar, stirring well. Cover and chill at least 2 hours. Drain and set aside.

Beat shortening at medium speed of an electric mixer until fluffy; gradually add ½ cup sugar, beating well. Add egg yolks; beat well.

Combine flour, baking powder, and salt. Add to shortening mixture alternately with milk, beginning and ending with flour mixture. Mix at low speed after each addition until blended. Stir in vanilla. Pour batter into two greased 8-inch round cakepans.

Beat egg whites at high speed until foamy. Gradually add remaining ½ cup sugar, 1 tablespoon at a time, beating until stiff peaks form and sugar dissolves (2 to 4 minutes). Place small dollops on top of batter; spread evenly over batter, leaving a 1-inch border around edges. Bake at 350° for 25 minutes. To serve, top with reserved strawberries and whipped cream. Yield: 12 servings.

Food for Thought
The Junior League of Birmingham, Alabama

Caramel-Pecan Crunch Ice Cream

Ice cream has never had it so good! Buttery pecans and ribbons of caramel are waiting for a big bowl and a spoon.

2 tablespoons butter or
   margarine, melted
1 cup chopped pecans
½ cup sugar
8 cups half-and-half

1 cup firmly packed brown
   sugar
2 (12-ounce) jars caramel
   topping
1 tablespoon vanilla extract

Combine first 3 ingredients in an 8-inch cast-iron skillet, and cook over medium heat, stirring constantly, 12 to 14 minutes or until sugar is golden. Pour mixture onto greased wax paper. Let cool completely; break into small pieces. Set aside.

Combine half-and-half and remaining 3 ingredients; stir until brown sugar and caramel topping dissolve. Pour mixture into freezer container of a 6-quart hand-turned or electric freezer. Add reserved pecan crunch pieces. Freeze according to manufacturer's instructions.

Pack freezer with additional ice and rock salt, and let stand 1 hour before serving. Yield: 15 cups. Sue Lewis

Note: You can use a 4-quart electric freezer, but a small amount of ice cream may leak from top.

Briarwood Recipes to Crown Your Table
Women's Ministries of Briarwood Presbyterian Church
Birmingham, Alabama

Peach Sorbet

Succulent fresh peaches in this refreshing sorbet announce summer's relief.

2 fresh peaches, peeled and chopped
¾ cup orange juice

¼ cup sugar
2 tablespoons lemon juice

Place peaches in container of an electric blender or food processor; process until smooth, stopping once to scrape down sides.

Combine peach puree, orange juice, sugar, and lemon juice; stir well. Pour into an 8-inch square dish. Cover and freeze 40 minutes or until almost firm, stirring occasionally.

Spoon mixture into a bowl, and beat at medium speed of an electric mixer until slushy. Return to dish; cover and freeze until firm, stirring occasionally. Yield: 1¾ cups. Ratana Tak

Note: This recipe can be doubled.

A Culinary Quilt
Edison/Computech P.T.S.A.
Fresno, California

Frosty Chocolate-Peanut Butter Loaf

A chocoholic's dream! Layers of buttery cookies, rich chocolate, and creamy peanut butter are drizzled with even more chocolate. Yum!

1 cup crushed vanilla wafers (about 30 wafers)
½ cup chopped peanuts
2 tablespoons powdered sugar
3 tablespoons butter or margarine, melted
1 cup chocolate syrup
½ cup sweetened condensed milk

1 teaspoon vanilla extract
2 cups whipping cream, divided
1 (3-ounce) package cream cheese, softened
¾ cup sifted powdered sugar
⅓ cup creamy peanut butter
⅓ cup milk
Chocolate syrup

Line a 9- x 5- x 3-inch loafpan with aluminum foil. Set aside.

Combine first 4 ingredients in a small bowl. Firmly press ¾ cup mixture in bottom of prepared loafpan. Cover and freeze. Reserve remaining crumb mixture.

Combine 1 cup chocolate syrup and condensed milk in a saucepan. Cook over medium heat until mixture comes to a boil, stirring often. Remove from heat, and stir in vanilla. Let cool. Cover and chill thoroughly. Beat 1½ cups whipping cream until soft peaks form. Gently fold whipped cream into chocolate mixture.

Divide chocolate mixture in half. Spoon half of chocolate mixture into prepared crust; cover and freeze 1 hour. Cover and chill remaining chocolate mixture.

Beat cream cheese at medium speed of an electric mixer until creamy. Gradually add ¾ cup powdered sugar, beating well. Add peanut butter and milk, beating well. Beat remaining ½ cup whipping cream until soft peaks form. Gently fold whipped cream into peanut butter mixture; spoon over frozen chocolate mixture. Freeze 1 hour.

Spoon remaining chilled chocolate mixture over frozen peanut butter mixture. Sprinkle with reserved crumb mixture. Cover and freeze at least 8 hours.

Let stand 10 minutes before serving. Invert onto a large serving platter. Remove and discard foil. Serve with chocolate syrup. Yield: 10 servings.

Shera Shirley

Making a Memory
Hospice Circle of Love
Enid, Oklahoma

Eggs & Cheese

Tomato and Basil Tart, page 157

Wine Eggs Mornay

An elegant breakfast awaits–poached eggs topped with a buttery wine sauce rest upon toasted English muffins.

3 English muffins, split
Butter or margarine, softened
3 tablespoons butter or margarine
3 tablespoons all-purpose flour
1 cup half-and-half
¼ cup dry white wine
⅓ cup (1.3 ounces) shredded Swiss cheese
¾ teaspoon salt

¼ teaspoon ground nutmeg
Dash of pepper
6 large eggs
1 tablespoon butter or margarine
6 slices Canadian bacon
Finely chopped green pepper (optional)
Chopped fresh chives (optional)

Spread cut sides of muffins with softened butter. Broil 5½ inches from heat (with electric oven door partially opened) until lightly browned. Set aside.

Melt 3 tablespoons butter in a heavy saucepan over low heat; add flour, stirring until smooth. Cook 1 minute, stirring constantly. Gradually add half-and-half and wine; cook over medium heat, stirring constantly, until mixture is thickened and bubbly. Add cheese, salt, nutmeg, and pepper; stir until cheese melts. Set sauce aside, and keep warm.

Lightly grease a large saucepan; add water to depth of 2 inches. Bring to a boil; reduce heat, and maintain at a simmer. Working with 2 eggs at a time, break eggs, one at a time, into a saucer; slip eggs into water. Simmer 5 minutes or to desired degree of doneness. Remove with a slotted spoon; trim edges, if desired. Repeat procedure with remaining 4 eggs. Set aside, and keep warm.

Melt 1 tablespoon butter in a large skillet over medium-high heat. Add Canadian bacon, and cook until browned on both sides.

Place a slice of Canadian bacon on each muffin half; top with a poached egg, and cover with sauce. If desired, sprinkle with green pepper or chives. Yield: 6 servings.   Nancy Apgar

Applause! Oklahoma's Best Performing Recipes
Oklahoma City Orchestra League
Oklahoma City, Oklahoma

Good Mornin' Oklahoma Brunch

A breakfast of warm cornbread smothered with a mock hollandaise sauce and topped with crispy bacon, green onions, and melted cheese gets you going.

1 cup yellow cornmeal
⅓ cup all-purpose flour
1 teaspoon baking powder
¼ teaspoon baking soda
½ teaspoon salt
1 large egg, beaten
1 cup buttermilk
3 tablespoons butter or margarine
3 tablespoons all-purpose flour

2 cups milk
¼ teaspoon salt
⅛ teaspoon pepper
½ cup mayonnaise
6 hard-cooked large eggs, peeled and coarsely chopped
½ cup cooked crumbled bacon
½ cup chopped green onions
½ cup shredded Cheddar cheese

Combine first 5 ingredients in a bowl; add beaten egg and buttermilk, stirring well. Pour batter into a greased 8-inch square pan. Bake at 400° for 20 minutes or until golden. Cut warm cornbread into 9 squares. Keep warm.

Melt butter in a heavy saucepan over low heat; add 3 tablespoons flour, stirring until smooth. Cook 1 minute, stirring constantly. Gradually add milk; cook over medium heat, stirring constantly, until mixture is thickened and bubbly. Stir in salt, pepper, mayonnaise, and chopped eggs.

To serve, place cornbread squares on individual serving plates. Spoon egg mixture evenly over cornbread. Sprinkle bacon, green onions, and cheese over egg mixture. Yield: 9 servings.

Cafe Oklahoma
The Junior Service League of Midwest City, Oklahoma

Breakfast Burritos

Sausage and eggs wrapped in a tortilla are a filling breakfast on-the-run.

½ cup butter or margarine, divided
¾ cup chopped onion
½ cup chopped green pepper

1 pound ground pork sausage
12 large eggs, lightly beaten
12 (7-inch) flour tortillas
Picante sauce

Melt ¼ cup butter in a large skillet over medium-high heat. Add onion and pepper; cook, stirring constantly, until vegetables are crisp-tender. Remove from skillet, and set aside.

Brown sausage in skillet, stirring until it crumbles; drain. Wipe drippings from skillet with a paper towel.

Melt remaining ¼ cup butter in skillet over medium heat. Add onion mixture, sausage, and eggs. Cook, without stirring, until egg mixture begins to set on bottom. Draw a spatula across bottom of skillet to form large curds. Continue cooking until eggs are firm, but still moist (do not stir constantly). Set aside.

Wrap tortillas tightly in aluminum foil; bake at 350° for 15 minutes. Spoon about ½ cup egg mixture down center of each warm tortilla. Roll up tortillas. Serve immediately with picante sauce. Yield: 12 burritos.

Joyce Barnes

Family Favorites
Optimist Clubs of Alabama/Mississippi District
Montgomery, Alabama

Jalapeño Omelet

10 slices bacon
1 cup chopped onion
2½ cups sliced fresh mushrooms
6 large eggs, lightly beaten
½ cup milk
1 tablespoon white wine Worcestershire sauce

3 jalapeño peppers, seeded and chopped
½ cup (2 ounces) shredded Monterey Jack cheese
½ cup (2 ounces) shredded extra sharp Cheddar cheese

Cook bacon in a large skillet until crisp; remove bacon, reserving 2 tablespoons drippings in skillet. Crumble bacon, and set aside.

Cook onion in drippings in skillet over medium-high heat, stirring constantly, until crisp-tender. Add mushrooms, and cook, stirring constantly, until tender.

Combine eggs and next 3 ingredients. Add egg mixture to mushroom mixture in skillet. As mixture starts to cook, gently lift edges of omelet with a spatula, and tilt pan so uncooked portion flows underneath. Sprinkle with cheeses. Cover and cook 2 to 3 additional minutes to allow uncooked portion on top to set. Sprinkle with bacon. Cut into fourths; serve immediately. Yield: 4 servings.

Tasteful Treasures
Docent Guild, Bowers Museum of Cultural Art
Santa Ana, California

Eggplant and Sweet Pepper Frittata

The original recipe made two thin frittatas, but we cooked it all in one large skillet to make a frittata big enough to cut into wedges. You'll enjoy the colorful red and green peppers and sublime eggplant.

⅔ **cup chopped sweet red pepper**
⅔ **cup chopped green pepper**
¾ **cup peeled and chopped eggplant**
3 **tablespoons olive oil**

10 **large eggs**
½ **cup milk**
1 **teaspoon salt**
¼ **teaspoon ground red pepper**
2 **tablespoons freshly grated Parmesan cheese**

Cook first 3 ingredients in oil in an ovenproof 10-inch nonstick skillet over medium-high heat, stirring constantly, 3 minutes or until vegetables are tender.

Combine eggs and next 3 ingredients in a large bowl; stir well. Add egg mixture to skillet. As mixture starts to cook, gently lift edges of frittata with a spatula, and tilt pan so uncooked portion flows underneath. Cover and cook over low heat 10 to 12 minutes to allow uncooked portion on top to set. Uncover, sprinkle with cheese, and broil 3 inches from heat (with electric oven door partially opened) 2 minutes or until golden. Cut into wedges. Serve immediately. Yield: 6 servings.

Around Our Table: California Cooks Kosher
Jewish Family Service of Los Angeles, California

Artichoke Brunch Casserole

There's a lot to love in this savory breakfast casserole—fresh mushrooms, artichokes, and olives layered with plenty of melted sharp Cheddar cheese.

1½ cups chopped onion
½ cup butter or margarine, melted and divided
12 large eggs, beaten
4 cups (16 ounces) shredded sharp Cheddar cheese
1 (8-ounce) package sliced fresh mushrooms
2 (14-ounce) cans artichoke hearts, drained and quartered

½ cup sliced ripe olives
3 tablespoons minced fresh parsley
2 cloves garlic, minced
¾ teaspoon dried oregano
½ teaspoon dried thyme
¼ teaspoon ground red pepper
¾ cup fine, dry breadcrumbs

Cook onion in ¼ cup plus 1 tablespoon butter in a large skillet over medium-high heat, stirring constantly, until tender.

Combine onion mixture, eggs, and next 9 ingredients in a large bowl; stir well. Pour into an ungreased 13- x 9- x 2-inch pan.

Combine remaining 3 tablespoons melted butter and breadcrumbs in a small bowl; stir well. Sprinkle over egg mixture. Bake at 350° for 40 to 45 minutes or until set and golden. Let stand 10 minutes before serving. Yield: 10 servings.

Food for the Journey
St. Francis Xavier College Church Choir
St. Louis, Missouri

Tomato and Basil Tart

Fresh Roma tomatoes and fragrant basil pair perfectly for this quiche-like tart.

1½ cups all-purpose flour	2 tablespoons chopped fresh chives
½ cup butter or margarine, cut into pieces	3 large eggs, lightly beaten
1 large egg	¾ cup half-and-half
1 cup (4 ounces) shredded mozzarella cheese	½ teaspoon ground mustard
4 Roma tomatoes, thinly sliced	¼ teaspoon salt
¼ cup slivered fresh basil	¼ teaspoon pepper
	Garnish: fresh basil

Position knife blade in food processor bowl; add flour and butter. Process until mixture is crumbly. Add 1 egg; process until mixture forms a ball.

Press dough on bottom and up sides of a 9-inch tart pan. Prick with a fork. Bake at 350° for 20 minutes. Cool completely on a wire rack.

Sprinkle mozzarella cheese over prepared pastry shell; top with sliced tomato, basil, and chives. Combine 3 eggs and next 4 ingredients; stir well. Pour over chives.

Bake at 400° for 30 minutes or until set. Remove from oven, and let cool on a wire rack 10 minutes. Garnish, if desired. Yield: 6 servings.

Simply Classic
The Junior League of Seattle, Washington

Chicken-Pecan Quiche

Wow! We loved this Southern take on quiche with its Cheddar cheese, chicken, pecan filling, and savory Cheddar crust so much we gave it our highest rating.

1 cup all-purpose flour
1 cup (4 ounces) shredded sharp Cheddar cheese
¾ cup chopped pecans
½ teaspoon salt
¼ teaspoon paprika
⅓ cup vegetable oil
1 cup sour cream
½ cup chicken broth
¼ cup mayonnaise

3 large eggs, lightly beaten
2 cups finely chopped cooked chicken
½ cup (2 ounces) shredded sharp Cheddar cheese
¼ cup minced onion
¼ teaspoon dried dillweed
3 drops of hot sauce
¼ cup pecan halves

Combine first 5 ingredients in a medium bowl; stir well. Add oil; stir well. Firmly press mixture on bottom and up sides of a 9-inch deep-dish pieplate. Bake at 350° for 12 minutes. Cool completely.

Combine sour cream, broth, mayonnaise, and eggs; stir with a wire whisk until smooth. Stir in chicken, ½ cup cheese, onion, dillweed, and hot sauce. Pour chicken mixture over prepared crust. Arrange pecan halves over chicken mixture. Bake at 350° for 55 minutes or until set. Let stand 10 minutes before serving. Yield: one 9-inch quiche.

True Grits: Tall Tales and Recipes from the New South
The Junior League of Atlanta, Georgia

Crustless California Quiche

1 cup chopped fresh mushrooms
½ cup finely chopped celery
½ cup finely chopped green onions
2 tablespoons butter or margarine, melted
6 large eggs
1½ cups half-and-half
¼ cup all-purpose flour

1 teaspoon paprika
½ teaspoon seasoned salt
½ teaspoon hot sauce
1 cup finely chopped cooked ham
3 tablespoons dry white wine
1 cup (4 ounces) shredded Swiss cheese
1 cup (4 ounces) shredded Cheddar cheese

Cook first 3 ingredients in butter in a large skillet over medium-high heat, stirring constantly, 2 minutes or until crisp-tender. Set aside.

Beat eggs and half-and-half at medium speed of an electric mixer until blended. Add flour and next 3 ingredients, beating well. Stir in vegetable mixture, ham, and remaining ingredients. Pour into a greased 10-inch quiche dish. Bake at 350° for 50 minutes or until a knife inserted in center comes out clean. Let stand 10 minutes before serving. Yield: one 10-inch quiche.

Celebrating California
Children's Home Society of California
San Diego, California

Breakfast Cloud Popover

If you like a Dutch Baby–puffy and golden browned in a skillet–you'll love this. Serve it with fresh berries and a dollop of whipped cream for a delicious Sunday breakfast.

½ **cup all-purpose flour**   3 **large eggs**
¼ **teaspoon salt**   2 **tablespoons butter or**
½ **cup milk**   **margarine**

Combine first 4 ingredients in a mixing bowl; beat at low speed of an electric mixer just until smooth.

Melt butter in a 10-inch cast-iron skillet. Pour batter into hot skillet. Bake at 450° for 10 to 12 minutes or until puffed and browned. Serve immediately. Yield: 4 servings.

Maine Ingredients
The Junior League of Portland, Maine

Fabulous French Toast

A luscious honey-pecan topping glazes thick slices of fabulous French toast.

2 large eggs	6 slices barbecue bread
¾ cup milk	2 tablespoons butter or
1 teaspoon vanilla extract	margarine, divided
¾ cup pancake mix	Pecan Nut Topping

Combine first 3 ingredients in a medium bowl; beat well with a wire whisk. Add pancake mix, beating until smooth. Pour mixture into a 13- x 9- x 2-inch baking dish. Place bread slices in egg mixture; turn slices to coat evenly. Let stand 5 minutes or until all liquid is absorbed.

Melt 1 tablespoon butter in a large skillet. Add 3 slices bread; cook over medium heat 3 minutes on each side or until golden. Remove from pan, and keep warm. Repeat procedure with remaining butter and bread slices. Serve immediately with Pecan Nut Topping. Yield: 6 servings.

Pecan Nut Topping

½ cup butter or margarine,	⅓ cup chopped pecans,
softened	toasted
½ cup honey	

Combine butter and honey, stirring until smooth. Add nuts, and stir well. Yield: 1 cup.   Mary Jo Hieb

The Museum Cookbook
Longport Historical Society
Longport, New Jersey

Italian Ricotta

Ready for a new cooking venture? Try this homemade cheese, a slightly sweet version of ricotta. It makes dreamy lasagna.

8 cups milk	1 teaspoon salt
2 cups whipping cream	¼ cup white vinegar
1 tablespoon sugar	

Combine first 4 ingredients in a large Dutch oven. Bring to a boil, stirring often. Remove from heat. Add vinegar, stirring well. Let stand 10 minutes.

Line a strainer with four layers of cheesecloth. Pour cheese mixture into strainer; discard liquid. Place strainer in a bowl. Cover loosely with plastic wrap; chill up to 3 hours or until cheese reaches desired consistency. Spoon into bowl; discard liquid. Cover and store in refrigerator up to 2 weeks. Yield: about 3 cups.   Lori Bronco

Literally Delicious
Friends of the Gates Public Library
Rochester, New York

Rose's Crab Fondue

The seventies are back–dig out your fondue pot and disco music!

1½ cups (6 ounces) grated Gruyère cheese	¼ cup sherry
1 (8-ounce) package cream cheese	1 pound fresh crabmeat, drained and flaked
½ cup half-and-half	1 (16-ounce) loaf French bread, cut into 1-inch cubes

Combine first 4 ingredients in top of a double boiler; bring water to a boil. Reduce heat to medium; cook until cheeses melt, stirring occasionally. Add crabmeat. Cook 5 to 10 minutes or until bubbly, stirring often. Pour into fondue pot. Serve fondue with bread cubes. Yield: 4 cups.   Rose Seward

Dock 'n Dine in Dorchester
Long Wharf Lighthouse Committee
Cambridge, Maryland

Chile Cheese Soufflé

This mock soufflé is a lazy make-ahead casserole that's laced with Cheddar cheese and green chiles.

8 slices white bread
½ cup butter or margarine,
   melted
1 cup (4 ounces) shredded
   Cheddar cheese
1 (4.5-ounce) can chopped
   green chiles

8 large eggs, separated
¼ teaspoon salt
¼ teaspoon pepper
2 cups milk

Trim crusts from bread; cut bread into ½-inch cubes, and place in a large bowl. Pour butter over bread cubes; toss well. Spread in a lightly greased 13- x 9- x 2-inch baking dish; top with cheese, and sprinkle with chiles.

Beat egg whites at high speed of an electric mixer until stiff peaks form. Beat yolks, salt, and pepper at medium speed; gradually stir in milk. Fold in beaten egg white. Pour egg mixture over cheese mixture. Cover and chill 8 hours. Bake at 325° for 40 minutes or until soufflé is set and lightly browned. Let stand 10 minutes before serving. Yield: 8 servings.

Carol Rozhon Raby

The Guild Cookbook, Volume IV
The Valparaiso University Guild
Valparaiso, Indiana

Cheese and Onion Pudding

Onions sizzle to sweet caramelized perfection before baking in this savory cheese pudding.

2 medium onions, sliced
2 tablespoons butter or
   margarine
2 cups milk
1 cup soft breadcrumbs

1 cup (4 ounces) shredded
   Cheddar cheese
3 large eggs, lightly beaten
½ teaspoon salt
⅛ teaspoon pepper

Cook onion in butter in a large skillet over medium heat 30 minutes, stirring constantly, until golden. Stir in milk. Combine milk mixture and breadcrumbs in a large bowl. Stir in cheese and remaining ingredients. Spoon onion mixture into a greased 1½-quart casserole. Bake at 375° for 30 minutes or until golden. Serve immediately. Yield: 6 servings.   Sybil Chandler

The Stoney Creek Recipe Collection:
A Treasury of Culinary Favorites and Historical Vignettes
Stoney Creek Presbyterian Foundation
Beaufort, South Carolina

Apple and Cheddar Gratin

Tart apples and extra sharp Cheddar cheese make a classic combination that's delightful as a dessert with vanilla ice cream or as an accompaniment with roast pork, chicken, or ham.

2 **pounds Granny Smith apples, peeled and cut into ¼-inch slices**
½ **cup raisins**
½ **teaspoon ground cinnamon**
¼ **cup fresh lemon juice**
¾ **cup firmly packed brown sugar**

½ **cup all-purpose flour**
⅛ **teaspoon salt**
¼ **cup unsalted butter, cut into small pieces**
1 **cup (4 ounces) finely shredded extra sharp Cheddar cheese**

Arrange apple slices in a buttered 11- x 7- x 1½-inch baking dish; sprinkle with raisins, cinnamon, and lemon juice.

Combine sugar, flour, and salt in a bowl. Cut in butter with pastry blender until mixture is crumbly. Add cheese; toss well. Sprinkle cheese mixture over apple mixture. Bake at 350° for 40 to 45 minutes or until apple is tender. Yield: 6 servings.   Jane Brannon

Cooking with Class
Park Maitland School
Maitland, Florida

Baja Quesadillas

Fresh avocado, asparagus, and white Cheddar cheese lend trendy California appeal to the typical Tex-Mex quesadilla.

3 fresh asparagus spears
1 large Anaheim chile pepper
1 small leek
1 medium potato, peeled and diced
1½ cups chopped onion
¼ cup butter or margarine, melted and divided
½ teaspoon salt
¼ teaspoon pepper
4 (8-inch) flour tortillas
1 cup chopped avocado
¼ cup chopped fresh cilantro
1 cup (4 ounces) shredded white Cheddar cheese
Salsa
Garnish: fresh cilantro sprigs

Snap off tough ends of asparagus. Remove scales with a vegetable peeler, if desired. Cut into ½-inch pieces. Set aside.

Wash and dry chile pepper; place on an aluminum foil-lined baking sheet. Broil pepper 5½ inches from heat (with electric oven door partially opened) about 5 minutes on each side or until pepper looks blistered.

Place pepper in a heavy-duty, zip-top plastic bag; close bag, and let stand 10 minutes. Peel pepper; remove core and seeds. Chop pepper; set aside.

Remove and discard root, tough outer leaves, and top of leek to where dark green begins to pale. Cut leek into ¼-inch slices. Cook leek, potato, and onion in 2 tablespoons butter in a large skillet over medium-high heat, stirring constantly, until tender. Stir in asparagus and chopped pepper; cook 3 minutes. Stir in salt and pepper.

Place 2 tortillas on a baking sheet; brush 1 side of each tortilla with 1 tablespoon butter. Turn tortillas over; spread half of potato mixture over each tortilla; sprinkle evenly with avocado, cilantro, and cheese. Place remaining tortillas on top of cheese. Brush with remaining 1 tablespoon butter. Bake at 400° for 6 minutes.

Broil 3 inches from heat (with electric oven door partially opened) 1 minute or until golden. Cut each tortilla in half. Serve warm with salsa. Garnish, if desired. Yield: 4 servings.

Seaport Savories
TWIG Junior Auxiliary of Alexandria Hospital
Alexandria, Virginia

Fish & Shellfish

Cape Fear Crab Cakes with Lemon-Dill Sauce, page 177

Crisp Parmesan Catfish with Garden Salsa

Vibrant tomato, zucchini, and yellow squash are splashed with tequila and sherry vinegar to make a cheeky partner for crispy baked catfish.

1 cup plus 2 tablespoons freshly grated Parmesan cheese
¼ cup plus 2 tablespoons all-purpose flour
½ teaspoon salt
½ teaspoon freshly ground pepper
¼ teaspoon ground red pepper
1 large egg, beaten
2 tablespoons milk
6 farm-raised catfish fillets (about 1½ pounds)
Garden Salsa

Combine first 5 ingredients in a shallow dish. Combine egg and milk in another shallow dish.

Dip fillets in egg mixture; dredge in flour mixture. Place fillets in a greased 13- x 9- x 2-inch pan. Bake at 500° for 14 minutes or until fish flakes easily when tested with a fork. Serve with Garden Salsa. Yield: 6 servings.

Garden Salsa

2 cups finely chopped zucchini
2 cups finely chopped yellow squash
3 fresh tomatillos, husked and chopped
1 medium tomato, seeded and chopped
½ cup finely chopped purple onion
1 medium carrot, scraped and finely chopped
2 jalapeño peppers, seeded and finely chopped
2 tablespoons chopped fresh cilantro
3 tablespoons tequila
2 tablespoons sherry vinegar
1 teaspoon ground cumin
½ teaspoon salt
½ teaspoon sugar
⅛ teaspoon freshly ground pepper

Combine all ingredients in a large bowl; stir well. Cover and chill 8 hours. Yield: 5 cups.

The Artful Table
Dallas Museum Art League
Dallas, Texas

Clara Wentraub's Cod Creole

Creole's familiar culinary "holy trinity" of onion, peppers, and celery embellishes this fish.

Vegetable cooking spray
1 large onion, coarsely chopped
2 medium-size green peppers, seeded and chopped
1 clove garlic, minced
1 (14.5-ounce) can whole tomatoes, undrained and chopped
1 (8-ounce) package sliced fresh mushrooms

2 medium tomatoes, peeled and coarsely chopped
½ cup chopped celery
1 jalapeño pepper, finely chopped
½ teaspoon sugar
1 pound cod fillets, cut into 4 pieces

Coat a large nonstick skillet with cooking spray; place over medium-high heat until hot. Add onion, green pepper, and garlic; cook, stirring constantly, until vegetables are crisp-tender. Add canned tomatoes and next 5 ingredients. Bring to a boil. Cover, reduce heat, and simmer 15 minutes. Uncover and simmer 10 minutes.

Place fillets in a 13- x 9- x 2-inch baking dish coated with cooking spray. Pour tomato mixture over cod. Bake, uncovered, at 400° for 20 minutes or until fish flakes easily when tested with a fork. Yield: 4 servings.

Ethel Green

Beyond Brisket
Sisterhood of Temple Israel
Natick, Massachusetts

Stuffed Flounder

Plumped with crabmeat filling and bathed in a white wine sauce, these fish bundles are decidedly company fare.

¼ cup chopped onion
¼ cup plus 3 tablespoons
   butter or margarine, melted
   and divided
1 (4-ounce) can sliced
   mushrooms
½ pound fresh crabmeat,
   drained and flaked
½ cup crumbled saltine
   crackers (about 12 crackers)
2 tablespoons chopped fresh
   parsley

8 (6-ounce) flounder fillets
¼ teaspoon salt
¼ teaspoon pepper
3 tablespoons all-purpose flour
¼ teaspoon salt
1 cup milk
⅓ cup dry white wine
1 cup (4 ounces) shredded
   Swiss cheese
Paprika

Cook onion in ¼ cup butter in a large skillet over medium-high heat, stirring constantly, until tender. Drain mushrooms, reserving liquid. Chop mushrooms, and add to onion in skillet. Add crabmeat, cracker crumbs, and parsley to onion mixture; stir well. Spread onion mixture evenly over each fillet; roll up fillets, and place, seam side down, in a greased 13- x 9- x 2-inch baking dish. Sprinkle with ¼ teaspoon salt and pepper.

Melt remaining 3 tablespoons butter in a heavy saucepan over low heat; add flour and ¼ teaspoon salt, stirring until smooth. Cook 1 minute, stirring constantly. Combine reserved mushroom liquid and enough milk to equal 1½ cups. Gradually add milk mixture to pan; cook over medium heat, stirring constantly, until thickened and bubbly. Stir in wine, and cook 2 additional minutes. Pour sauce over fillets. Bake, uncovered, at 400° for 25 minutes. Sprinkle with cheese and paprika. Bake 5 additional minutes or until fish flakes easily when tested with a fork. Yield: 8 servings.

Feed My Sheep
Signal Mountain Presbyterian Church
Signal Mountain, Tennessee

Lemon-Broiled Orange Roughy

Dijon mustard masterminds the familiar lemon-butter sauce in this recipe. Brush the sauce over fillets for an entrée in minutes.

3 tablespoons lemon juice
1 tablespoon Dijon mustard
1 tablespoon reduced-calorie margarine, melted
¼ teaspoon coarsely ground pepper

4 (4-ounce) orange roughy fillets
Coarsely ground pepper
Garnish: lemon slices

Combine lemon juice, mustard, margarine, and ¼ teaspoon pepper; stir well.

Place fillets on a lightly greased rack in broiler pan. Brush half of lemon juice mixture on fillets. Broil 5½ inches from heat (with electric oven door partially opened) 10 to 12 minutes or until fish flakes easily when tested with a fork. Transfer fillets to a serving platter. Drizzle remaining half of lemon juice mixture over fillets. Sprinkle with pepper; garnish, if desired. Yield: 4 servings.

Amazing Graces: Meals and Memories from the Parsonage
Texas Conference United Methodist Minister's Spouses Association
Palestine, Texas

Baked Salmon with Wine

Sweeter than most white wine, the Sauterne accentuates the earthy hickory-smoked salt found in the spice section of your supermarket.

5 (6-ounce) salmon fillets
¾ cup Sauterne
¼ cup vegetable oil
3 large cloves garlic, minced
2 tablespoons soy sauce

1 teaspoon salt
Vegetable cooking spray
¾ teaspoon hickory-smoked
   salt, divided

Place fillets in a large heavy-duty, zip-top plastic bag. Combine wine and next 4 ingredients in container of an electric blender; process 30 seconds. Pour ¾ cup marinade over fillets. Seal bag securely; marinate in refrigerator 3 hours, turning occasionally. Chill remaining marinade for basting.

Remove fillets from marinade, discarding marinade. Place fillets in a 13- x 9- x 2-inch baking dish coated with cooking spray; sprinkle with ¼ teaspoon hickory-smoked salt. Bake at 350° for 15 minutes or until fish flakes easily when tested with a fork, basting twice with reserved marinade and sprinkling with remaining ½ teaspoon hickory-smoked salt. Yield: 5 servings.   Ines Kiffer

Favorite Recipes from Our Best Cooks
Senior Center of Ketchikan, Alaska

Grilled Salmon with Galliano Beurre Blanc

Indulge salmon fillets with this sweet licorice-flavored butter sauce.

½ cup butter, divided
2 tablespoons grated orange
   rind
1 tablespoon chopped fresh
   parsley
1 tablespoon chopped shallot
⅔ cup fresh orange juice

¼ cup Galliano liqueur or
   other anise-flavored liqueur
¼ cup plus 2 tablespoons
   whipping cream
Vegetable cooking spray
6 (8-ounce) salmon fillets

Melt 1 tablespoon butter in a medium saucepan over medium-high heat. Add orange rind, parsley, and shallot; cook, stirring constantly, until shallot is tender. Add orange juice and liqueur. Bring to a boil; reduce heat, and simmer, uncovered, 2 minutes or until liquid is reduced by half.

Add whipping cream. Bring to a boil; reduce heat, and simmer, uncovered, 7 minutes or until liquid is reduced by half. Remove from heat, and add remaining ¼ cup plus 3 tablespoons butter, stirring until butter melts. Cover and keep warm.

Coat grill rack with cooking spray; place rack on grill over medium-hot coals (350° to 400°). Place fillets on rack, and grill 7 to 9 minutes on each side or until fish flakes easily when tested with a fork. To serve, spoon butter sauce over fillets. Yield: 6 servings.

Sailing Through Dinner
Three Squares Press
Stonington, Connecticut

Spiced Cold Salmon

Marinated in a plucky mix of vinegar, allspice, and peppercorns, the salmon takes on a spicy-sweet flavor.

4 cups water
2 teaspoons salt, divided
6 (6-ounce) salmon steaks
1½ teaspoons whole black
   peppercorns

1½ teaspoons whole allspice
½ cup white wine vinegar

Combine water and 1 teaspoon salt in a fish poacher or large skillet. Add steaks; cover and cook over low heat 30 minutes or until fish flakes easily when tested with a fork. Remove steaks from poaching liquid, reserving liquid; drain steaks on paper towels.

Combine 1¼ cups reserved poaching liquid, remaining 1 teaspoon salt, peppercorns, allspice, and vinegar in a saucepan; bring to a boil. Reduce heat, and simmer 5 minutes. Place steaks in a 13- x 9- x 2-inch baking dish; pour vinegar mixture over steaks. Cover and chill 8 hours. Remove steaks from vinegar mixture to serve; discard vinegar mixture. Yield: 6 servings.

Cooking with Fire
Fairfield Historical Society
Fairfield, Connecticut

Italian Baked Scrod

2 pounds scrod fillets
1 medium onion, sliced
½ teaspoon salt
⅛ teaspoon pepper
1 (14½-ounce) can Italian-style stewed tomatoes, drained and chopped
1 (2¼-ounce) can sliced ripe olives

2 tablespoons chopped fresh basil
2 tablespoons chopped fresh parsley
1 clove garlic, minced
2 tablespoons clam juice or tomato juice

Wash fillets, and pat dry. Arrange onion in a 13- x 9- x 2-inch baking dish. Place fillets over onion. Sprinkle with salt and pepper. Add tomatoes, olives, basil, parsley, and garlic. Sprinkle with clam juice.

Bake fillets, uncovered, at 375° for 20 minutes or until fish flakes easily when tested with a fork. Serve fish with a slotted spoon. Yield: 4 servings.

Paul Newman

As You Like It
Williamstown Theatre Festival Guild
Williamstown, Massachusetts

Baked Snapper with Ginger-Cilantro Butter

Butter rosettes melt temptingly atop warm seasoned snapper steaks.

½ cup butter, softened
2 teaspoons chopped fresh cilantro
1 teaspoon ground ginger
½ cup all-purpose flour

½ teaspoon salt
¼ teaspoon ground white pepper
4 (5-ounce) red snapper steaks
2 tablespoons olive oil, divided

Combine first 3 ingredients, stirring well. Spoon butter mixture into a decorating bag fitted with a large star tip. Pipe mixture into 12 rosettes on a wax paper-lined baking sheet. Cover and freeze until butter mixture is firm.

Combine flour, salt, and pepper; dredge steaks in flour mixture. Heat 1 tablespoon oil in a large skillet over medium-high heat. Add steaks, and cook 2 minutes on each side or until browned.

Brush remaining 1 tablespoon olive oil on a rack in broiling pan; place steaks on rack. Bake at 350° for 10 minutes or until fish flakes easily when tested with a fork. Serve immediately with butter rosettes. Yield: 4 servings. Peter C. Moret

The Collection
Mountain Brook Baptist Church
Birmingham, Alabama

Mexican Lime Snapper

Sprite lime dances with green onions, green chiles, and tomatoes. Serve the snapper with warm tortillas and rice to catch all of the south-of-the-border flavor.

¼ cup chopped green onions
2 tablespoons butter or margarine, melted
2 cups seeded and chopped tomato
1 tablespoon chopped fresh parsley
3 tablespoons fresh lime juice

2 tablespoons canned chopped green chiles, drained
⅛ teaspoon salt
⅛ teaspoon garlic salt
Dash of pepper
2 (8-ounce) red snapper fillets
Lime wedges

Cook green onions in butter in a large skillet over medium-high heat, stirring constantly, until tender. Stir in chopped tomato and next 6 ingredients. Bring to a boil; reduce heat, and simmer, uncovered, 10 minutes.

Place fillets in skillet. Spoon tomato mixture evenly over fillets. Bring to a boil; cover, reduce heat, and simmer 10 minutes or until fish flakes easily when tested with a fork. Serve with lime wedges. Yield: 2 servings. Donna Bales

Cooking from the Hip
Calvary Bible Evangelical Free Church, Mothers of Preschoolers
Boulder, Colorado

Stuffed Sole Fillets with Nutmeg Sauce

A sublime wine sauce with a touch of nutmeg complements the rice-stuffed fillets.

1 green onion, chopped
⅓ cup shredded carrot
2 tablespoons unsalted butter, divided
½ cup cooked rice
1 teaspoon grated lemon rind, divided
1 teaspoon fresh lemon juice, divided
½ teaspoon ground nutmeg, divided

½ teaspoon salt
¼ teaspoon pepper
4 small sole fillets (about 10 ounces)
1 tablespoon plus 1 teaspoon all-purpose flour
¾ cup canned low-sodium chicken broth, undiluted
¼ cup dry white wine
1 tablespoon chopped fresh parsley

Cook onion and carrot in 1 tablespoon melted butter in a heavy skillet over medium heat 3 to 5 minutes or until tender, stirring occasionally. Stir in rice, ½ teaspoon lemon rind, ½ teaspoon lemon juice, ¼ teaspoon nutmeg, salt, and pepper.

Spoon one-fourth of rice mixture onto end of each fillet; roll up fillets, and place, seam side down, in a lightly greased 11- x 7- x 1½-inch baking dish. Bake at 350° for 20 minutes or until fish flakes easily when tested with a fork. Keep warm.

Melt remaining 1 tablespoon butter in a heavy saucepan over low heat; add flour, stirring until smooth. Cook 1 minute, stirring constantly. Gradually add chicken broth; cook over medium heat, stirring constantly, until mixture is thickened and bubbly. Stir in remaining ½ teaspoon lemon rind, ½ teaspoon lemon juice, and ¼ teaspoon nutmeg. Stir in wine and parsley; cook until thoroughly heated. Serve over fillets. Yield: 2 servings.   Rebecca Sigler

History, Memories & Recipes
Fox River Grove Diamond Jubilee Committee
Fox River Grove, Illinois

Grilled Swordfish with Ocean Club Sauce

Touted as being served to President Bill Clinton, this thick swordfish steak with pungent caper sauce is worthy of presidential accolades.

2½ pounds swordfish steaks
    (about ½ inch thick)
½ cup fresh orange juice
¼ cup fresh lemon juice

¼ cup olive oil
¼ teaspoon salt
¼ teaspoon pepper
Ocean Club Sauce

Place steaks in a large heavy-duty, zip-top plastic bag. Combine orange juice and next 4 ingredients in a small bowl; stir well. Pour marinade over steaks. Seal bag; marinate in refrigerator 3 hours, turning occasionally.

Remove steaks from marinade, discarding marinade. Grill, covered, over medium-hot coals (350° to 400°) 5 minutes on each side or until fish flakes easily when tested with a fork. Serve with Ocean Club Sauce. Yield: 4 servings.

Ocean Club Sauce

½ cup extra virgin olive oil
2 tablespoons fresh lemon
    juice
2 tablespoons minced garlic
2 tablespoons drained capers

2 tablespoons soy sauce
1 tablespoon minced anchovies
¼ teaspoon coarsely ground
    pepper

Combine all ingredients in a small bowl, stirring well with a wire whisk. Yield: 1 cup.   V. Jaime Schilcher

A Quest for Good Eating
Cape Cod Questers
Yarmouth Port, Massachusetts

Capered Trout

Bake these trout fillets in a lemony sea of pungent capers and breadcrumbs.

⅓ cup mayonnaise
2 tablespoons capers, drained
1 tablespoon fresh lemon juice
1 tablespoon Dijon mustard

2 (4-ounce) trout fillets
2 tablespoons soft
  breadcrumbs

Combine first 4 ingredients, stirring well; set aside.

Place trout in a lightly greased 11- x 7- x 1½-inch baking dish. Spoon mayonnaise mixture evenly over fillets; sprinkle with breadcrumbs. Bake at 350° for 25 minutes or until fish flakes easily when tested with a fork. Yield: 2 servings.

Gathered at the Gables: Then and Now
The House of the Seven Gables
Salem, Massachusetts

Lemon-Basil Tuna Grill

Lyrical lemon and fragrant basil join in chorus for a grilled tuna steak that sings.

6 (4-ounce) tuna steaks
  (1½ inches thick)
1 large lemon
¼ cup chopped fresh basil

¼ cup olive oil
1 teaspoon salt
½ teaspoon pepper
Vegetable cooking spray

Place steaks in an 11- x 7- x 1½-inch baking dish.

Grate lemon rind, and squeeze juice from lemon. Combine lemon juice, lemon rind, basil, and next 3 ingredients; pour over steaks. Cover and marinate in refrigerator 1½ hours, turning once.

Coat grill rack with cooking spray; place rack on grill over medium-hot coals (350° to 400°). Place steaks on rack, and grill, covered, 6 minutes on each side or until fish flakes easily when tested with a fork. Yield: 6 servings.   Kim Williams

Seasonings
20th Century Club Juniors of Park Ridge, Illinois

Cape Fear Crab Cakes with Lemon-Dill Sauce

A pert Lemon-Dill Sauce awakens the fresh crab cakes that are fried to a golden hue.

¾ cup mayonnaise
½ cup buttermilk
2 tablespoons chopped fresh dill
1 tablespoon minced fresh parsley
1 tablespoon grated lemon rind
2 teaspoons fresh lemon juice
1 clove garlic, minced
1 green onion, finely chopped
1 clove garlic, minced
2 tablespoons finely chopped sweet red pepper
3 tablespoons butter or margarine, melted and divided
⅛ teaspoon ground red pepper
3 tablespoons whipping cream
1 tablespoon Dijon mustard
1 large egg, beaten
1 teaspoon minced fresh basil
1 teaspoon minced fresh parsley
1 cup fine, dry breadcrumbs, divided
1 pound fresh lump crabmeat, drained
¼ cup grated Parmesan cheese
2 tablespoons vegetable oil

Combine first 7 ingredients; stir well. Cover sauce, and chill.

Cook green onion, 1 minced garlic clove, and sweet red pepper in 1 tablespoon butter in a large skillet over medium-high heat until vegetables are crisp-tender, stirring occasionally. Add ground red pepper, whipping cream, and mustard; stir well. Let cool slightly.

Combine vegetable mixture, egg, basil, 1 teaspoon minced parsley, and ½ cup breadcrumbs; stir in crabmeat. Shape mixture into 12 (2-inch) patties. Cover and chill at least 1 hour.

Combine remaining ½ cup breadcrumbs and Parmesan cheese; dredge patties in crumb mixture.

Cook patties in hot oil and remaining 2 tablespoons butter in a large skillet over medium heat 3 minutes on each side or until golden. Remove from skillet. Serve crab cakes with sauce. Yield: 6 servings.

Dining by Fireflies: Unexpected Pleasures of the New South
The Junior League of Charlotte, North Carolina

Grilled Soft-Shell Crabs

Certainly a delicacy, soft-shell crab's tender meaty flesh is enhanced by the butter and lemon juice in this recipe.

12 fresh soft-shell crabs	¼ teaspoon soy sauce
½ cup butter	Dash of hot sauce
¾ cup chopped fresh parsley	Vegetable cooking spray
1 teaspoon lemon juice	Garnish: lemon wedges
¼ teaspoon ground nutmeg	

To clean crabs, remove spongy substance (gills) that lies under the tapering points on either side of back shell. Place crabs on back, and remove the small piece at lower part of shell that terminates in a point (the apron). Wash crabs thoroughly; drain well.

Combine butter and next 5 ingredients in a small saucepan. Cook over medium heat until butter melts.

Coat grill rack with cooking spray; place rack on grill over medium-hot coals (350° to 400°). Place crab on rack, and grill, covered, 3 minutes on each side or until crabmeat flakes easily when tested with a fork, basting crab with butter mixture. Garnish, if desired. Yield: 6 servings.

Very Virginia: Culinary Traditions with a Twist
The Junior League of Hampton Roads
Newport News, Virginia

Basil-Tomato Mussels

Slices of crusty French bread are a must to soak up the tomato juices in these saucy mussels.

3½ pounds raw mussels in shells	½ teaspoon freshly ground black pepper
¾ cup chopped onion	¼ teaspoon dried crushed red pepper
1 tablespoon minced garlic	½ cup chopped fresh flat-leaf parsley
¼ cup olive oil	
2 (14.5-ounce) cans Italian-style diced tomatoes	¼ cup chopped fresh basil
¼ cup red wine vinegar	French bread
½ teaspoon dried oregano	

Scrub mussels with a brush, removing beards. Discard opened, cracked, or heavy mussels (they're filled with sand); set aside.

Cook onion and garlic in oil in a large Dutch oven over medium-high heat, stirring constantly, until tender. Add tomatoes and next 4 ingredients. Bring to a boil; cover, reduce heat, and simmer 5 minutes. Add mussels, parsley, and basil. Cover and cook 4 minutes or until mussels open, shaking pot several times. Discard any unopened mussels. To serve, ladle mussels into individual soup bowls. Serve with French bread. Yield: 12 cups.

Maine Ingredients
The Junior League of Portland, Maine

Easy Baked Oysters

A simple dressing of breadcrumbs and butter makes these oysters so easy and so delicious.

⅓ **cup butter or margarine, melted**
1 **large egg**
¼ **cup milk**
¼ **teaspoon salt**
⅛ **teaspoon pepper**
1 **(10-ounce) container Select oysters, drained**

½ **cup fine, dry breadcrumbs**
¼ **cup (1 ounce) shredded Monterey Jack cheese**
1 **tablespoon chopped fresh parsley**
⅛ **teaspoon paprika**

Pour melted butter into an 11- x 7- x 1½-inch baking dish; set aside.

Combine egg, milk, salt, and pepper in a small bowl; beat with a wire whisk until blended. Dip each oyster in egg mixture, and dredge in breadcrumbs. Place oysters in baking dish; turn to coat with butter. Top oysters evenly with cheese, parsley, and paprika.

Bake at 425° for 10 to 12 minutes or until lightly browned. Yield: 4 servings. W. Clifton Pritchett

Note: Melt butter in baking dish in microwave at HIGH 1 minute or until melted, if desired.

Dock 'n Dine in Dorchester
Long Wharf Lighthouse Committee
Cambridge, Maryland

Scallops in Mustard-Dill Sauce

Spooned into avocado shells, these delicate scallops guarantee a showy presentation.

2½ pounds bay scallops
½ cup Dijon mustard
¼ cup sugar
¼ cup white wine vinegar
1 tablespoon plus 1 teaspoon
 dry mustard

⅛ teaspoon salt
⅔ cup vegetable oil
½ cup chopped fresh dill
4 avocados
8 toast points

Cook scallops in simmering water to cover 4 minutes or until white. Drain; rinse under cold water, and drain. Cover and chill thoroughly.

Combine Dijon mustard and next 4 ingredients. Gradually add oil in a thin stream, stirring constantly with a wire whisk, until blended. Stir in dill. Cover and chill.

Peel, halve, and seed avocados. Pour sauce over scallops, tossing mixture gently to coat. Spoon scallop mixture evenly into avocado halves. Serve with toast points. Yield: 4 servings.　　　　Sally Byrd

A Continual Feast
St. Mary's Guild of St. Clement's Episcopal Church
Berkeley, California

Oven-Fried Scallops

A light breading bathed with butter on these scallops mimics the golden coat of deep-frying.

12 sea scallops (about 1 pound)
2 tablespoons vegetable oil
2 tablespoons lemon juice
1 large egg, lightly beaten
2 tablespoons water
½ cup fine, dry breadcrumbs
½ teaspoon salt

Dash of pepper
Dash of paprika
¼ cup butter or margarine,
 melted
Lemon wedges (optional)
Tartar sauce (optional)

Place scallops in a small heavy-duty, zip-top plastic bag. Combine oil and lemon juice. Pour over scallops. Seal bag securely; marinate in refrigerator 30 minutes, turning occasionally.

Remove scallops from marinade, discarding marinade. Combine egg and water; stir well. Combine breadcrumbs and next 3 ingredients. Dip each scallop in egg mixture; dredge in breadcrumb mixture. Place scallops in an ungreased 8-inch square baking pan. Drizzle butter over scallops. Bake, uncovered, at 450° for 15 to 20 minutes or until scallops are white. If desired, serve with lemon wedges and tartar sauce. Yield: 4 servings.   Judy Ingram

Feeding Our Flocks
The Shepherd's Fund
Hollis, New Hampshire

Fiery Shrimp

Don't let this recipe title fool you; delicate palates need not be wary of this sweet-and-sour shrimp bake. But if you're a daredevil, splash on a few more drops of the feisty hot sauce to deliver a flaming punch.

1 cup butter, melted	2 teaspoons salt
1 cup margarine, melted	4 cloves garlic, minced
½ cup Worcestershire sauce	3 pounds unpeeled large fresh
¼ cup lemon juice	shrimp
1 teaspoon hot sauce	2 lemons, thinly sliced
¼ cup chopped green pepper	French bread

Combine first 8 ingredients. Pour half of butter mixture into a 15- x 10- x 2-inch baking dish. Add shrimp and lemon slices. Pour remaining sauce over shrimp. Bake, uncovered, at 400° for 20 minutes or until shrimp turn pink, stirring occasionally. Drain. Serve with French bread. Yield: 6 servings.   Ann Schwanekamp

Appetizers from A to Z
Christ Child Society
Phoenix, Arizona

Edouard Manet's Magnificent Shrimp With Mango in Grand Marnier Sauce

A brilliant orange mango sauce adds a fruity edge to the plump shrimp swimming in a Grand Marnier cream.

2½ pounds unpeeled large
    fresh shrimp
2 peeled ripe mangoes
½ cup sugar
¼ cup plus 2 tablespoons fresh
    lime juice
1 teaspoon chopped fresh
    cilantro
5 shallots, chopped
2 cloves elephant garlic,
    chopped
½ cup canola oil, divided
1 cup chicken broth
⅔ cup Grand Marnier or other
    orange-flavored liqueur

½ teaspoon dry mustard
½ teaspoon Worcestershire
    sauce
3 drops of hot sauce
½ cup plus 2 tablespoons
    whipping cream
⅛ teaspoon salt
⅛ teaspoon pepper
2 tablespoons onion powder
½ pound shiitake mushrooms,
    sliced
4 cups cooked rice

Peel shrimp, and devein, if desired. Set aside.

Position knife blade in food processor bowl; add mangoes, sugar, lime juice, and cilantro. Process until smooth, stopping once to scrape down sides. Cover and chill.

Cook shallot and garlic in ¼ cup oil in a large skillet over medium-high heat, stirring constantly, until tender. Add chicken broth and next 4 ingredients, stirring well. Bring to a boil; reduce heat, and simmer, uncovered, 15 minutes or until reduced by half. Add whipping cream, stirring constantly with a wire whisk. Cook over medium-low heat until sauce is reduced by half, stirring often. Add salt and pepper. Set aside, and keep warm.

Sprinkle shrimp with onion powder. Cook shrimp in remaining ¼ cup oil in a skillet over medium-high heat, stirring constantly, until shrimp turn pink. Add mushrooms; cook 1 minute.

Pour cream sauce over shrimp mixture, stirring well. Serve with rice, and top shrimp with mango mixture. Yield: 8 servings.

Cuisine for Connoisseurs: Food Among the Fine Arts
Boca Raton Museum of Art
Boca Raton, Florida

Shrimp and Cashew Stir-Fry

Delicate shreds of spinach, mushrooms, and onions twirl through this shrimp stir-fry sprinkled with skillet-roasted cashews.

1 pound unpeeled medium-size fresh shrimp
1 teaspoon cornstarch
¼ cup chicken broth
2 tablespoons soy sauce
⅓ cup dry roasted cashews
3 tablespoons peanut oil
1 medium onion, cut into very thin strips
½ cup thinly sliced celery
6 ounces fresh mushrooms, sliced
1 clove garlic, minced
2 cups loosely packed shredded fresh spinach
4 ounces fresh snow pea pods
⅛ teaspoon salt
Hot cooked brown rice

Peel shrimp, and devein, if desired. Set aside.

Combine cornstarch, broth, and soy sauce in a small bowl, stirring until smooth. Set aside.

Cook cashews in peanut oil in a large skillet 1 to 2 minutes or until cashews begin to brown. Remove cashews to a small bowl; set aside.

Add onion and celery to skillet. Cook over medium-high heat, stirring constantly, 5 minutes or until tender. Add mushrooms; cook 1 minute, stirring constantly. Add shrimp and garlic; cook 2 minutes or until shrimp turn pink, stirring occasionally. Add spinach and snow peas; cook 1 minute. Add reserved cornstarch mixture and salt, stirring just until thickened. Sprinkle with reserved cashews. Serve over rice. Yield: 4 servings.

Elizabeth Ingram

The Sampler
Association for the Preservation of Tennessee Antiquities,
Hardeman County Chapter
Bolivar, Tennessee

Shrimp and Leek Pizza

Homemade hits a home run with this gourmet pizza topped with gutsy feta, Gruyère, and Parmesan cheeses, ripe tomato, and delicious shrimp.

1 large tomato, peeled, seeded, and diced
¾ teaspoon salt
1½ cups thinly sliced leek
2 tablespoons butter or margarine
2 tablespoons olive oil
¼ pound unpeeled medium-size fresh shrimp
1½ tablespoons olive oil
Dash of salt
Dash of pepper
1 (10-ounce) can refrigerated pizza crust
2 teaspoons olive oil
1 cup (4 ounces) crumbled feta cheese
¼ cup (1 ounce) grated Gruyère cheese
3 tablespoons grated Parmesan cheese
1½ tablespoons minced fresh mint

Combine tomato and ¾ teaspoon salt in a small bowl. Cover and let stand 30 minutes. Drain tomato, and gently press between paper towels to remove excess moisture. Set aside.

Cook leeks in butter and 2 tablespoons olive oil in a large skillet over medium heat, stirring constantly, 10 minutes or until leek is tender. Set aside.

Peel shrimp, and devein, if desired. Cut each shrimp in half lengthwise. Combine shrimp, 1½ tablespoons olive oil, and a dash each of salt and pepper. Cover and let stand 15 minutes.

Pat pizza dough evenly into a lightly greased 12-inch pizza pan. Brush with 2 teaspoons olive oil. Sprinkle feta and Gruyère over dough. Top with leek and tomato.

Bake at 425° for 10 minutes. Drain shrimp, and arrange over pizza. Bake 3 to 5 additional minutes or until crust is golden and shrimp turn pink. Sprinkle with Parmesan cheese and mint. Serve immediately. Yield: 6 servings.

Cindy Nagle

A New Taste of Yardley
Makefield Women's Association
Yardley, Pennsylvania

Meats

Beef Tenderloin with Port-Walnut Stuffing, page 187

Marinated Beef Roast

This may be the most tender eye-of-round roast we've ever tasted. The succulent meat is well versed in flavor with its marinade of soy sauce, lime juice, and sherry.

1 (3½-pound) eye-of-round roast	3 tablespoons minced garlic
⅓ cup soy sauce	2 tablespoons vegetable oil
⅓ cup lime juice	1 tablespoon minced fresh ginger
⅓ cup sherry	1 tablespoon maple syrup
¼ cup chopped fresh cilantro	

Place roast in a large heavy-duty, zip-top plastic bag. Combine soy sauce and remaining 7 ingredients. Pour over roast. Seal bag; marinate in refrigerator at least 8 hours, turning occasionally.

Remove roast from marinade, reserving marinade. Bring marinade to a boil. Set aside.

Place roast on a rack in a roasting pan. Bake, uncovered, at 350° for 1½ hours or until meat thermometer inserted in thickest part of roast registers 145° (medium-rare) or 160° (medium), basting every 30 minutes with reserved marinade. Yield: 10 servings.   Connie White

Angel Food
St. Vincent de Paul School
Salt Lake City, Utah

Beef Tenderloin with Port-Walnut Stuffing

A tender spiral of beef encircles a moist walnut stuffing.

¾ cup minced onion
3 tablespoons butter or
  margarine, melted
⅓ cup port wine
1½ cups chopped fresh parsley
¾ cup soft breadcrumbs
¾ cup finely chopped walnuts,
  toasted
1½ teaspoons dried thyme
1 tablespoon grated orange
  rind

¼ cup egg substitute
1 (4-pound) beef tenderloin,
  trimmed
¼ cup Dijon mustard
½ teaspoon salt
¼ teaspoon freshly ground
  pepper
⅓ cup butter or margarine,
  melted

Cook onion in 3 tablespoons butter in a large skillet over medium-high heat, stirring constantly, until tender. Add wine; cook 5 minutes or until liquid evaporates. Remove from heat. Add parsley and next 5 ingredients; stir well.

Slice tenderloin lengthwise to, but not through, the center, leaving 1 long side connected. Make another lengthwise cut down center of each cut side, cutting to, but not through, the center of each side. Press tenderloin open to flatten.

Combine mustard, salt, and pepper; spread mixture on both sides of tenderloin. Spoon stuffing mixture over cut side of tenderloin, leaving a 1-inch border on all sides. Gently roll up tenderloin, starting at long side; tie securely with heavy string at 2-inch intervals.

Place tenderloin, seam side down, on a rack in a greased roasting pan. Insert meat thermometer into thickest part of tenderloin; brush with ⅓ cup melted butter. Bake at 400° for 50 minutes or until thermometer registers 145° (medium-rare) or 160° (medium), basting occasionally with butter. Let stand 10 minutes before serving. Yield: 10 servings.

Carolyn Grimme

Plain & Fancy Favorites
Montgomery Woman's Club
Cincinnati, Ohio

Filet Gorgonzola

Gutsy Gorgonzola cheese massages these tenderloin steaks with pungent flavor. Serve them with humble side dishes that won't compete with Gorgonzola's bold personality.

8 (6-ounce) beef tenderloin steaks
2 tablespoons olive oil
1 tablespoon unsalted butter
2 shallots, minced
¼ cup brandy

8 ounces Gorgonzola cheese, crumbled
3 cups beef broth
¼ teaspoon salt
¼ teaspoon pepper

Cook steaks in hot oil in a large skillet over medium-high heat to desired degree of doneness. Remove steaks from pan; keep warm. Add butter and shallot to pan; cook, stirring constantly, until minced shallots are tender. Add brandy and cheese, stirring constantly, until cheese melts. Add beef broth, salt, and pepper. Bring to a boil; reduce heat, and simmer, uncovered, 45 minutes or until slightly thickened. Return steaks to pan, and cook over low heat just until thoroughly heated. Yield: 8 servings.

Minnesota Times and Tastes, Recipes and Menus Seasoned with History from the Minnesota Governor's Residence
1006 Summit Avenue Society
St. Paul, Minnesota

Filet Mignon with Mustard-Caper Sauce

6 (6-ounce) beef tenderloin steaks
3 tablespoons butter or margarine, melted
½ cup dry vermouth
2 tablespoons chopped green onions
½ cup water

½ cup whipping cream
2 tablespoons capers
2 tablespoons prepared mustard
½ teaspoon salt
½ teaspoon pepper
1 beef-flavored bouillon cube
Watercress (optional)

Cook steaks in butter in a large skillet over medium-high heat 4 to 6 minutes on each side or to desired degree of doneness. Remove from skillet; keep warm. Add vermouth; cook over high heat, deglazing skillet by scraping particles that cling to bottom. Add green onions and next 7 ingredients. Bring to a boil; reduce heat, and simmer 5 minutes or until sauce is reduced to 1 cup. Serve steaks with sauce, and watercress, if desired. Yield: 6 servings.   Ellen Hill

A New Taste of Yardley
Makefield Women's Association
Yardley, Pennsylvania

Beef Medaillons with Lingonberries and Port Sauce

Lingonberries, found in the jams and jellies section of your supermarket, deliver a charming tartness to this robust port sauce. If they're not available in your area, you can substitute whole-berry cranberry sauce.

2 cups beef broth
⅓ cup port wine
2 tablespoons instant-blending
   flour
½ teaspoon dry mustard
½ teaspoon salt
¼ teaspoon pepper

3 shallots, finely chopped
1 cup sliced fresh mushrooms
3 tablespoons olive oil, divided
½ cup lingonberries in sugar
6 beef tenderloin steaks (1 inch
   thick)

Combine first 6 ingredients in a medium bowl, stirring until smooth. Set aside.

Cook shallot and mushrooms in 1½ tablespoons olive oil in a large skillet over medium-high heat 2 minutes, stirring constantly. Gradually add broth mixture, stirring until smooth. Bring to a boil; reduce heat, and simmer, uncovered, 18 minutes or until sauce is reduced by one-third. Stir in lingonberries.

Cook steaks in remaining 1½ tablespoons oil in a large skillet 4 minutes on each side or to desired degree of doneness. Serve sauce with steaks. Yield: 6 servings.

Sterling Performances
Guilds of the Orange County Performing Arts Center
Costa Mesa, California

Herbed Steak with Red Pepper-Saffron Cream Sauce

Saffron sports its signature burnt orange color in the delicate cream sauce. The full-bodied sauce is ready when it's reduced by half. Measure before and during cooking by standing a wooden spoon on its handle end in the saucepan.

1 teaspoon kosher salt
4 (8-ounce) rib-eye steaks (1 inch thick)
2½ teaspoons coarsely ground pepper
2 teaspoons chopped fresh thyme
1 teaspoon chopped fresh rosemary

½ teaspoon garlic powder
1½ tablespoons extra light olive oil
Red Pepper-Saffron Cream Sauce
Garnish: fresh rosemary or thyme sprigs

Sprinkle salt on both sides of steaks; let stand 10 minutes. Combine pepper and next 3 ingredients; rub mixture on both sides of steaks.

Heat olive oil in a large skillet over medium-high heat. Add steaks; reduce heat, and cook 4 minutes on each side or to desired degree of doneness. Serve with Red Pepper-Saffron Cream Sauce. Garnish, if desired. Yield: 4 servings.

Red Pepper-Saffron Cream Sauce

1 (7-ounce) jar diced pimiento, drained
⅔ cup beef broth

½ cup whipping cream
½ teaspoon threads of saffron
2 teaspoons lemon juice

Combine first 4 ingredients in a small saucepan. Bring to a boil; reduce heat, and simmer, uncovered, until mixture is reduced by half. Cool slightly. Pour mixture into container of an electric blender. Add lemon juice; process until smooth. Yield: ¾ cup.   Karen Davis

Applause! Oklahoma's Best Performing Recipes
Oklahoma City Orchestra League
Oklahoma City, Oklahoma

Beef Stroganoff

We couldn't resist this family favorite with its chunky beef and creamy-smooth mushroom sauce.

1½ cups all-purpose flour
1½ teaspoons salt
½ teaspoon pepper
2 pounds sirloin steak, cut into
   1-inch cubes
1½ cups butter or margarine,
   melted
3 cups sliced fresh mushrooms

1 cup chopped onion
2 cloves garlic, minced
½ cup dry white wine
3 cups beef broth
2 tablespoons tomato paste
2½ cups sour cream
Hot cooked noodles

Combine flour, salt, and pepper in a large heavy-duty, zip-top plastic bag; add steak. Seal bag, and shake until meat is coated.

Brown meat in butter in a large skillet, stirring occasionally. Remove meat from skillet; keep warm. Add mushrooms, onion, and garlic to drippings in skillet; cook, stirring constantly, until tender. Remove from pan; keep warm.

Add wine to skillet; cook over high heat, deglazing skillet by scraping particles that cling to bottom. Cook until wine is reduced by half. Add beef broth and tomato paste, stirring until smooth. Cook over medium heat, stirring constantly, until thickened. Add meat and mushroom mixture; cook until thoroughly heated. Stir in sour cream; cook just until mixture is hot, stirring constantly. Serve over noodles. Yield: 10 servings.

Jerry Perkins

To Serve with Love
Christian Women's Fellowship of the First Christian Church
Duncan, Oklahoma

Beef Enchiladas

For authentic Mexican flavor use traditional corn tortillas instead of flour tortillas in this extra saucy, extra cheesy weeknight favorite.

1 pound ground chuck	8 large flour tortillas
1 clove garlic, minced	Sauce
1 tablespoon chili powder	1 cup (4 ounces) shredded
1 tablespoon tequila	Cheddar cheese
2 teaspoons salt	Sour cream (optional)
1 (16-ounce) can pinto beans	Guacamole (optional)

Brown ground chuck and garlic in a large nonstick skillet, stirring until meat crumbles. Drain well. Wipe pan drippings from skillet with a paper towel. Return meat mixture to skillet; stir in chili powder and next 3 ingredients, mixing well.

Place about ½ cup meat mixture down center of each tortilla; roll up, and place, seam side down, in a 13- x 9- x 2-inch baking dish. Top with Sauce; sprinkle with cheese. Bake at 350° for 25 minutes. If desired, serve with sour cream and guacamole. Yield: 8 servings.

Sauce

1 beef-flavored bouillon cube	2 (16-ounce) cans stewed
1 cup boiling water	tomatoes, undrained
1 clove garlic, minced	1 (4.5-ounce) can chopped
¼ cup chopped green pepper	green chiles
½ cup chopped onion	½ teaspoon salt
3 tablespoons vegetable oil	⅛ teaspoon pepper
3 tablespoons all-purpose flour	⅛ teaspoon cumin

Dissolve bouillon cube in boiling water; set aside.

Cook garlic, green pepper, and onion in oil in a large skillet over medium-high heat, stirring constantly, until tender. Add flour, stirring well. Add tomatoes and bouillon. Cook over medium heat, stirring constantly, until mixture comes to a boil. Add chiles and remaining ingredients. Reduce heat, and simmer 10 minutes, stirring occasionally. Yield: 6 cups.
Marabeth Loomis

A Cook's Tour of Libertyville
Main Street Libertyville
Libertyville, Illinois

Miniature Meat Pies

These little pastries are mini meals and can be tucked away in the freezer until ready to bake.

4½ cups all-purpose flour
2 teaspoons salt
1½ cups shortening
¾ cup beer
3 egg yolks
2 pounds ground chuck
2 cups beer, divided
2 teaspoons salt

½ teaspoon pepper
¼ teaspoon dried thyme
1 large clove garlic, minced
2½ cups chopped onion
1½ cups finely chopped carrot
2 cups sliced zucchini
3 tablespoons all-purpose flour

Combine 4½ cups flour and 2 teaspoons salt; cut in shortening with pastry blender until mixture is crumbly. Add ¾ cup beer and egg yolks to flour mixture; stir with a fork until dry ingredients are moistened. Shape into a ball; wrap in wax paper, and chill.

Brown ground chuck in a large skillet, stirring until it crumbles. Drain well. Return meat to skillet. Add 1 cup beer, 2 teaspoons salt, and next 3 ingredients. Bring to a boil; cover, reduce heat, and simmer 15 minutes. Add onion and carrot; cover and simmer 15 minutes. Add zucchini; cover and simmer 10 to 15 minutes or until vegetables are tender. Combine remaining 1 cup beer and 3 tablespoons flour, stirring until smooth. Add to vegetable mixture, stirring until thickened. Set aside, and let cool.

Divide pastry into 18 portions. Roll out each portion of dough to ⅛-inch thickness on a lightly floured surface. Spoon a rounded ⅓ cup beef mixture on one-half of each dough circle. Moisten edges with water. Fold circles in half; press edges with a fork dipped in flour to seal. Transfer to baking sheets. Make slits in top of dough to allow steam to escape. Bake at 425° for 20 minutes or until golden. Yield: 1½ dozen.

Mary Ruland

Note: You can freeze unbaked pies, and then bake, without thawing, at 425° for 25 to 30 minutes or until golden.

Home Cookin'
American Legion Auxiliary, Department of Wyoming
Torrington, Wyoming

Sensational Spaghetti

Meat rules supremely in this hearty spaghetti dish. Beef, veal, and pork are the reigning triumvirate flavorfully served by a slow-cooking sauce.

1 cup diced onion	2 (6-ounce) cans tomato paste
2 cloves garlic, minced	½ cup dry red wine
½ pound ground chuck	1 tablespoon sugar
½ pound ground pork	1½ teaspoons aromatic bitters
½ pound ground veal	1½ teaspoons Worcestershire
¼ cup butter or margarine,	sauce
melted	½ teaspoon celery salt
1 tablespoon olive oil	½ teaspoon salt
½ pound fresh mushrooms,	¼ teaspoon black pepper
chopped	Dash of ground red pepper
½ cup chopped green pepper	2 bay leaves
1 (28-ounce) can Italian-style	1 (16-ounce) package spaghetti
stewed tomatoes	Freshly grated Parmesan cheese

Cook first 5 ingredients in butter and oil in a large Dutch oven over medium heat until meat is browned, stirring to crumble meat; drain. Add mushrooms and next 12 ingredients; stir well. Bring to a boil; reduce heat, and simmer, uncovered, 1 hour. Discard bay leaves.

Cook spaghetti according to package directions; drain well. Place spaghetti evenly on individual serving plates. Spoon sauce evenly over spaghetti. Sprinkle with cheese. Yield: 7 servings.   Judy Graham

Fanconi Anemia Family Cookbook
Fanconi Anemia Research Fund
Eugene, Oregon

Veal à l'Orientale

2½ pounds veal cutlets	2 teaspoons lemon juice
½ teaspoon salt	1½ teaspoons grated fresh
¼ teaspoon freshly ground	ginger
pepper	1 clove garlic, minced
2 tablespoons all-purpose flour	¾ teaspoon dried tarragon
¼ cup butter or margarine,	⅓ cup finely chopped fresh
melted	parsley, divided
½ cup dry white wine	1 small lemon, thinly sliced

Place veal between two sheets of wax paper; flatten veal to ¼-inch thickness, using a meat mallet or rolling pin. Sprinkle veal with salt, pepper, and flour. Cook veal in butter in a large skillet over medium heat 1 minute on each side or until browned. Remove veal, reserving drippings in skillet. Set veal aside; keep warm.

Combine wine and next 4 ingredients; add 3 tablespoons parsley. Add wine mixture to skillet; cook over high heat, deglazing skillet by scraping particles that cling to bottom. Add veal to skillet; top with lemon slices. Cover, reduce heat, and cook 5 minutes. Transfer veal to a serving platter; pour sauce over veal. Sprinkle with remaining parsley. Yield: 6 servings.

Silver Selections
Catawba School Alumni
Rock Hill, South Carolina

Sautéed Veal Scallops with Marsala Sauce

1 cup all-purpose flour	3 tablespoons olive oil, divided
1 teaspoon salt	½ cup dry Marsala wine
½ teaspoon pepper	½ cup beef broth, divided
1½ pounds veal cutlets	
¼ cup butter or margarine, melted and divided	

Combine flour, salt, and pepper. Dredge veal in flour mixture. Brown half of veal in 1 tablespoon melted butter and 1½ tablespoons oil in a large skillet over medium-high heat. Remove veal to a serving platter. Repeat procedure with remaining veal, adding 1 tablespoon melted butter and 1½ tablespoons oil as needed.

Add Marsala and ¼ cup broth to skillet. Bring to a boil over high heat; cook 1 minute, stirring constantly. Return veal to skillet; cover, reduce heat, and simmer 10 minutes. Transfer veal to a platter.

Add remaining ¼ cup broth to skillet; cook 1 minute, stirring constantly. Remove from heat; stir in 2 tablespoons butter. Drizzle Marsala Sauce over veal. Yield: 6 servings.   Virginia G. Peco

Food for the Spirit
St. Thomas Aquinas Home & School Association
Hammond, Louisiana

Veal Sentino

At first glance you'd think this was Veal Oscar with its slender veal cutlets and tender asparagus tucked under a blanket of Swiss cheese. But buttery mushrooms take the sensible place of pricey crabmeat for an entrée prepared to sensory satisfaction.

8 fresh asparagus spears	2 cups sliced fresh mushrooms
4 veal cutlets (about 12 ounces)	4 (1-ounce) slices Swiss cheese
½ teaspoon salt	2 tablespoons fresh lemon
⅛ teaspoon pepper	juice
¼ cup all-purpose flour	Hot buttered noodles
¼ cup plus 3 tablespoons	
butter or margarine, melted	
and divided	

Snap off tough ends of asparagus. Remove scales with a vegetable peeler, if desired. Cook asparagus in a small amount of boiling water 4 minutes or until crisp-tender. Drain and set aside.

Place veal between two sheets of heavy-duty plastic wrap, and flatten, using a meat mallet or rolling pin. Sprinkle cutlets with salt and pepper; dredge veal in flour. Cook veal in 2 tablespoons melted butter in a large skillet over medium-high heat until browned on both sides. Remove from skillet, and place in a 13- x 9- x 2-inch pan; set aside. Cook mushrooms in remaining ¼ cup plus 1 tablespoon butter in skillet, stirring constantly, until tender. Top veal with sautéed mushrooms, reserving pan drippings. Arrange asparagus spears over mushrooms, and top with Swiss cheese slices.

Broil 5½ inches from heat (with electric oven door partially opened) 2 minutes or until cheese melts. Transfer to a serving platter. Mix lemon juice with reserved drippings in skillet; pour over veal. Serve with noodles. Yield: 4 servings.   Martha Durr Lemon

Homecoming: Special Foods, Special Memories
Baylor University Alumni Association
Waco, Texas

Butterflied Lamb Leg with Orange Sauce

The acid in the citrusy orange marinade mellows the lamb's distinct flavor.

1 (5-pound) boneless leg of lamb, butterflied
2⅔ cups orange juice, divided
½ cup butter or margarine
½ cup orange marmalade

½ teaspoon grated fresh ginger
¼ teaspoon dry mustard
1 tablespoon cornstarch
2 tablespoons lemon juice

Trim fat from lamb. Place lamb in a large heavy-duty, zip-top plastic bag. Add 2 cups orange juice; seal bag securely, and shake until coated. Marinate in refrigerator at least 2 hours, turning bag occasionally.

Melt butter in a small saucepan over medium-high heat. Add remaining ⅔ cup orange juice, orange marmalade, ginger, and mustard. Cook until marmalade melts.

Combine cornstarch and lemon juice in a bowl, stirring until smooth. Stir into orange mixture. Cook over medium heat, stirring constantly, until mixture thickens and boils. Boil 1 minute, stirring constantly. Remove from heat. Reserve half of Orange Sauce.

Grill lamb over medium coals (300° to 350°) 20 minutes, basting often with remaining half of Orange Sauce; turn lamb, and insert meat thermometer into thickest part. Grill 20 minutes or until thermometer registers 150° (medium-rare), basting often with sauce. Let stand 10 minutes. Slice diagonally across grain into thin slices. Serve with reserved half of Orange Sauce. Yield: 8 servings.   Patti Hanafourde

A Cook's Tour of Gautier
Gautier Garden Club
Gautier, Mississippi

Roast Lamb with Herbs and Pistachios

6 slices white bread, divided,
   and crusts removed
2 cloves garlic
3 tablespoons chopped fresh
   parsley
2 teaspoons chopped fresh
   chives
1 teaspoon dried thyme
1 teaspoon dried rosemary
½ teaspoon salt
⅛ teaspoon pepper
¼ cup shelled pistachio nuts
1 (6½-pound) boneless leg of
   lamb, butterflied

Position knife blade in food processor bowl; add 4 bread slices. Process 20 seconds or until bread is crumbly. Remove breadcrumbs from food processor, and set aside.

Drop garlic through food chute with processor running; process 5 seconds or until garlic is minced. Add remaining 2 bread slices, parsley, and next 6 ingredients; process 15 seconds or until nuts are finely chopped.

Remove excess fat from lamb. Spread herb mixture over inner surface of lamb. Roll roast, starting at shortest end, and tie securely with heavy string at 2-inch intervals.

Coat entire surface of lamb with reserved breadcrumbs, patting to secure crumbs.

Place lamb on a rack in a roasting pan, seam side down. Bake at 425° for 30 minutes. Reduce heat to 350°; bake 2½ hours or until a meat thermometer inserted in thickest part registers 150° (medium-rare). Remove from oven; cover loosely with aluminum foil, and let stand 20 minutes before serving. Yield: 6 servings.

Gourmet Our Way
Cascia Hall Preparatory School Parent Faculty Association
Tulsa, Oklahoma

Lamb and Pear Stir-Fry

1½ pounds boneless leg of
   lamb
¼ cup dark sesame oil
6 cloves garlic, minced
½ cup chopped fresh basil
½ cup chopped fresh mint
2 teaspoons dried marjoram
¼ teaspoon salt
¼ teaspoon pepper
1 sweet red pepper, cut into
   very thin strips
¾ cup sliced green onions
2 large ripe pears, cut into thin
   wedges
1 tablespoon soy sauce
Hot cooked rice

Trim and discard fat from lamb, and slice diagonally across grain into thin slices.

Heat oil in a large skillet. Add lamb, garlic, and next 5 ingredients. Stir-fry 3 minutes or until lamb is no longer pink. Add red pepper and green onions. Stir-fry 1 minute. Add pears and soy sauce. Stir-fry 20 seconds. Serve immediately with rice. Yield: 4 servings.

Maine Ingredients
The Junior League of Portland, Maine

Sosaties (Lamb Kabobs)

3 medium onions, cut into
  1-inch-thick slices
1 tablespoon vegetable oil
9 ounces dried apricot halves,
  (1½ cups)
1 cup hot water
1 pound boneless leg of lamb,
  cut into 1-inch cubes
¼ cup plus 1 tablespoon
  apricot preserves

3 cloves garlic, chopped
2 bay leaves
2 tablespoons curry powder
2 tablespoons firmly packed
  brown sugar
2 tablespoons white vinegar
2½ teaspoons salt
1 teaspoon pepper
Vegetable cooking spray
Hot cooked rice

Separate onion slices into rings. Cook onion in oil in a large skillet over medium-high heat 3 minutes, stirring constantly. Drain well on paper towels, and set aside.

Combine apricots and hot water; let stand 5 minutes, and drain.

Place onion, apricots, and lamb cubes in a large heavy-duty, zip-top plastic bag. Combine preserves and next 7 ingredients; pour over lamb mixture. Seal bag, and shake to coat. Marinate in refrigerator 8 hours.

Remove lamb mixture from marinade, reserving marinade. Alternately thread lamb, onion, and apricots onto eight 12-inch metal skewers. Coat grill rack with cooking spray; place rack on grill over medium-hot coals (350° to 400°). Place kabobs on rack; grill, covered, 12 minutes or to desired degree of doneness, turning occasionally.

Discard bay leaves from reserved marinade; bring marinade to a boil in a saucepan. Serve kabobs and sauce over rice. Yield: 4 servings.

Delicious Developments
Friends of Strong Memorial Hospital
Rochester, New York

Pork Tenderloin with Molasses Barbecue Sauce and Mango Salsa

1 small onion, finely chopped
1 jalapeño pepper, seeded and
    minced
1 clove garlic, minced
2 teaspoons olive oil
½ cup molasses
½ cup cider vinegar
¼ cup Dijon mustard
1 tablespoon reduced-sodium
    soy sauce
2 (¾-pound) pork tenderloins
Hickory chunks
Vegetable cooking spray
Mango Salsa

Cook first 3 ingredients in olive oil in a saucepan over medium-high heat, stirring constantly, until tender. Stir in molasses and next 3 ingredients. Bring to a boil; reduce heat, and simmer, uncovered, 5 minutes, stirring occasionally. Let cool.

Place tenderloins in a large heavy-duty, zip-top plastic bag. Pour marinade over tenderloins. Seal bag; marinate in refrigerator 3 hours, turning occasionally.

Soak hickory chunks in water to cover at least 30 minutes, and drain chunks.

Prepare charcoal fire in smoker; let burn 15 to 20 minutes. Place hickory chunks on coals. Remove tenderloins from marinade, reserving marinade. Place water pan in smoker; add reserved marinade and water to pan to fill line. Coat grill rack with cooking spray. Place rack in smoker. Place tenderloins on food rack; cover with smoker lid.

Cook 2½ hours or until meat thermometer inserted in thickest portion of tenderloin registers 160° (medium). (Add additional coals and wood chunks to maintain an internal smoker temperature of 200° to 225°.) Serve with Mango Salsa. Yield: 6 servings.

Mango Salsa

3 cups peeled and diced mango
    (about 3 large)
⅓ cup minced purple onion
3 jalapeño peppers, seeded
    and minced
¼ cup chopped fresh cilantro
3 tablespoons fresh lime juice
1 tablespoon brown sugar
2 teaspoons minced fresh
    ginger
½ teaspoon salt
¼ teaspoon pepper

Combine all ingredients in a medium bowl, and toss well. Serve within 1 hour. Yield: 3½ cups.

Note: Do not use the color of the meat as a test for doneness when smoking. The outside of the tenderloins will be pinkish red and the inside will be pink. Be sure to use a reliable meat thermometer to test for the correct internal temperature of the meat.

Texas Tapestry
The Junior Woman's Club of Houston, Texas

Pork with Red Plum Sauce

Irresistibly tender and heightened with a lavish plum sauce, this pork roast received our best rating.

1 (4-pound) rolled boneless
  pork loin roast
¼ teaspoon onion salt
¼ teaspoon garlic salt
1 cup water
¾ cup chopped onion
2 tablespoons butter or
  margarine, melted
1 (10-ounce) jar red plum
  preserves

½ cup firmly packed brown
  sugar
⅓ cup chili sauce
¼ cup soy sauce
2 tablespoons lemon juice
2 teaspoons prepared mustard
3 drops of hot sauce

Remove strings from roast; trim fat. Sprinkle roast with onion salt and garlic salt. Reroll roast, tying securely with heavy string at 2-inch intervals. Place roast on a rack in a roasting pan; add water to pan. Cover with aluminum foil, and bake at 325° for 2 hours. Drain and discard drippings.

Cook onion in butter in a medium saucepan over medium-high heat, stirring constantly, until tender. Add plum preserves and remaining 6 ingredients. Cook over medium heat, uncovered, 15 minutes, stirring often.

Pour half of sauce over roast. Bake, uncovered, 20 additional minutes or until meat thermometer inserted in thickest part of roast registers 160° (medium), basting with half of remaining sauce. Transfer roast to a serving platter; let stand 10 minutes before serving. Serve remaining sauce with roast. Yield: 16 servings.

A Southern Collection, Then and Now
The Junior League of Columbus, Georgia

Fantastic Pork Fajitas

1 (1-pound) pork tenderloin
2 cloves garlic, minced
2 tablespoons orange juice
2 tablespoons white vinegar
1 teaspoon dried oregano
1 teaspoon ground cumin
1 teaspoon seasoned salt
½ teaspoon hot sauce

4 (8-inch) flour tortillas
1 medium onion, sliced
1 medium-size green pepper,
  cored and sliced
1 tablespoon vegetable oil
Sliced green onions (optional)
Shredded lettuce (optional)
Salsa (optional)

Slice pork diagonally across grain into ¼-inch strips, and place in a heavy-duty, zip-top plastic bag.

Combine garlic and next 6 ingredients, stirring well. Add marinade to pork; seal bag securely, and shake to coat. Marinate in refrigerator up to 1 hour.

Heat tortillas according to package directions; keep warm.

Cook pork, onion, and green pepper in oil in a heavy skillet over medium heat, stirring constantly, 3 to 5 minutes or until pork is done. Spoon pork mixture evenly down centers of tortillas; if desired, top with sliced green onions, shredded lettuce, and salsa. Serve immediately. Yield: 4 servings.

Jon Howard

Living off the Land: Arkansas Style
Howard County 4-H Foundation
Nashville, Arkansas

Ross's Prized Deep-Dish Pizza Pie

Chicago's got nothing on this whopper of a pizza! Mile-high homemade pizza crust hosts a harvest of squash, peppers, mushrooms, and a generous helping of homemade pesto. You'll need a knife and fork for this hearty dish!

8 ounces hot Italian sausage
2 cups warm water
  (105° to 115°)
1 teaspoon vegetable oil
1 teaspoon sugar
1 teaspoon salt
½ teaspoon garlic powder

1 package active dry yeast
5 cups all-purpose flour
Pesto Sauce
Squash Filling
2 cups (8 ounces) shredded
  mozzarella cheese
1 (14-ounce) jar pizza sauce

Remove casings from sausage. Cook sausage in a skillet over medium heat until browned, stirring until meat crumbles; drain and set aside.

Combine water and next 4 ingredients; sprinkle yeast over mixture, stirring until dissolved. Gradually add flour, mixing well after each addition. Turn dough out onto a floured surface; knead until smooth and elastic (about 8 minutes). Shape into a ball; place in a greased bowl, turning to grease top. Cover and let rise in a warm place (85°), free from drafts, 1 hour or until doubled in bulk.

Punch dough down; divide in half. Lightly grease hands; pat one half of dough in bottom and up sides of a greased 12-inch cast-iron skillet. Spread Pesto Sauce over crust; spread Squash Filling over pesto layer. Spoon reserved sausage over Squash Filling. Sprinkle mozzarella cheese over top.

Roll remaining dough into a 12-inch circle; transfer to top of pizza. Fold edges under, and flute. Spread pizza sauce over dough. Bake at 400° for 30 minutes. Yield: one 12-inch deep-dish pizza.

Pesto Sauce

1 cup loosely packed fresh basil
⅓ cup extra virgin olive oil
¼ cup pine nuts, toasted
¼ cup grated Parmesan cheese

3 cloves garlic, chopped
½ teaspoon salt
¼ teaspoon pepper

Position knife blade in food processor bowl; add all ingredients. Process until smooth. Yield: ¾ cup.

Squash Filling

3 yellow squash, thinly sliced
3 zucchini, thinly sliced
½ purple onion, sliced
½ sweet red pepper, sliced

2 cloves garlic, minced
1 (8-ounce) package sliced fresh mushrooms
3 tablespoons olive oil

Cook first 6 ingredients in hot oil in a large skillet over medium-high heat until tender, stirring occasionally. Yield: 5 cups.

The Roaring Fork
Gloria J. Deschamp Donation Fund
Grand Junction, Colorado

Pork Chops with Caramelized Onions and Smoked Gouda

1 cup all-purpose flour
1¼ teaspoons salt, divided
1¼ teaspoons pepper, divided
8 (1-inch-thick) rib pork chops
½ cup plus 1 tablespoon vegetable oil, divided
1 tablespoon plus 1 teaspoon sweet Hungarian paprika, divided
8 cups sliced onion (4 large)
1 teaspoon sugar
1 tablespoon plus 1 teaspoon minced garlic
2 cups beef broth
¾ cup (3 ounces) shredded smoked Gouda cheese
3 tablespoons butter or margarine
¼ cup plus 1 tablespoon all-purpose flour

Combine flour, 1 teaspoon salt, and 1 teaspoon pepper in a large heavy-duty, zip-top plastic bag. Add chops; seal bag, and shake to coat.

Heat 3 tablespoons oil in a heavy skillet over medium-high heat until hot; add 4 chops. Cook 3 minutes on each side or until browned. Transfer to a 15- x 10- x 2-inch baking dish. Repeat procedure. Sprinkle with 1 teaspoon paprika. Wipe skillet with a paper towel.

Heat remaining 3 tablespoons oil in skillet until hot. Add onion; sprinkle with sugar. Cook, stirring constantly, 20 minutes or until tender and golden. Add garlic; cook 1 minute. Remove from heat; add remaining 1 tablespoon paprika; stir well. Spoon onion over chops. Pour broth over onion mixture. Cover and bake at 350° for 45 minutes.

Remove from oven, and transfer chops to a serving platter. Pour onion mixture through a wire-mesh strainer into a 4-cup liquid measuring cup. Add enough water to broth mixture to measure 2½ cups, if necessary. Set aside. Return solids in strainer to baking dish; top with chops. Sprinkle with cheese. Bake 5 additional minutes or until cheese melts. Set aside, and keep warm.

Melt butter in a heavy saucepan over low heat; add ¼ cup plus 1 tablespoon flour, stirring until smooth. Cook 1 minute, stirring constantly. Gradually add reserved broth mixture; cook over medium heat, stirring constantly, until thickened and bubbly. Stir in remaining ¼ teaspoon salt and ¼ teaspoon pepper. Serve chops and onion with sauce. Yield: 8 servings.

Mary Gentile

Sunflowers and Samovars Recipe Collection
St. Nicholas Orthodox Church
Kenosha, Wisconsin

Pasta, Rice & Grains

Lasagna with Sausage and Colorful Peppers, page 210

Pasta with Korean Sesame Sauce

Hot bean paste, found in Asian markets, provides the peppery heat of this pasta temptation, while dark sesame oil and ginger impart their spicy-sweet lure.

10 ounces angel hair pasta, uncooked
3 tablespoons white vinegar
2 tablespoons hot bean paste
2 tablespoons soy sauce
1 tablespoon dark sesame oil
3 tablespoons sliced green onions

2 cloves garlic, minced
2 teaspoons grated fresh ginger
1 teaspoon sugar
1 teaspoon freshly ground pepper
2 tablespoons sesame seeds
1 medium cucumber, thinly sliced

Cook pasta according to package directions; drain well. Set aside, and keep warm.

Combine vinegar and next 8 ingredients, stirring well.

Place a large skillet over medium heat until hot; add sesame seeds. Cook, stirring constantly, 2 to 3 minutes or until sesame seeds are golden. Add pasta and vinegar mixture to skillet; toss until coated. Serve with cucumber. Yield: 6 servings.   Rossanna Groom

H.E.A.L. of Michiana Cookbook: A Collection of Health Conscious Recipes
Human Ecology Action League of Michiana
Stevensville, Michigan

Crab Cannelloni

Lavishly dressed in premium crabmeat and rich cheese, these stuffed pasta shells show off for company.

2 (8-ounce) packages cannelloni shells
¾ cup plus 1 tablespoon butter or margarine, divided
½ cup all-purpose flour
5 cups milk
1 teaspoon ground nutmeg
2 egg yolks, lightly beaten
1 pound fresh lump crabmeat, drained
1 pound mozzarella cheese, cubed
½ teaspoon salt
½ teaspoon pepper
3 tablespoons tomato paste
1 cup grated Parmesan cheese, divided
1 pound fresh mushrooms, sliced
1 tablespoon dried sage
3 tablespoons butter or margarine, melted

Cook cannelloni according to package directions; drain. Toss pasta with 1 tablespoon butter; set aside.

Melt remaining ¾ cup butter in a heavy saucepan over low heat; add flour, stirring until smooth. Cook 1 minute, stirring constantly. Gradually add milk; cook over medium heat, stirring constantly, until mixture is thickened and bubbly. Stir in nutmeg. Set aside half of sauce.

Add egg yolks to remaining sauce, stirring well. Stir in crabmeat, mozzarella cheese, salt, and pepper. Stuff each cannelloni shell with an equal amount of crab mixture; place stuffed shells in two lightly greased 13- x 9- x 2-inch baking dishes. Add tomato paste and ½ cup Parmesan cheese to reserved sauce; spoon over shells.

Cook mushrooms and sage in 3 tablespoons butter in a large skillet over medium heat until tender, stirring occasionally. Spoon mushrooms over sauce, and sprinkle with remaining ½ cup Parmesan cheese. Bake at 400° for 20 minutes. Yield: 14 servings.

Note: You can substitute 3 cups chopped cooked chicken for the crabmeat.

Take the Tour
St. Paul's Episcopal Church Women
Edenton, North Carolina

Fettuccine with Pistachio Sauce

Delicate pistachios cloaked in a garlic cream sauce dance in the arms of lanky fettuccine.

1 (16-ounce) package fettuccine
¾ pound roasted and salted pistachio nuts, shelled and coarsely chopped
2 cloves garlic, pressed
¼ cup olive oil
¾ cup whipping cream
¼ teaspoon salt
¼ teaspoon pepper

Cook fettuccine according to package directions. Drain well; place in a large bowl, and keep warm.

Cook pistachio nuts and garlic in oil in a large skillet over medium-high heat, stirring constantly, 3 minutes or until nuts are toasted. Add whipping cream, salt, and pepper. Cook 2 minutes, stirring constantly. Pour pistachio sauce over fettuccine; toss until fettuccine is coated. Yield: 8 servings.

Seaport Savories
TWIG Junior Auxiliary of Alexandria Hospital
Alexandria, Virginia

Pasta con Funghi (Pasta with Mushrooms)

3 tablespoons butter
1 clove garlic, pressed
¼ teaspoon dried basil
¼ teaspoon dried thyme
¼ teaspoon dried oregano
¼ teaspoon paprika
¼ teaspoon dried rosemary, crushed
¼ teaspoon salt

¼ teaspoon freshly ground pepper
1½ pounds fresh mushrooms, sliced
1 (16-ounce) package fettuccine
Simple Tomato Sauce
2 cups freshly grated Parmesan cheese

Melt butter in a large skillet over medium heat. Add garlic and next 7 ingredients; stir well. Add mushrooms, and stir to coat. Cook over medium heat 15 to 20 minutes or until mushrooms are tender.

Cook fettuccine according to package directions. Drain. Divide pasta evenly among six individual serving plates. Top with Simple Tomato Sauce. Spoon mushroom mixture over sauce, and serve with Parmesan cheese. Yield: 6 servings.

Simple Tomato Sauce

1 (28-ounce) can Italian-style tomatoes, undrained
1 medium-size green pepper, coarsely chopped
4 cloves garlic, pressed
1 medium onion, chopped
¼ cup olive oil
1 bay leaf

2 teaspoons chopped fresh parsley
½ teaspoon salt
½ teaspoon freshly ground pepper
¼ teaspoon dried oregano
¼ teaspoon dried basil
2 tablespoons dry red wine

Place tomatoes and green pepper in container of an electric blender; process until smooth.

Cook garlic and onion in oil in a Dutch oven over medium-high heat, stirring constantly, until tender. Add tomato mixture, bay leaf, and remaining ingredients. Bring to a boil; reduce heat, and simmer 1 hour. Discard bay leaf. Yield: 5¾ cups.   Laura Hutchinson Paye

Signature Edition
The Junior Woman's Club of Green Bay, Wisconsin

Lasagna with Sausage and Colorful Peppers

Tall cheesy layers of Italian sausage and red, green, and yellow peppers vibrantly elevate this lasagna to extraordinary.

1 pound sweet Italian sausage
8 ounces hot Italian sausage
1 large onion, sliced
2 sweet red peppers, sliced
2 green peppers, sliced
2 sweet yellow peppers, sliced
3 cloves garlic, chopped
½ cup chopped fresh parsley
⅛ teaspoon black pepper
12 lasagna noodles, uncooked
1 (8-ounce) can tomato sauce
1 (6-ounce) can tomato paste
4 cups (16 ounces) shredded part-skim mozzarella cheese
¼ cup grated Parmesan cheese

Remove casings from sausage. Cook sausage in a large skillet over medium heat until meat is browned, stirring until meat crumbles; drain. Add onion, sliced peppers, and garlic; cook over medium heat until vegetables are tender, stirring occasionally. Add parsley and pepper.

Cook lasagna noodles according to package directions; drain well, and set aside.

Combine tomato sauce and tomato paste; stir well. Spread half of tomato sauce mixture in a lightly greased 13- x 9- x 2-inch baking dish. Layer 4 lasagna noodles, half of sausage mixture, 1 cup mozzarella cheese, and 1 tablespoon Parmesan cheese. Repeat layers once. Top with remaining 4 lasagna noodles; spread remaining tomato sauce mixture over noodles. Top with remaining 2 cups mozzarella cheese; sprinkle with remaining 2 tablespoons Parmesan cheese. Bake, uncovered, at 350° for 40 to 45 minutes. Let stand 15 minutes. Yield: 8 servings.

Lil McKinnon Hicks

Recipes of Love
Alpha Delta Pi, Jackson Area Alumnae Association
Brandon, Mississippi

Linguine with Scallops in Cream Sauce

½ pound fresh spinach
1 (12-ounce) package linguine
4 quarts water
2 teaspoons salt, divided
1¼ pounds sea scallops
3 tablespoons butter or
    margarine, melted and
    divided
2 medium shallots, finely
    chopped

1 (8-ounce) package sliced
    fresh mushrooms
1¼ cups half-and-half
¾ cup chicken broth
1 tablespoon dry sherry
½ teaspoon pepper
2 cups cherry tomatoes, cut in
    half

Remove and discard spinach stems. Wash spinach, and pat dry with paper towels; slice thinly, and set aside.

Cook linguine according to package directions, using 4 quarts water and 1 teaspoon salt; drain. Set aside, and keep warm.

Cook half of scallops in 1 tablespoon butter in a large skillet over medium-high heat 3 minutes on each side. Remove from pan; cover and keep warm. Cook remaining half of scallops 3 minutes on each side. Remove from pan; cover and keep warm.

Cook shallot and mushrooms in remaining 2 tablespoons butter in skillet over medium-high heat 5 minutes. Add remaining 1 teaspoon salt, half-and-half, and next 3 ingredients to skillet. Bring to a boil over medium-high heat; cook, uncovered, 13 minutes or until liquid is reduced by half.

Add spinach, scallops, and cherry tomatoes to skillet; cook 3 minutes or until spinach wilts and mixture is thoroughly heated, stirring often. Pour scallop mixture over pasta; toss gently. Serve immediately. Yield: 6 servings.

Adair Horton

The Legal Aid Bureau Cookbook, Recipes for Slaw and Order
Legal Aid Bureau
Chicago, Illinois

Linguine with Tomato and Fresh Basil

When tossed, the warmth of the pasta softens the Brie in the fresh tomato-basil marinara to a yielding perfection.

1 (15-ounce) round Brie
1 cup plus 1 tablespoon olive oil, divided
2½ teaspoons salt, divided
4 large tomatoes, seeded and chopped
3 cloves garlic, minced

1 cup loosely packed fresh basil, thinly sliced
½ teaspoon freshly ground pepper
1½ pounds linguine, uncooked
6 quarts water
Freshly grated Parmesan cheese

Remove and discard rind from Brie, and tear cheese into bite-size pieces. Combine Brie, 1 cup olive oil, ½ teaspoon salt, tomato, and next 3 ingredients in a large serving bowl. Cover and marinate in refrigerator 2 hours.

Let Brie mixture stand, covered, at room temperature while preparing pasta.

Cook pasta in a large Dutch oven according to package directions, using 6 quarts water, remaining 1 tablespoon olive oil and remaining 2 teaspoons salt. Drain well, and add pasta to Brie mixture, tossing well. Sprinkle evenly with Parmesan cheese. Serve immediately. Yield: 8 servings.

Martha Beckwith

The Christ Church Cookbook
Christ Episcopal Church
Woodbury, Minnesota

Macaroni and Cheese Deluxe

Who doesn't yearn for the cheesy comfort of macaroni and cheese? Sour cream, cottage cheese, and ease of preparation boost this one above the status quo.

1 (8-ounce) package elbow macaroni
2 cups small-curd cottage cheese
2 cups (8 ounces) shredded sharp Cheddar cheese

1 (8-ounce) carton sour cream
1 large egg, lightly beaten
¾ teaspoon salt
Dash of pepper
Paprika

Cook macaroni according to package directions, and drain well. Combine macaroni, cottage cheese, and next 5 ingredients; stir well. Spoon mixture into a lightly greased 2-quart casserole. Sprinkle evenly with paprika. Bake at 350° for 45 minutes or until bubbly. Yield: 8 servings.   Jennifer McClam

First Family Favorites
First Baptist Church of Orlando, Florida

Greek Pasta

Provocative orzo is a refreshing understudy to rice. Its petite shape doesn't overwhelm its Mediterranean suitors–feta cheese, ripe olives, and fresh basil.

1½ cups orzo, uncooked
1 pound fresh broccoli
3 tablespoons pine nuts
¼ cup olive oil
½ teaspoon dried crushed red
   pepper

¾ cup crumbled feta cheese
1 (4¼-ounce) can chopped ripe
   olives, drained
½ cup grated Parmesan cheese
¼ cup chopped fresh basil

Cook orzo according to package directions; drain. Set aside.

Remove and discard broccoli leaves and tough ends of stalks. Wash broccoli thoroughly, and coarsely chop. Cook broccoli in a small amount of boiling water 8 minutes or until crisp-tender. Drain well.

Cook pine nuts in olive oil in a small skillet over medium heat 2 to 3 minutes or until browned, stirring often. Add red pepper; cook 1 minute, stirring constantly.

Combine orzo, broccoli, pine nuts, feta cheese, and remaining ingredients in a large bowl; toss gently. Serve immediately. Yield: 8 servings.   Patty Duncan

Charlie Daniel's Angels Cook Book
Mt. Juliet Tennis Association at Charlie Daniels Park
Old Hickory, Tennessee

Pasta with Asparagus, Prosciutto, and Wild Mushrooms

Brie adds its buttery goodness to a medley of fresh asparagus, salty prosciutto, and meaty shiitake mushrooms.

1 (16-ounce) package spaghetti
1 teaspoon olive oil
1 pound fresh asparagus spears
¼ cup diced shallot
2 tablespoons minced garlic
¼ cup olive oil
3 ounces prosciutto, cut into thin strips
1 (3½-ounce) package shiitake mushrooms, sliced
1 cup chicken broth
¼ cup plus 2 tablespoons dry white wine
½ teaspoon salt
¼ teaspoon pepper
4 ounces Brie cheese, cut into thin slices

Cook spaghetti according to package directions; drain. Add 1 teaspoon olive oil; toss. Set spaghetti aside, and keep warm.

Snap off tough ends of asparagus. Remove scales with a vegetable peeler, if desired. Cut asparagus into 1-inch pieces. Set aside.

Cook shallot and minced garlic in ¼ cup olive oil in a large skillet over medium-high heat, stirring constantly, until golden.

Add asparagus and prosciutto. Cook 3 minutes, stirring constantly. Add mushrooms; cook 5 minutes, stirring constantly. Add broth, wine, salt, and pepper; cook 2 minutes, stirring constantly.

Combine prosciutto mixture and reserved spaghetti in a large bowl, and toss gently. Add cheese slices, and toss gently. Serve immediately. Yield: 6 servings.   Patricia Hitner

Irish Children's Summer Program 10th Anniversary Cookbook
Irish Children's Summer Program
Greenville, South Carolina

Three-Cheese Tetrazzini

Cream cheese and cottage cheese provide a velvety contrast to the meaty sauce in this make-ahead dinner. Parmesan completes the cheesy trio atop the spaghetti casserole.

½ cup chopped onion
1 tablespoon butter or
    margarine, melted
1½ pounds ground chuck
1 teaspoon salt
¼ teaspoon pepper
1 (15-ounce) can tomato sauce
8 ounces spaghetti, uncooked

1 (8-ounce) package cream
    cheese
1 cup cottage cheese
¼ cup sour cream
¼ cup chopped green pepper
¼ cup sliced green onions
¼ cup freshly grated Parmesan
    cheese

Cook chopped onion in butter in a large skillet over medium-high heat, stirring constantly, until tender. Add ground chuck; cook, stirring constantly, until meat crumbles. Drain.

Return meat and onion to skillet; add salt, pepper, and tomato sauce. Cook 10 minutes over medium-low heat, stirring occasionally.

Cook spaghetti according to package directions. Drain and set aside.

Combine cream cheese, cottage cheese, and sour cream; stir well. Stir in green pepper and green onions. Add spaghetti; stir well. Spoon spaghetti mixture into a greased 13- x 9- x 2-inch baking dish. Pour meat sauce over top. Sprinkle with Parmesan cheese. Bake at 325° for 30 minutes. Yield: 8 servings.   Virginia Irene Crowe

Amazing Graces: Meals and Memories from the Parsonage
Texas Conference United Methodist Minister's Spouses Association
Palestine, Texas

Oriental Stir-Fry Pasta Salad

8 ounces vermicelli, uncooked
3 tablespoons lemon juice
3½ tablespoons vegetable oil, divided
3 tablespoons soy sauce, divided
2 tablespoons minced fresh parsley
1¼ teaspoons sesame oil
1 teaspoon sugar
1 clove garlic, minced
8 ounces turkey breast cutlets, cut into thin strips
4 ounces fresh snow pea pods, cut into very thin strips
1 medium carrot, scraped and cut into very thin strips
1 tablespoon water

Cook vermicelli according to package directions; drain. Keep warm.

Combine lemon juice, 2½ tablespoons vegetable oil, 2 tablespoons soy sauce, parsley, and next 3 ingredients; stir well. Pour mixture over pasta; toss gently. Set aside, and keep warm.

Cook turkey in remaining 1 tablespoon vegetable oil in a wok or large skillet over medium-high heat 2 minutes, stirring constantly. Add snow peas, carrot, and water, and cook 2 minutes, stirring constantly. Add remaining 1 tablespoon soy sauce; stir well. Spoon turkey mixture over pasta; toss gently. Serve immediately. Yield: 4 servings.

Joan Klause

Colony Club Concoctions
Colony Club
Ocean City, New Jersey

Kusherie (Egyptian Rice and Lentils)

This meatless main dish is surprisingly easy and delicious.

1¼ cups dried lentils
2 tablespoons vegetable oil
4 cups canned vegetable broth, divided
1 teaspoon salt
⅛ teaspoon black pepper
1½ cups long-grain rice, uncooked
3 cups coarsely chopped tomato
1 cup chopped green pepper

¾ cup tomato paste
¼ cup chopped celery leaves
1 tablespoon sugar
1 teaspoon ground cumin
½ teaspoon salt
¼ teaspoon ground red pepper
3 medium-size onions, sliced
4 cloves garlic, minced
2 tablespoons vegetable oil
Plain lowfat yogurt (optional)

Cook lentils in 2 tablespoons oil in a large saucepan over medium-high heat, stirring constantly, 3 minutes or until browned. Add 3 cups broth, 1 teaspoon salt, and ⅛ teaspoon pepper. Bring to a boil; cover, reduce heat, and simmer 15 minutes.

Stir in rice and remaining 1 cup broth; bring to a boil. Cover, reduce heat, and simmer 25 minutes or until liquid is absorbed and rice is tender; set aside, and keep warm.

Combine chopped tomato and next 7 ingredients in a medium saucepan. Bring to a boil; reduce heat, and simmer, uncovered, 25 minutes. Set aside, and keep warm.

Cook onion and garlic in 2 tablespoons oil in a large skillet over medium-high heat, stirring constantly, until tender.

To serve, spoon lentil mixture onto a serving platter. Spoon tomato mixture over lentils. Top with onion mixture. Serve immediately with yogurt, if desired. Yield: 6 servings.   Harriette Sturges

Helpings of Hope
Franklin County Habitat for Humanity
Louisburg, North Carolina

Green Rice

Curry distinguishes this marinated side dish medley of rice and vegetables. It's an updated substitute for potato salad or coleslaw, and with chopped cooked chicken, makes a filling one-dish meal.

4 cups chicken broth
2 cups long-grain rice, uncooked
3 (6-ounce) cans marinated artichokes
5 green onions, chopped
1 medium-size green pepper, chopped

3 stalks celery, chopped
¼ cup chopped fresh parsley
1 (3-ounce) jar pimiento-stuffed olives, drained and chopped
2 cups mayonnaise
1 teaspoon curry powder
¼ teaspoon pepper

Bring chicken broth to a boil in a medium saucepan; add rice. Cover, reduce heat, and simmer 20 minutes or until liquid is absorbed and rice is tender. Set aside.

Drain artichokes, reserving marinade. Chop artichokes. Combine rice, artichokes, green onions, and next 4 ingredients; stir well. Combine reserved artichoke marinade, mayonnaise, curry powder, and pepper; stir well. Add marinade mixture to rice mixture; stir well. Cover and chill at least 8 hours. Yield: 10 servings.   Neal Haskew

Briarwood Recipes to Crown Your Table
Women's Ministries of Briarwood Presbyterian Church
Birmingham, Alabama

Risotto Cabrillo

3 cups chicken broth
1½ cups Arborio or other
   short-grain rice, uncooked
½ cup chopped onion
2 tablespoons butter, melted
3 medium tomatoes, diced
2 cups chopped fresh spinach
⅓ cup shredded carrot
⅓ cup shredded zucchini
3 green onions, chopped

1 ounce dried porcini
   mushrooms, stemmed
3 tablespoons olive oil
¼ cup dry white wine
¼ cup whipping cream
1 teaspoon dried basil
¾ cup freshly grated Parmesan
   cheese
¼ teaspoon salt
⅛ teaspoon pepper

Bring chicken broth to a boil in a small saucepan. Cover, reduce heat to low, and keep warm.

Cook rice and onion in butter in a 3-quart saucepan over medium-high heat 8 minutes, stirring constantly. Add 1½ cups chicken broth, stirring well. Cover, reduce heat, and simmer 10 minutes.

Cook tomato and next 5 ingredients in oil in a large skillet over medium-high heat, stirring constantly, 8 minutes or until crisp-tender.

Add remaining chicken broth, vegetables, wine, whipping cream, and basil to rice mixture, stirring well. Cover and simmer 10 minutes or until most of liquid is absorbed, stirring twice. Stir in cheese, salt, and pepper. Yield: 7 servings.

Feast of Eden
The Junior League of Monterey County
Monterey, California

Eggplant with Bulgur

1 large eggplant, peeled and
   cut into 1-inch cubes
1 cup chopped onion
2 cloves garlic, minced
2 tablespoons olive oil
1 cup bulgur wheat, uncooked
2½ cups vegetable juice or
   tomato juice
½ cup sliced almonds
1½ teaspoons dried oregano
¼ cup chopped fresh parsley
½ teaspoon salt
¼ teaspoon pepper

Cook eggplant in boiling water to cover 3 minutes. Drain and set aside. Cook onion and garlic in olive oil in a large skillet until onion is tender, stirring occasionally. Add eggplant, bulgur, and remaining ingredients to skillet. Bring to a boil; reduce heat, and simmer, uncovered, 3 minutes.

Spoon eggplant mixture into a lightly greased 11- x 7- x 1½-inch baking dish. Bake at 350° for 30 minutes. Yield: 6 servings.

Delicious Developments
Friends of Strong Memorial Hospital
Rochester, New York

Tabbouleh Primavera

Tamari imparts a flavor similar to soy sauce to the vinaigrette that dresses this minted vegetable-bulgur side salad.

1 cup bulgur wheat, uncooked
2 cups boiling water
1⅓ cups chopped tomato
   (about 2 medium)
½ cup currants
½ cup salted dry roasted
   sunflower kernels
⅓ cup shredded carrot
2 green onions, chopped
1 clove garlic, minced
2 tablespoons chopped fresh
   mint
1 tablespoon chopped fresh
   basil
Pinch of dried oregano
Vinaigrette

Combine bulgur and water in a large bowl; cover and let stand 20 minutes or until liquid is absorbed and bulgur is tender.

Add tomato and next 8 ingredients to bulgur; toss well. Add Vinaigrette; toss. Cover and chill at least 2 hours. Yield: 5 servings.

Vinaigrette

¼ cup red wine vinegar   ¼ cup olive oil
¼ cup tamari

Combine all ingredients in a small bowl, stirring well with a wire whisk. Yield: ¾ cup.   Miki Roth and Clara McNay

A Culinary Tour of Homes
Big Canoe Chapel Women's Guild
Big Canoe, Georgia

Vegetable Couscous

Chunks of red pepper, carrot, and zucchini fleck this tender grain side dish with color and crunch.

1 large onion, coarsely   2¼ cups chicken broth
  chopped   1 cup golden raisins
2 tablespoons olive oil   ¾ teaspoon ground cinnamon
1 large sweet red pepper,   ½ teaspoon salt
  coarsely chopped   ¼ teaspoon pepper
4 medium carrots, scraped and   ¼ teaspoon ground turmeric
  coarsely chopped   1 (10-ounce) package couscous
2 medium zucchini, quartered
  lengthwise and cut into
  ½-inch slices

Cook onion in olive oil in a large saucepan over medium-high heat 5 minutes, stirring constantly, until tender. Add red pepper and carrot; cook 5 minutes. Add zucchini, and cook 5 minutes. Add broth and next 5 ingredients. Bring to a boil; slowly stir in couscous. Remove from heat; cover and let stand 10 minutes. Fluff with a fork. Yield: 8 servings.

Everybody Bring a Dish, Cooking in the Spirit of Shalom
Shalom United Church of Christ
Richland, Washington

Rosemary-Mushroom Grits

Aromatic rosemary and premium Parmigianno Reggiano perfume homey grits to sophistication. We give two serving suggestions—one in individual custard cups, the other akin to polenta squares.

2 (14.5-ounce) cans beef broth
¾ cup grits, uncooked
1 clove garlic, minced
¾ cup grated Parmigianno Reggiano cheese
2½ tablespoons butter or margarine
1 teaspoon freshly ground pepper
1 clove garlic, minced
1 tablespoon olive oil

1 fresh rosemary sprig, chopped
2 cups sliced fresh shiitake mushrooms
2 tablespoons chopped fresh parsley
½ teaspoon salt
¼ teaspoon freshly ground pepper
Vegetable cooking spray

Bring broth to a boil in a medium saucepan. Stir in grits and 1 clove garlic. Cover, reduce heat, and simmer 20 minutes, stirring occasionally. Remove from heat; add cheese, butter, and 1 teaspoon pepper. Stir until cheese melts.

Cook 1 clove garlic in olive oil in a large skillet over medium-high heat, stirring constantly, until tender. Add rosemary and mushrooms; cook over medium heat 10 minutes or until browned. Remove from heat. Stir in parsley, salt, and ¼ teaspoon pepper; let cool.

Lightly coat a 13- x 9- x 2-inch baking dish with cooking spray. Spoon half of grits mixture into prepared dish; sprinkle with mushroom mixture, and top with remaining grits mixture. Cover and chill 8 hours. Cut into squares. To serve hot, broil 5½ inches from heat (with electric oven door partially opened) 5 minutes or until lightly browned. Yield: 8 servings.

Note: You can also make individual servings. Spoon ½ cup of mixture into each of eight 6-ounce custard cups.

True Grits: Tall Tales and Recipes from the New South
The Junior League of Atlanta, Georgia

Pies & Pastries

Lemon Tart with Butter Pecan Crust, page 233

Spicy Harvest Pie

Shreds of apple, zucchini, and carrot laced with cinnamon and nutmeg deliver a fall indulgence.

1½ cups firmly packed brown sugar
¼ cup butter or margarine, melted
1 tablespoon lemon juice
2 teaspoons ground cinnamon
1 teaspoon vanilla extract
1 teaspoon grated orange rind
½ teaspoon ground nutmeg
¼ teaspoon salt
2 large eggs
2 cups shredded unpeeled apple

1 cup shredded unpeeled zucchini
1 cup shredded carrot
½ cup chopped walnuts
3 tablespoons all-purpose flour
1 (15-ounce) package refrigerated piecrust
1 large egg
1 tablespoon water
1 cup whipped cream

Combine first 8 ingredients in a medium bowl; stir well. Add 2 eggs, beating well with a wire whisk; set aside.

Combine apple and next 4 ingredients, tossing gently. Pour egg mixture over apple mixture; stir well.

Unfold 1 piecrust, and press out fold lines; sprinkle with flour, spreading over surface. Roll into a 9½-inch circle. Place piecrust, floured side down, in a 9-inch deep-dish pieplate; fold edges under, and flute. Spoon in filling. Roll remaining piecrust to press out fold lines. Cut 3 leaves with a 4-inch leaf-shaped cutter, and mark veins, using a pastry wheel or knife. Arrange pastry leaves on top of filling.

Combine remaining 1 egg and 1 tablespoon water in a small bowl; beat well with a wire whisk. Brush pastry with egg mixture. Bake at 425° for 35 to 40 minutes or until set. (Cover edges of pastry with strips of aluminum foil after 15 minutes to prevent excessive browning, if necessary.) Cool completely on a wire rack. Serve with a dollop of whipped cream. Yield: one 9-inch pie.   Gloria Titus

Colony Club Concoctions
Colony Club
Ocean City, New Jersey

The Famous Stuart Hall Brown Sugar Pie

½ cup butter or margarine,
 melted
2 cups firmly packed brown
 sugar

3 large eggs
1 teaspoon vanilla extract
1 unbaked 9-inch pastry shell

Beat butter, sugar, eggs, and vanilla in a large mixing bowl at medium speed of an electric mixer until blended. Pour into pastry shell. Bake at 350° for 45 minutes. Let cool completely on a wire rack. Yield: one 9-inch pie.   Blakeslee Chase

Saints Alive!
Ladies' Guild of St. Barnabas Anglican Church
Atlanta, Georgia

French Cranapple Pie

4 cups peeled, sliced cooking
 apple (about 4 large)
2 cups fresh or frozen
 cranberries, thawed
¾ cup sugar
¼ cup all-purpose flour
¼ cup firmly packed brown
 sugar
½ teaspoon ground cinnamon

¼ teaspoon ground nutmeg
1 unbaked 9-inch pastry shell
½ cup all-purpose flour
⅓ cup firmly packed brown
 sugar
¼ teaspoon ground cinnamon
Dash of nutmeg
¼ cup butter or margarine
⅓ cup chopped pecans

Combine apple and cranberries in a large bowl. Combine ¾ cup sugar and next 4 ingredients; add to cranberry mixture, tossing gently. Spoon mixture into pastry shell.

Combine ½ cup flour, ⅓ cup brown sugar, ¼ teaspoon cinnamon, and dash of nutmeg; stir well. Cut in butter with pastry blender until mixture is crumbly. Stir in pecans. Sprinkle crumb mixture over apple mixture. Bake at 375° for 45 minutes. Serve warm or at room temperature. Yield: one 9-inch pie.   Francis Radke

Madison County Cookbook
St. Joseph Church
Winterset, Iowa

Sweet Potato Praline Pie

A luscious praline layer baked in the crust elevates this classic sweet potato pie to a new level.

1⅓ cups all-purpose flour
½ teaspoon salt
½ cup shortening
3 to 4 tablespoons cold water
3 tablespoons butter or
   margarine, softened
⅓ cup firmly packed dark
   brown sugar
⅓ cup chopped pecans
3 large eggs, lightly beaten
1 cup evaporated milk

1½ cups cooked, mashed sweet
   potato
½ cup sugar
½ cup firmly packed dark
   brown sugar
1 teaspoon salt
1 teaspoon ground cinnamon
¼ teaspoon ground cloves
¼ teaspoon ground nutmeg
Whipped cream (optional)

Combine flour and ½ teaspoon salt; cut in shortening with pastry blender until mixture is crumbly. Sprinkle cold water (1 tablespoon at a time) evenly over surface; stir with a fork until dry ingredients are moistened. Shape into a ball; cover and chill.

Roll dough into a 12-inch circle on a lightly floured surface. Place in a 10-inch pieplate; trim off excess pastry along edges. Fold edges under, and flute.

Combine butter and ⅓ cup brown sugar; stir in pecans. Press mixture over pastry shell. Bake at 425° for 5 minutes. Let cool on a wire rack. Reduce oven temperature to 350°.

Combine eggs and next 8 ingredients in a large mixing bowl; beat at medium speed of an electric mixer until blended. Pour mixture over praline layer in pastry shell. Bake at 350° for 50 minutes or until pie is set. Let cool on wire rack. Top with whipped cream, if desired. Yield: one 10-inch pie.

Viola Goldberg

Historic Spanish Point: Cooking Then and Now
Gulf Coast Heritage Association
Osprey, Florida

Colonial Pumpkin Pie

Pastry
¾ cup sugar, divided
1 (16-ounce) can pumpkin
**1½ pounds cooking apples,
    peeled, cored, and cut into
    ½-inch slices (about 3
    medium apples)**

**2 tablespoons butter or
    margarine**
1 tablespoon milk

Roll half of Pastry to ⅛-inch thickness on a heavily floured surface. Place in a 9-inch pieplate; sprinkle with 2 tablespoons sugar. Spoon pumpkin into pastry; sprinkle ¼ cup sugar over pumpkin. Arrange apple slices over pumpkin layer. Sprinkle with ¼ cup plus 1 tablespoon sugar. Dot with butter.

Roll remaining half of pastry to ⅛-inch thickness; transfer to top of pie. Trim off excess pastry along edges. Fold edges under, and crimp. Brush milk over top of pie, and sprinkle with remaining tablespoon sugar. Cut slits in top of pastry to allow steam to escape. Bake at 375° for 1 hour or until fruit is tender. Serve warm. Yield: one 9-inch pie.

Pastry

2 cups all-purpose flour
1 teaspoon salt
⅔ cup butter, cut into pieces

¼ cup shortening
2 egg whites, lightly beaten
2 teaspoons water

Position knife blade in food processor bowl; add flour, salt, butter, and shortening; process until mixture is crumbly. Add egg whites and water to mixture; process just until dough begins to form a ball (dough will be sticky). Remove dough from bowl with floured hands. Shape dough into a ball, and flatten into a round disc on plastic wrap. Cover and chill at least 15 minutes. Yield: enough pastry for a 9-inch double-crust pie.

Cooking with Fire
Fairfield Historical Society
Fairfield, Connecticut

Heavenly Red Raspberry Meringue

A fluffy white meringue shell provides the "crust" for the ruby-red fresh raspberry filling.

4 egg whites
¼ teaspoon cream of tartar
1 cup sugar
4 cups fresh raspberries, divided
¾ cup sugar, divided
2½ tablespoons cornstarch
¼ teaspoon salt
⅓ cup water
2½ tablespoons fresh lemon juice
2 tablespoons lemon-flavored gelatin
1 tablespoon unsalted butter
Sweetened whipped cream

Beat egg whites and cream of tartar at high speed of an electric mixer until foamy. Gradually add 1 cup sugar, 1 tablespoon at a time, beating until stiff peaks form and sugar dissolves (2 to 4 minutes). Spread meringue into a lightly oiled pieplate, covering bottom and sides of pieplate. Make a large indentation in center of meringue. Bake at 250° for 1 hour and 30 minutes to 1 hour and 45 minutes. Turn oven off; let cool in oven 1 hour with electric oven door partially opened.

Position knife blade in food processor bowl; add ¼ cup raspberries, ¼ cup sugar, cornstarch, salt, water, and lemon juice. Process until smooth, stopping once to scrape down sides. Transfer mixture to a large heavy saucepan; cook over medium heat, stirring constantly, until thickened. Remove from heat; add gelatin, butter, and remaining ½ cup sugar. Stir until gelatin dissolves. Let cool.

Spread a thin layer of glaze over bottom of meringue shell. Fold 2¾ cups raspberries into remaining glaze in bowl. Spoon raspberry mixture over glaze in meringue shell. Top with remaining 1 cup raspberries. Dollop with whipped cream. Yield: one 9-inch pie.

Saint Louis Days, Saint Louis Nights
The Junior League of St. Louis, Missouri

White Chocolate-Banana Cream Pie

Feathery pillows of whipped cream endowed with white chocolate cushion generous banana slices for an out-of-this-world cream pie.

1 cup milk
½ teaspoon vanilla extract
3 egg yolks
⅓ cup sugar
2 tablespoons cornstarch
1 tablespoon butter or
   margarine
3 ounces premium white
   chocolate baking squares,
   finely chopped
1½ tablespoons crème de
   banane

1½ tablespoons white crème de
   cacao
4 ripe bananas, sliced
1 tablespoon lemon juice
1 cup whipping cream,
   whipped
1 baked 9-inch pastry shell
Garnishes: white chocolate
   curls, cocoa

Combine milk and vanilla in a medium saucepan; cook over medium heat until warm. Combine egg yolks, sugar, and cornstarch. Gradually stir about one-fourth of hot mixture into yolk mixture; add to remaining hot mixture, stirring constantly. Cook, stirring constantly, 3 minutes or until thickened and bubbly. Add butter and chopped white chocolate; stir until smooth. Gently stir in crème de banane and crème de cacao. Cover and chill thoroughly.

Toss banana slices in lemon juice. Gently fold banana slices and whipped cream into custard mixture; spoon mixture into prepared pastry shell. Cover pie, and chill 2 hours. Garnish, if desired. Yield: one 9-inch pie.   Barbara Gillispie

Cookin' in the Canyon
Gallatin Canyon Women's Club
Big Sky, Montana

Fresh Peach Pie

Tempt your senses with summer's bounty of sweet peaches. This pie takes you back to the lazy days of porch swings and warm breezes.

5 to 6 medium-size ripe peaches (about 2¼ pounds)	¼ teaspoon ground nutmeg
1 cup sugar	1 tablespoon fresh lemon juice
3 tablespoons cornstarch	1 baked 9-inch pastry shell
	Whipped cream (optional)

Peel peaches, and remove and discard pits. Mash 2½ peaches. Combine mashed peaches, sugar, cornstarch, and nutmeg in a large saucepan. Bring to a boil; reduce heat, and simmer, stirring constantly, until thickened. Remove from heat, and stir in lemon juice. Cover and let cool to room temperature.

Slice remaining peaches, and add to cooled peach mixture in pan, stirring gently. Spoon mixture into prepared pastry shell; cover and chill at least 3 hours. Serve with whipped cream, if desired. Yield: one 9-inch pie. Carolyn Gargasz

Feeding Our Flocks
The Shepherd's Fund
Hollis, New Hampshire

Cool White Chocolate-Pecan Pie

Chunky pecans wade in a velvety sea of white chocolate whipped cream.

2 tablespoons butter or margarine	¼ cup milk
2 cups chopped pecans	2 cups whipping cream
8 ounces white chocolate, broken into pieces	½ cup sugar
	1 tablespoon vanilla extract
	1 baked 9-inch pastry shell

Melt butter in a large skillet over medium-high heat. Add pecans, and cook until toasted, stirring often. Let cool completely on paper towels.

Position knife blade in food processor bowl; add chocolate pieces. Process until finely chopped. Place chocolate and milk in top of a double boiler over hot, not boiling, water, stirring constantly until chocolate melts. Let cool.

Beat whipping cream until foamy; gradually add sugar and vanilla, beating until soft peaks form. Fold in chocolate mixture and pecans.

Spoon filling into pastry shell. Cover and chill at least 3 hours. Yield: one 9-inch pie.

Virginia Fare
The Junior League of Richmond, Virginia

Raspberry-Lemon Pie

Luscious scarlet raspberries sit pristinely atop a lively lemon filling.

1 **(9-inch) graham cracker crust**	2 **egg yolks, lightly beaten**
1 **egg white, lightly beaten**	1½ **tablespoons butter**
1 **cup sugar**	¼ **cup lemon juice**
⅛ **teaspoon salt**	1 **tablespoon grated lemon rind**
2 **tablespoons cornstarch**	1 **cup fresh raspberries**
2 **tablespoons all-purpose flour**	**Garnishes: fresh mint sprigs,**
1 **cup water**	**lemon rind strips**

Brush crust with egg white, and bake at 400° for 5 minutes. Let cool completely.

Combine sugar and next 3 ingredients in a medium saucepan; slowly add water, stirring well. Cook over medium heat 3 minutes, stirring constantly. Remove from heat, and gradually stir about one-fourth of hot mixture into yolks; add to remaining hot mixture, stirring constantly. Cook 2 additional minutes over medium heat. Remove from heat, and add butter, lemon juice, and grated lemon rind; stir well. Pour into prepared crust; cover and chill 2 hours. Top with raspberries just before serving. Garnish, if desired. Yield: one 9-inch pie.

En Pointe: Culinary Delights from Pittsburgh Ballet Theatre
Pittsburgh Ballet Theatre School
Pittsburgh, Pennsylvania

Strawberries 'n' Cream Pie

1 (8-ounce) package cream
  cheese, softened
⅓ cup sugar
¼ teaspoon almond extract
1 cup whipping cream,
  whipped
1 baked 9-inch pastry shell

4 cups fresh strawberries,
  hulled
3 (1-ounce) squares semisweet
  chocolate
1 tablespoon butter or
  margarine

Beat cream cheese at medium speed of an electric mixer until creamy; gradually add sugar and almond extract, beating well. Fold in whipped cream. Spoon mixture into pastry shell. Arrange strawberries, stem side down, over whipped cream mixture.

Melt chocolate and butter in a small heavy saucepan over low heat, stirring constantly. Remove from heat, and let cool.

Spoon melted chocolate mixture into a large heavy-duty, zip-top plastic bag or a decorating bag fitted with a No. 2 round tip; seal plastic bag. Snip a tiny hole in one corner of plastic bag, using scissors. Pipe chocolate mixture in a decorative design over strawberries. Cover and chill 3 hours. Yield: one 9-inch pie.   Sally Edwards

Simply Irresistible
The Junior Auxiliary of Conway, Arkansas

Berries and Cream Tart

Plump juicy blueberries bathe in a raspberry jam and crown a smooth layer of cream cheese with a texture akin to a creamy cheesecake.

1 cup graham cracker crumbs
½ cup finely chopped pecans
2½ tablespoons sugar
¼ cup unsalted butter, melted
1 (8-ounce) package cream
  cheese, softened
⅓ cup sifted powdered sugar
1 teaspoon vanilla extract

2 tablespoons Grand Marnier
  or other orange-flavored
  liqueur
1 cup whipping cream,
  whipped
4 cups fresh blueberries
½ cup raspberry jam

Position knife blade in food processor bowl. Add first 4 ingredients; process 10 seconds. Press crumb mixture in bottom and up sides of an ungreased 11-inch tart pan with a removable bottom. Bake at 350° for 8 minutes. Let cool completely.

Beat cream cheese and powdered sugar at medium speed of an electric mixer until fluffy. Add vanilla and liqueur; beat well. Fold in whipped cream. Spoon filling into crust.

Place blueberries and raspberry jam in a small saucepan. Cook over low heat 5 minutes or until jam melts and blueberries are glazed, stirring occasionally. Spoon blueberry mixture over filling. Cover and chill 6 hours. Yield: one 11-inch tart.

Charted Courses
Child and Family Agency of Southeastern Connecticut
New London, Connecticut

Lemon Tart with Butter Pecan Crust

1¼ cups all-purpose flour
3 tablespoons sifted powdered
  sugar
¼ teaspoon salt
½ cup butter
1 egg yolk
⅓ cup finely chopped pecans
3 large eggs, beaten

1 cup sugar
1 tablespoon all-purpose flour
1 tablespoon grated lemon rind
3 tablespoons fresh lemon
  juice
3 cups fresh raspberries
⅓ cup red currant jelly, melted
Garnish: lemon rind curls

Combine first 3 ingredients in a large bowl; cut in butter with pastry blender until mixture is crumbly. Add egg yolk and pecans, stirring with a fork until dough forms a ball. Firmly press dough in bottom and up sides of an ungreased 9-inch tart pan with a removable bottom. Bake at 350° for 10 minutes. Let cool on a wire rack.

Combine beaten eggs, 1 cup sugar, 1 tablespoon flour, lemon rind, and lemon juice in a bowl; stir well. Pour mixture into prepared crust. Bake at 350° for 20 to 25 minutes or until filling is set. Let cool completely on wire rack. Cover tart with raspberries, and brush with melted jelly. Garnish, if desired. Yield: one 9-inch tart.

The Artful Table
Dallas Museum Art League
Dallas, Texas

Apple Pastry Squares

¼ cup firmly packed brown
   sugar
2 tablespoons cornstarch
1 cup water
5 cups peeled and thinly sliced
   apple
½ teaspoon ground cinnamon
¼ teaspoon ground nutmeg
1 tablespoon lemon juice
2 cups all-purpose flour

½ teaspoon salt
⅔ cup shortening
2 egg yolks, lightly beaten
¼ cup cold water
1 tablespoon lemon juice
½ cup sifted powdered sugar
1 tablespoon butter or
   margarine, softened
1 tablespoon milk
½ teaspoon vanilla extract

Combine first 3 ingredients in a large saucepan; add apple, and stir well. Bring to a boil, stirring constantly; reduce heat, and simmer 5 minutes, stirring occasionally. Remove from heat; stir in cinnamon, nutmeg, and 1 tablespoon lemon juice. Set aside.

Combine flour and salt; cut in shortening with pastry blender until mixture is crumbly. Combine egg yolks, water, and 1 tablespoon lemon juice; sprinkle mixture evenly over surface. Stir mixture with a fork until dry ingredients are moistened. Divide dough in half.

Roll half of pastry into a 15- x 11-inch rectangle on a lightly floured surface. Place in bottom and up sides of a 13- x 9- x 2-inch pan; spoon apple mixture into pastry. Roll remaining pastry into a 13- x 9-inch rectangle; transfer to top of pan. Fold edges under, and crimp. Cut slits in top to allow steam to escape. Bake at 400° for 40 minutes. Remove to a wire rack.

Combine powdered sugar and remaining 3 ingredients in a small bowl; stir until smooth. Drizzle glaze over warm pastry. Cut into 24 squares. Yield: 2 dozen. Verna Wahl

Years and Years of Goodwill Cooking
Goodwill Circle of New Hope Lutheran Church
Upham, North Dakota

Date-Nut Cheese Pastries

Cookie-like pastry dotted with cheese surrounds a delectable filling of dates and pecans–it'll be hard to eat just one.

2 cups all-purpose flour
1 teaspoon baking powder
2 cups (8 ounces) shredded
  sharp Cheddar cheese
1 cup butter or margarine
¼ cup cold water

1 (8-ounce) package chopped
  dates
1 cup chopped pecans
1 (12-ounce) jar orange
  marmalade

Combine first 3 ingredients; cut in butter with pastry blender until mixture is crumbly. Sprinkle cold water (1 tablespoon at a time) evenly over surface; stir with a fork until dry ingredients are moistened. Shape into a ball; cover and chill.

Combine dates, pecans, and marmalade; stir well.

Roll pastry to ⅛-inch thickness on a lightly floured surface; cut into 2-inch circles. Place 1 heaping teaspoon date mixture on half of each pastry circle. To seal pastries, dip fingers in water, and moisten edges of pastry circles; fold circles in half, making sure edges are even. Press edges of filled pastry firmly together, using a fork dipped in flour.

Place pastries on lightly greased baking sheets. Bake at 400° for 10 to 12 minutes or until golden. Remove to wire racks, and let cool completely. Yield: about 5 dozen.   Doris Davis

Helpings of Hope
Franklin County Habitat for Humanity
Louisburg, North Carolina

Cream Horns

These spiral pastries stuffed to creamy plumpness are elegant edible art.

1 cup butter, divided
1¾ cups all-purpose flour
½ cup cold water
1 large egg, separated

2 tablespoons milk
1 teaspoon water
3 tablespoons sugar, divided
Cream Filling

Cut in 1 tablespoon butter into flour with pastry blender until mixture is crumbly. Sprinkle ½ cup cold water (1 tablespoon at a time) evenly over surface; stir with a fork until flour is moistened. Knead 2 minutes or until smooth; shape into a ball. Using a sharp knife, score 2 (½-inch-deep) slits in top of ball, forming an X; wrap in wax paper. Chill 15 minutes.

Knead remaining ¾ cup plus 3 tablespoons butter with hands until pliable. (If heat from hands begins to melt butter, rinse hands under cold water.) Shape butter into a 6-inch square on wax paper; freeze 5 minutes.

Roll pastry into a 20- x 8-inch rectangle on a lightly floured surface; place chilled butter square on pastry 2 inches from one of the short sides. Fold other short side over butter.

Working quickly so butter does not melt, roll pastry into a 20- x 8-inch rectangle on a lightly floured surface. Fold rectangle into thirds, beginning with short side; fold into thirds again, beginning with short side. Roll pastry into another 20- x 8-inch rectangle; fold rectangle into thirds and again into thirds. Wrap pastry in wax paper, and chill 1 hour. Repeat rolling, folding, and chilling process 3 times.

Divide dough in half. Roll half of pastry dough into a 15- x 8-inch rectangle on a lightly floured surface, keeping remaining half of dough chilled. Cut into eight 15- x 1-inch strips. Starting at tip of mold, wrap one strip around an ungreased 4-inch metal cream horn mold, winding strip spiral-fashion and overlapping edges about ¼ inch. Place on a lightly greased baking sheet, end of strip down. Repeat with remaining strips. Combine egg yolk and milk; brush over entire pastry.

Bake at 425° for 12 minutes or until puffed and golden. Remove from oven, and gently slide molds from pastry. Combine egg white and 1 teaspoon water; brush over entire pastry, and sprinkle evenly with half of sugar. Bake 3 additional minutes. Remove from oven, and let cool completely on a wire rack. Repeat procedure with remaining pastry dough, egg mixtures, and sugar.

Spoon Cream Filling into a decorating bag fitted with metal tip No. 8. Pipe filling into pastry horns. Chill until ready to serve. Yield: 16 servings.

Cream Filling

½ cup sugar	1¾ cups milk
1½ tablespoons cornstarch	1 large egg, lightly beaten
1 tablespoon all-purpose flour	2 tablespoons butter
¼ teaspoon salt	1 teaspoon vanilla extract

Combine first 4 ingredients in a large saucepan, stirring well. Gradually stir in milk and egg. Cook over medium heat, stirring constantly, until mixture comes to a boil; boil 1 minute or until thickened, stirring constantly. Remove from heat, and stir in butter and vanilla. Cover tightly with plastic wrap, and let cool slightly. Chill thoroughly. Yield: 2 cups.

A Taste of Toronto: Ohio, That Is
Toronto High School Alumni Association
Toronto, Ohio

Too-Easy Peach Cobbler

Bread slices encrusted with a sugar-butter coating are the quick secret to this simple cobbler.

6 medium-size fresh ripe peaches	½ cup butter or margarine, melted
5 slices white bread	2 tablespoons all-purpose flour
1 cup sugar	1 large egg, lightly beaten

Blanch peaches in boiling water 1 minute. Drain and rinse under cold water until cool. Drain. Peel skins from peaches, and slice peaches. Place peach slices in a greased 8-inch square baking dish.

Remove and discard crust from bread; cut each bread slice into 5 rectangular strips. Arrange evenly over peach slices.

Combine sugar, butter, flour, and egg; stir well. Pour over bread. Bake at 350° for 30 to 35 minutes or until golden. Let stand 10 minutes before serving. Yield: 6 servings.

Food for Thought
The Junior League of Birmingham, Alabama

Apple Crisp with Orange Juice

4 medium-size cooking apples, cored and sliced
¼ cup orange juice
1 cup sugar
¾ cup all-purpose flour
½ teaspoon ground cinnamon
¼ teaspoon ground nutmeg
Dash of salt
⅓ cup butter or margarine
Whipping cream

Place sliced apple in a buttered 8-inch square baking dish; drizzle with orange juice. Combine sugar and next 4 ingredients; cut in butter with pastry blender until mixture is crumbly, and sprinkle over apple mixture. Bake at 375° for 45 minutes or until apple is tender and topping is golden. Serve warm with whipping cream. Yield: 4 servings.

Barbara Bush

Take Note! Band Boosters Community Cookbook
Pinconning Area Schools Band Boosters
Pinconning, Michigan

Pear-Cranberry Crisp

8 firm ripe pears, peeled, cored, and sliced (about 3 pounds)
2 (12-ounce) packages fresh or frozen cranberries, thawed
⅔ cup sugar
1 teaspoon ground cinnamon, divided
1½ cups regular oats, uncooked
1⅓ cups firmly packed brown sugar
1 cup all-purpose flour
Pinch of salt
1 cup butter or margarine, cut into ½-inch pieces

Combine pear slices, cranberries, ⅔ cup sugar, and ½ teaspoon cinnamon in a large bowl; toss gently. Spoon mixture into a lightly greased 13- x 9- x 2-inch baking dish.

Combine oats, brown sugar, flour, salt, and remaining ½ teaspoon cinnamon; cut in butter with pastry blender until mixture is crumbly. Sprinkle mixture over fruit mixture. Bake at 375° for 40 to 45 minutes or until topping is golden. Let stand 10 minutes. Yield: 10 servings.

Everybody Bring a Dish, Cooking in the Spirit of Shalom
Shalom United Church of Christ
Richland, Washington

Poultry

Chicken Pie, page 241

Roast Chicken with Artichokes, Tomatoes, and Peppers

Tender roasted chicken gains classy distinction from the artichoke rub massaged under its skin.

1 medium-size green pepper
1 (14-ounce) can artichoke
   hearts, drained and divided
2 cloves garlic, peeled
1 tablespoon olive oil, divided
½ teaspoon salt
¼ teaspoon freshly ground
   black pepper

1 (3½-pound) broiler-fryer
Salt and black pepper to taste
½ lemon, quartered
3 sprigs fresh rosemary
1 (14½-ounce) can whole
   tomatoes, drained and
   coarsely chopped
⅛ teaspoon ground red pepper

Wash and dry green pepper; place on an aluminum foil-lined baking sheet. Broil 5½ inches from heat (with electric oven door partially opened) about 5 minutes on each side or until pepper looks blistered.

Place pepper in a heavy-duty, zip-top plastic bag; seal bag, and let stand 10 minutes. Peel pepper; remove core and seeds. Cut pepper into 1½-inch strips. Set aside.

Position knife blade in food processor bowl; add 4 artichoke hearts, garlic, 2 teaspoons olive oil, ½ teaspoon salt, and ¼ teaspoon black pepper. Process until smooth, stopping once to scrape down sides.

Loosen skin from chicken breast without totally detaching skin; rub artichoke mixture under skin on chicken. Rub remaining 1 teaspoon oil over outside of chicken; sprinkle with salt and pepper to taste.

Insert remaining artichoke hearts, lemon, and rosemary in cavity. Tie ends of legs together with string. Lift wing tips up and over back, and tuck under bird. Place chicken, breast side up, on a lightly greased rack in a shallow roasting pan. Insert meat thermometer into meaty portion of thigh, making sure it does not touch bone. Bake at 450° for 35 minutes.

Combine tomatoes, pepper strips, and red pepper. Spoon mixture over chicken. Bake 35 additional minutes or until thermometer registers 180°, basting once with pan juices. (Cover with foil the last 10 minutes of baking to prevent excessive browning, if necessary.) Let stand 10 minutes before serving. Yield: 4 servings.   Lois Lipson

Hand in Hand, Heart to Heart
Sisterhood Temple Beth El
Allentown, Pennsylvania

Chicken Pie

1 (2½- to 3-pound) broiler-fryer
1 medium onion, quartered
1 stalk celery, cut into 1-inch
  pieces
1 bay leaf
1 teaspoon salt
1 teaspoon dried thyme
1 teaspoon dried rosemary
1 teaspoon dried basil
1 cup peeled, chopped potato
⅓ cup butter or margarine
1 cup chopped celery
1 cup chopped onion
1 cup chopped carrot
½ cup all-purpose flour
1½ cups half-and-half
¾ teaspoon salt
¼ teaspoon pepper
3 cups all-purpose flour
1 teaspoon salt
1 cup shortening
1 large egg, lightly beaten
1 tablespoon white vinegar
¼ cup plus 2 tablespoons water
1 large egg, lightly beaten
1 tablespoon milk

Combine first 8 ingredients in a large Dutch oven; add water to cover. Bring to a boil; cover, reduce heat, and simmer 1 hour. Remove chicken from broth, reserving broth; let chicken cool. Bone chicken, and coarsely chop meat. Set aside. Strain broth, reserving 1½ cups.

Cook potato in butter in a large skillet over medium-high heat 5 minutes, stirring constantly. Add celery, onion, and carrot; cook 5 additional minutes, stirring constantly. Add ½ cup flour, stirring well; cook 1 minute, stirring constantly. Gradually add reserved 1½ cups broth and half-and-half; cook over medium heat, stirring constantly, until mixture is thickened and bubbly. Stir in ¾ teaspoon salt, pepper, and reserved chicken. Set aside.

Combine 3 cups flour and 1 teaspoon salt; cut in shortening with pastry blender until mixture is crumbly. Combine egg, vinegar, and water; sprinkle evenly over surface. Stir with a fork until dry ingredients are moistened. Shape into a ball.

Roll two-thirds of pastry to ⅛-inch thickness on a floured surface. Fit pastry into a 2½-quart casserole. Spoon chicken mixture into prepared pastry. Roll remaining pastry to ⅛-inch thickness; cut into ¾-inch strips. Arrange strips in a lattice design over chicken mixture. Seal pastry edges. Combine remaining egg and milk; brush over pastry. Bake at 400° for 30 minutes or until golden and chicken mixture is hot and bubbly. Yield: 6 servings.

Catherine Hicks

The Heritage Cookbook
St. George's Episcopal Church
Fredericksburg, Virginia

Forty-Garlic Chicken

Yes, 40 cloves of garlic! Long roasting mellows garlic's intensity.
Spread the softened cloves on French bread for a savory topping.

1 (3- to 3½-pound) broiler-
  fryer, cut up
1½ teaspoons salt, divided
¼ teaspoon pepper
Dash of nutmeg
40 cloves garlic
3 tablespoons olive oil

3 tablespoons butter or
  margarine, melted
2 stalks celery, thinly sliced
¼ cup minced fresh parsley
½ cup whipping cream
½ cup sherry

Sprinkle chicken with 1 teaspoon salt, pepper, and nutmeg; set aside.
Place garlic in boiling water to cover; cook 30 seconds. Drain; remove and discard skins.
Combine oil and butter; pour 1 tablespoon into a 3-quart baking dish, coating bottom and sides. Dip chicken in remaining mixture. Layer half of garlic in dish; add half each of celery and parsley. Sprinkle with ¼ teaspoon salt. Add half of chicken. Layer remaining garlic, celery, parsley, ¼ teaspoon salt, and chicken. Pour cream and sherry over chicken. Bake at 350° for 1 hour and 15 minutes or until done, basting occasionally. Yield: 4 servings.   Donna Fox

Bountiful Blessings
St. Luke's United Methodist Church
Orlando, Florida

Beer-Batter Chicken

2 (3-pound) broiler-fryers,
  cut up
1 large onion, chopped
4 stalks celery
2 teaspoons salt
½ teaspoon pepper
1½ cups all-purpose flour

1½ teaspoons baking powder
1½ teaspoons salt
1½ teaspoons sugar
1 (12-ounce) bottle beer
1 large egg, lightly beaten
Vegetable oil

Combine first 5 ingredients in a large Dutch oven; cover with water. Bring to a boil; cover, reduce heat, and simmer 20 minutes. Drain chicken, reserving broth for another use; let chicken cool.

Combine flour and next 3 ingredients in a large bowl; add beer and egg. Stir until smooth. Dip chicken in batter to cover.

Pour oil to depth of 6 inches into a Dutch oven; heat to 375°. Fry chicken, in batches, in hot oil 4 to 6 minutes or until chicken is done. Drain on paper towels. Yield: 8 servings.   Jo Wischer

Recipes and Remembrances
Newport Bicentennial Commission
Newport, Kentucky

Chicken Burgundy

1 (3½-pound) package chicken pieces	1 tablespoon minced fresh parsley
1 teaspoon salt	1 clove garlic, minced
½ teaspoon pepper	½ cup dry red wine
2 tablespoons vegetable oil	¼ teaspoon dried rosemary
1 chicken-flavored bouillon cube	1 bay leaf
¼ cup warm water	1 tablespoon cornstarch
2 tablespoons minced onion	2 tablespoons cold water
1 tablespoon minced celery	Salt and pepper to taste

Sprinkle chicken with 1 teaspoon salt and ½ teaspoon pepper. Brown in oil in a large skillet over medium-high heat. Place chicken, skin side up, in a lightly greased 13- x 9- x 2-inch baking dish.

Dissolve bouillon cube in ¼ cup water. Add bouillon, onion, celery, parsley, and garlic to skillet. Cook over medium-high heat 1 minute, stirring constantly. Add wine, rosemary, and bay leaf. Pour wine mixture over chicken.

Cover and bake at 325° for 45 minutes or until chicken is done. Remove chicken to a serving platter, reserving drippings in dish. Set chicken aside, and keep warm. Remove and discard bay leaf.

Combine cornstarch and 2 tablespoons water. Add to pan drippings, stirring well. Cover and bake 5 additional minutes. Sprinkle with salt and pepper to taste. Spoon warm sauce over chicken. Yield: 8 servings.   Isa Louise Byers Blaney

Queen Anne Goes to the Kitchen
Episcopal Church Women of St. Paul's Parish
Centreville, Maryland

Chicken Mandarin with Three Happiness Orange-Almond Rice

1 (2½-pound) package chicken pieces, skinned
½ teaspoon salt
½ teaspoon pepper
1 cup chopped onion
1 clove garlic, pressed
1 tablespoon butter or margarine, melted
1 cup chicken broth
1 (11-ounce) can mandarin oranges, undrained
⅓ cup orange marmalade
¼ cup ketchup
2 tablespoons soy sauce
2 teaspoons dry mustard
1 green pepper, seeded and cut into thin strips
Three Happiness Orange-Almond Rice

Sprinkle chicken with salt and pepper. Place in a lightly greased 13- x 9- x 2-inch pan. Bake at 350° for 30 minutes.

Cook onion and garlic in butter in a large skillet over medium-high heat until tender. Add chicken broth and next 5 ingredients, stirring well. Bring to a boil; reduce heat, and simmer 10 minutes. Spoon broth mixture over chicken. Bake 20 additional minutes.

Stir in green pepper, and bake 5 additional minutes. Serve chicken and warm sauce over Three Happiness Orange-Almond Rice. Yield: 6 servings.

Three Happiness Orange-Almond Rice

2 cups orange juice
1 cup water
¼ cup plus 2 tablespoons butter or margarine
2 teaspoons salt
1½ cups long-grain rice, uncooked
½ cup sliced almonds, toasted
⅓ cup chopped fresh parsley

Combine first 4 ingredients in a medium saucepan, and bring to a boil. Add rice; cover, reduce heat, and simmer 30 minutes or until liquid is absorbed and rice is tender. Add almonds and parsley, stirring well. Yield: 5 cups.   Mona Williams and Kelly Strand

History, Memories & Recipes
Fox River Grove Diamond Jubilee Committee
Fox River Grove, Illinois

Yogurt Chicken Curry

Garlic, ginger, cinnamon, and cloves spice up inexpensive chicken thighs for a one-dish meal that's easy to make–and easy to love.

2 medium onions, chopped
1 tablespoon butter or
   margarine, melted
1 large clove garlic, minced
2 teaspoons minced fresh
   ginger
1½ teaspoons curry powder
1 teaspoon salt
¾ teaspoon ground turmeric

½ teaspoon ground cloves
¼ teaspoon ground cinnamon
¼ teaspoon pepper
1 cup peeled, seeded, and
   diced tomato
1 cup plain yogurt
8 skinned chicken thighs
3 cups cooked rice
¼ cup chopped fresh parsley

Cook onion in butter in a large skillet over medium-high heat, stirring constantly, until tender. Stir in garlic and next 7 ingredients; cook 1 minute, stirring constantly. Stir in tomato and yogurt.

Place chicken thighs on top of tomato mixture. Bring to a boil; cover, reduce heat, and simmer 30 minutes. Uncover, turn chicken, and simmer 15 minutes or until chicken is tender.

Combine rice and parsley in a medium bowl; toss gently. Serve chicken over parsley rice. Yield: 4 servings.   Carina Amaya

Calvert Street School 1995 Cookbook
Calvert Street School
Woodland Hills, California

Mexican Chicken Kiev

Monterey Jack cheese and green chiles mingle discreetly inside crispy coated chicken breasts. When cut, the buttery essence of the cheese and chiles oozes onto your dinner plate. You can make this dish ahead for company or treat your family to an ethnic delight.

8 large skinned and boned
   chicken breast halves
1 (4.5-ounce) can chopped
   green chiles, drained
4 ounces Monterey Jack
   cheese, cut into 8 strips
½ cup fine, dry breadcrumbs
½ cup grated Parmesan cheese

1 tablespoon chili powder
½ teaspoon ground cumin
½ teaspoon salt
⅛ teaspoon pepper
¼ cup plus 2 tablespoons
   butter or margarine, melted
Salsa

Place chicken between two sheets of heavy-duty plastic wrap, and flatten to ¼-inch thickness, using a meat mallet or rolling pin. Place chiles and cheese evenly on top of chicken breasts. Roll up chicken, starting with short end; secure with wooden picks.

Combine breadcrumbs and next 5 ingredients. Dip chicken rolls in melted butter; dredge in breadcrumb mixture. Place in a lightly greased 13- x 9- x 2-inch baking dish. Cover and chill 8 hours.

Bake at 400° for 30 minutes or until chicken is done; discard wooden picks. Serve chicken with salsa. Yield: 8 servings.

Entertaining in Kingwood
Kingwood Women's Club
Kingwood, Texas

Chicken Breasts Stuffed with Dried Tomatoes, Feta, Olives, and Pine Nuts

Tangy feta cheese, tempting olives, and toasted pine nuts stuff the side pockets of these chicken breasts. We recommend buying large chicken breasts to accommodate the chunky filling.

½ cup finely chopped purple
   onion
1½ teaspoons minced garlic
2 tablespoons olive oil, divided
1 cup crumbled feta cheese
½ cup pitted ripe olives, sliced
½ cup oil-packed dried
   tomatoes, drained, and
   cut into thin strips

¼ cup pine nuts, toasted
2 tablespoons freshly grated
   Parmesan cheese
1 teaspoon dried marjoram
4 large skinned and boned
   chicken breast halves

Cook onion and garlic in 1 tablespoon oil in a large skillet over medium-high heat, stirring constantly, until tender. Let cool. Add feta cheese and next 5 ingredients; stir well.

Cut a pocket in each chicken breast half, cutting to, but not through, remaining side. Spoon feta mixture evenly into each pocket, and secure with wooden picks. Brown chicken in remaining 1 tablespoon oil in a large skillet over medium-high heat. Remove chicken to a lightly greased 8-inch square baking dish.

Bake at 350° for 30 minutes or until chicken is done. Discard wooden picks. Yield: 4 servings. Mrs. Paul M. Bowman

Emmanuel's Best in Cooking
Emmanuel Episcopal Church
Chestertown, Maryland

Chicken en Papillote

3 large carrots, scraped and cut into thin strips
3 medium zucchini, cut into thin strips
6 green onions, cut into 1-inch pieces
2 tablespoons minced fresh parsley
1 teaspoon salt
1½ teaspoons grated lemon rind
⅛ teaspoon pepper
Vegetable cooking spray
6 large skinned and boned chicken breasts halves
¼ cup plus 2 tablespoons butter or margarine

Combine first 7 ingredients in a large bowl; toss well, and set aside.

Cut six 12-inch squares of parchment paper; fold each square in half, and trim each into a large heart shape. Place parchment hearts on a baking sheet, and open out flat. Coat open side of parchment paper with cooking spray. Place 1 chicken breast half on parchment heart near the crease. Spoon vegetable mixture evenly over chicken; top each portion of vegetables with 1 tablespoon butter.

Fold paper edges over to seal securely. Starting with rounded edges of hearts, pleat and crimp edges of parchment to make an airtight seal. Bake at 375° for 20 minutes or until packets are puffed and lightly browned.

Place packets on six individual serving plates; cut an opening in the top of each packet. Fold paper back on packet. Serve immediately. Yield: 6 servings.

The Guild Cookbook, Volume IV
The Valparaiso University Guild
Valparaiso, Indiana

Colby's Cheesy Chicken

Your favorite barbecue sauce, green chiles, and melted cheese turn plain chicken into a southwestern meal in minutes.

8 skinned and boned chicken breast halves
¾ cup barbecue sauce
1 (4.5-ounce) can chopped green chiles, undrained
½ cup chopped green pepper
½ cup (2 ounces) shredded Monterey Jack cheese
½ cup (2 ounces) shredded Colby cheese

Place chicken in a lightly greased 13- x 9- x 2-inch baking dish. Brush chicken with barbecue sauce.

Bake, uncovered, at 375° for 15 minutes; sprinkle with green chiles and chopped green pepper. Bake 15 additional minutes or until chicken is done.

Place chicken on a serving platter, reserving drippings. Stir drippings until smooth, and pour over chicken; top with cheeses. Serve immediately. Yield: 8 servings.   Colby Cox

Discover Oklahoma Cookin'
Oklahoma 4-H Foundation
Stillwater, Oklahoma

Grilled Chicken with Summer Salsa

Summer's sweet abundance of fresh peaches, plums, pineapple, and red pepper gives grilled chicken a face-lift. You can also serve the colorful salsa with fish or pork.

1 **cup chopped fresh plums**
1 **cup peeled and chopped
   fresh peaches**
½ **cup chopped fresh
   pineapple**
¼ **cup chopped sweet red
   pepper**
2½ **tablespoons white wine
   vinegar**
1½ **tablespoons minced fresh
   cilantro**
1 **teaspoon sugar**
¼ **teaspoon chili powder**
6 **skinned and boned chicken
   breast halves**
¼ **teaspoon salt**
¼ **teaspoon pepper**
Vegetable cooking spray

Combine first 8 ingredients in a medium bowl, and toss well. Cover salsa, and chill at least 3 hours.

Sprinkle chicken breast halves with salt and pepper.

Coat grill rack with cooking spray; place rack on grill over medium-hot coals (350° to 400°). Place chicken on rack, and grill, covered, 5 minutes on each side or until chicken is done. Serve salsa with chicken. Serve immediately. Yield: 6 servings.   Marilyn Wyrick Ingram

Homecoming: Special Foods, Special Memories
Baylor University Alumni Association
Waco, Texas

Provolone Chicken

6 skinned and boned chicken
  breast halves
½ cup all-purpose flour
1 teaspoon salt
½ teaspoon minced fresh
  tarragon
¼ teaspoon pepper

¼ cup butter or margarine,
  melted and divided
¼ cup dry white wine
½ pound sliced fresh
  mushrooms
1 (6-ounce) package sliced
  provolone cheese

Place chicken between two sheets of heavy-duty plastic wrap, and flatten to ¼-inch thickness, using a meat mallet or rolling pin.

Combine flour and next 3 ingredients in a heavy-duty, zip-top plastic bag; add chicken. Seal bag, and shake to coat.

Cook 3 chicken breasts in 2 tablespoons butter in a large skillet over medium-high heat 4 minutes on each side or until done. Remove chicken from skillet, and place in a lightly greased 13- x 9- x 2-inch baking dish. Cover and keep warm. Repeat procedure with remaining 3 chicken breasts and 2 tablespoons butter.

Add wine to skillet; bring to a boil, deglazing skillet by scraping particles that cling to bottom. Add mushrooms; cook 3 minutes. Pour mixture over chicken. Top each breast with a cheese slice. Broil 5½ inches from heat (with electric oven door partially opened) 2 minutes or until cheese melts. Yield: 6 servings.   Norma Russell

Recipes From Colorado's Wine and Fruit Valley
Palisade Community Cookbook Association
Palisade, Colorado

Pecan Chicken

Buttery pecans roasted with the chicken lend crunch to the rich Dijon-sour cream sauce that distinguishes this dish.

8 skinned and boned chicken
  breast halves (about 2½
  pounds)
½ teaspoon salt
⅛ teaspoon pepper
½ cup butter or margarine,
  melted

¼ cup plus 2 tablespoons Dijon
  mustard, divided
1 cup coarsely chopped pecans
1 (16-ounce) carton sour cream
⅓ cup water (optional)

Sprinkle chicken with salt and pepper; place in a greased 13- x 9- x 2-inch baking dish. Combine butter and ¼ cup mustard; stir well. Pour over chicken; sprinkle pecans over top. Bake, uncovered, at 375° for 35 minutes or until chicken is done. Remove chicken to a serving platter, reserving drippings in dish; keep warm.

Combine remaining 2 tablespoons mustard, pan drippings, sour cream, and water, if desired for consistency, in a large saucepan; cook over medium heat until thoroughly heated, stirring often. To serve, pour sauce over chicken. Yield: 8 servings.

Entertaining Recipes II
Madison Zonta Club
Middleton, Wisconsin

Apple-Cheese Chicken Casserole

Warm brandy ignites the senses in this memorable casserole.

3 medium cooking apples, peeled, cored, and sliced	1 teaspoon salt
2 large onions, thinly sliced	¼ teaspoon pepper
¼ cup plus 1 tablespoon butter or margarine, melted and divided	1 cup (4 ounces) shredded Swiss cheese
6 skinned and boned chicken breast halves	½ cup grated Parmesan cheese
	¼ cup fine, dry breadcrumbs
	½ teaspoon dried thyme
	2 tablespoons brandy

Cook apple and onion in ¼ cup butter in a large skillet over medium heat 10 minutes or until tender, stirring occasionally. Coat a 13- x 9- x 2-inch baking dish with remaining 1 tablespoon butter. Spoon apple mixture into prepared baking dish.

Sprinkle chicken with salt and pepper; arrange over apple mixture. Combine cheeses, breadcrumbs, and thyme; sprinkle evenly over chicken. Bake at 350° for 45 minutes or until chicken is done.

Place brandy in a small long-handled saucepan; heat until warm (do not boil). Remove from heat. Ignite with a long match; pour over casserole. Serve immediately after flames die down. Yield: 6 servings.

Dining with Duke Cookbook
Badger Association of the Blind
Milwaukee, Wisconsin

Chicken Livers with Sage

White wine and prosciutto dress up plebeian chicken livers for a tempting dinner we recommend serving over rice.

1 pound chicken livers	¼ cup butter or margarine
1½ tablespoons chopped fresh sage	¼ cup minced prosciutto
½ teaspoon salt	¼ cup dry white wine
¼ teaspoon freshly ground pepper	

Sprinkle chicken livers with sage, salt, and pepper; set aside.

Heat butter in a skillet over medium-high heat until hot. Add prosciutto, and cook 1 minute. Stir in chicken livers, cook 5 to 6 minutes, stirring constantly. Add wine. Bring to a boil; reduce heat, and simmer 3 minutes. Yield: 4 servings.   Camille Codella

Cucina Classica, Maintaining a Tradition
Order Sons of Italy in America,
New York Grand Lodge Foundation
Bellmore, New York

Lemon-Sage Turkey

Fresh sage leaves tucked underneath the skin of this juicy turkey impart their musty mint aroma. This turkey's pan juices are delectable if you like to make your own homemade gravy.

2 tablespoons butter or margarine, softened	1 lemon, halved
2 tablespoons fresh lemon juice	1 teaspoon salt, divided
1 (12-pound) turkey	½ teaspoon freshly ground pepper, divided
8 to 10 fresh sage leaves	Lemon-Parmesan Stuffing
	2 cups dry white wine

Beat butter at medium speed of an electric mixer until creamy. Gradually beat in lemon juice, a few drops at a time. Set aside.

Remove giblets and neck from turkey; set giblets aside for use in stuffing. Reserve neck for other uses. Rinse turkey thoroughly with cold water, and pat dry with paper towels.

Carefully loosen skin from turkey at neck area, working down to breast and thigh area. Rub two-thirds butter mixture under skin. Place sage leaves between skin and meat. Rub inside of body and neck cavities with lemon halves. Sprinkle cavities with ½ teaspoon salt and ¼ teaspoon pepper.

Lightly stuff Lemon-Parmesan Stuffing into body and neck cavities of turkey. Tie ends of legs together with string. Lift wingtips up and over back, and tuck under turkey. Coat bird with remaining one-third lemon butter mixture; sprinkle with remaining ½ teaspoon salt and ¼ teaspoon pepper. Pour wine into a large roasting pan. Place turkey on a rack in pan. Insert meat thermometer into meaty portion of thigh, making sure it does not touch bone.

Bake, uncovered, at 325° for 4 hours or until thermometer registers 180°. Turkey is done when drumsticks are easy to move up and down. Let stand 15 minutes before carving. Yield: 12 servings.

Lemon-Parmesan Stuffing

2 **medium onions, coarsely chopped (about 2 cups)**
¼ **cup butter, melted**
Turkey giblets, chopped
1½ **cups dry white wine**
2 **lemons, peeled, seeded, and diced**
6 **cups day-old bread cubes**

⅔ **cup freshly grated Parmesan cheese**
¼ **cup chopped fresh parsley**
2 **tablespoons chopped fresh sage**
1 **teaspoon salt**
1 **teaspoon cracked pepper**

Cook onion in butter in a large skillet over medium-high heat, stirring constantly, until tender. Add giblets and wine. Bring to a boil; cover, reduce heat, and simmer 45 minutes or until giblets are tender. Add lemon, and cook, uncovered, 2 minutes.

Place bread cubes in a large bowl. Pour giblet mixture over bread cubes; add Parmesan cheese and remaining ingredients, tossing well. Yield: 6½ cups.

Everybody Bring a Dish, Cooking in the Spirit of Shalom
Shalom United Church of Christ
Richland, Washington

Turkey Breast Florentine

An easy filling of spinach, mushrooms, and creamy cheese spirals in this turkey breast roll. Keep the skin on the turkey to seal in its juices.

5 slices bacon
½ cup chopped onion
3 tablespoons all-purpose
    flour
1½ cups milk
½ teaspoon dried tarragon
¼ teaspoon pepper
1 (10-ounce) package frozen
    chopped spinach, thawed

1 (3-pound) boneless turkey
    breast
1 (2.5-ounce) jar sliced
    mushrooms, drained
1 tablespoon butter or
    margarine, melted
⅓ cup (1.3 ounces) shredded
    process American cheese

Chop 2 slices bacon. Cook chopped bacon in a large skillet until crisp. Drain, reserving drippings in skillet; set bacon aside. Add onion to drippings in skillet, and cook, stirring constantly, until tender. Add flour, stirring constantly. Gradually add milk; cook over medium heat, stirring constantly, until mixture is thickened and bubbly. Stir in tarragon and pepper. Reserve ½ cup sauce. Cover and chill remaining sauce.

Cook spinach according to package directions; drain and press between paper towels to remove excess moisture. Place in a large bowl; set aside.

Remove skin from turkey breast, reserving skin. Place turkey breast between two sheets of heavy-duty plastic wrap, and flatten to ½-inch thickness, using a meat mallet or rolling pin. Set aside.

Add cooked bacon, ½ cup reserved sauce, and mushrooms to spinach; mix well. Spread spinach mixture in center of turkey to within 1 inch of sides. Roll up turkey, jellyroll fashion, starting with long side. Wrap reserved turkey skin around turkey. Secure at 2-inch intervals with string.

Place turkey on a rack in a roasting pan. Brush with butter. Bake, uncovered, at 350° for 1½ hours. Remove string; arrange remaining 3 bacon slices crosswise over turkey. Bake 45 additional minutes or until meat thermometer registers 180°; let stand 10 minutes before slicing.

Combine remaining sauce and cheese in a small saucepan. Cook over medium heat, stirring constantly, until cheese melts. Serve cheese sauce with turkey. Yield: 6 servings.   Beth Ann Dague

The Best of Wheeling
The Junior League of Wheeling, West Virginia

Hot Brown

This classic open-face sandwich layers crisp bacon, sliced turkey, and tomato, and then smothers it all in a robust cheese sauce.

8 slices bacon
8 slices bread, crusts removed
   and toasted
1 pound sliced cooked turkey
   breast

4 slices tomato
Cheese Sauce
½ cup grated Parmesan cheese

Cook bacon in a large skillet over medium heat until partially crisp; remove bacon, and set aside.

Cut 4 slices of toast in half diagonally. Place 2 slices, cut side in, with one whole slice in the center, on an ovenproof plate or a 15- x 10- x 1-inch jellyroll pan. Repeat with remaining toast. Top with turkey, tomato, Cheese Sauce, bacon, and Parmesan cheese. Bake at 425° for 15 minutes or until bacon is crisp and sauce is bubbly. Yield: 4 servings.

Cheese Sauce

2 tablespoons butter or
   margarine
2 tablespoons all-purpose flour
2 cups milk
½ teaspoon Worcestershire
   sauce

¼ teaspoon salt
¼ cup (1 ounce) shredded
   sharp Cheddar cheese
¼ cup grated Parmesan cheese

Melt butter in a heavy saucepan over low heat; add flour, stirring until smooth. Cook 1 minute, stirring constantly. Gradually add milk, Worcestershire sauce, and salt; cook over medium heat, stirring constantly, until mixture is thickened and bubbly. Add cheeses, stirring until cheeses melt. Yield: 2¼ cups.

Recipes and Remembrances
Newport Bicentennial Commission
Newport, Kentucky

Turkey Picadillo

½ pound ground turkey
½ cup chopped onion
½ cup chopped green pepper
¼ cup chopped sweet red pepper
Dash of garlic powder
2 (14.5-ounce) cans stewed tomatoes

1 Granny Smith apple, peeled, cored, and chopped
¼ cup raisins
½ teaspoon ground cinnamon
½ teaspoon ground cumin
⅛ teaspoon ground cloves
4 cups hot cooked rice

Cook first 5 ingredients in a large nonstick skillet over medium-high heat, stirring constantly, until turkey crumbles and onion is tender; drain. Stir in tomatoes and next 5 ingredients. Bring to a boil; cover, reduce heat, and simmer 20 minutes. Serve over rice. Serve immediately. Yield: 4 servings.   Ruth Gehly

ABC of Cooking
McKean Elementary PTA
McKean, Pennsylvania

Honey-Glazed Cornish Hens with Dried Cranberries

1 cup chopped onion
¼ cup chopped fresh parsley
1 tablespoon vegetable oil
1 cup dried cranberries
1½ teaspoons ground cinnamon
1 teaspoon pepper
½ teaspoon salt

⅛ teaspoon ground cloves
4 (1-pound) Cornish hens
1 cup water
1 cup honey
2 tablespoons cornstarch
¼ cup water
Garnish: fresh parsley sprigs

Cook chopped onion and chopped parsley in oil in a large skillet over medium-high heat, stirring constantly, until onion is tender. Add cranberries and next 4 ingredients, stirring well. Set aside.

Remove giblets from hens, and reserve for other uses. Rinse hens thoroughly with cold water; pat dry with paper towels. Lift wing tips up and over back of hens, tucking wing tips under hens. Place hens, breast side up, on a lightly greased rack in a roasting pan. Lightly pack each hen with ¼ cup cranberry mixture. Close cavities; secure with wooden picks. Tie leg ends together with string. Sprinkle remaining cranberry mixture over hens. Bake, uncovered, at 350° for 40 minutes. Pour 1 cup water in pan. Brush hens with honey. Bake 45 additional minutes or until done. Remove to a serving platter, reserving drippings in pan. Set hens aside; keep warm.

Place drippings in a saucepan, adding enough water, if necessary, to measure 1¾ cups. Combine cornstarch and ¼ cup water; add to drippings, stirring well. Cook over medium heat, stirring constantly, until thickened. Spoon over hens. Garnish, if desired. Yield: 4 servings.

Jewish Cooking from Here & Far
Congregation Beth Israel
Carmel, California

Cornish Game Hens

2 (1½-pound) Cornish hens
½ teaspoon salt
¼ teaspoon pepper
3 tablespoons butter, melted
Vegetable cooking spray
1 (15-ounce) can dark sweet
  pitted cherries

1 tablespoon cornstarch
1 tablespoon brown sugar
1 teaspoon grated orange rind
½ teaspoon ground ginger
¼ teaspoon dried marjoram
1 (6-ounce) box long-grain and
  wild rice mix

Remove and discard giblets from hens; reserve for another use. Rinse hens thoroughly with cold water; pat dry with paper towels. Split each hen in half lengthwise. Sprinkle hens with salt and pepper; brush with butter. Place hens, breast side down, on broiler pan coated with cooking spray. Broil 8 inches from heat (with electric oven door partially opened) 30 minutes or until done, turning once. Keep warm.

Drain cherries, reserving liquid; add enough water to liquid to make 1 cup. Combine cornstarch and next 4 ingredients in a saucepan; gradually add reserved liquid. Bring to a boil, stirring constantly; cook 1 minute, stirring constantly, until thickened. Stir in cherries.

Prepare rice according to package directions. Serve hen halves over rice; top with sauce. Yield: 4 servings.   Rose Marie McWilliams

What's Cooking at Cathedral Plaza
Cathedral Plaza
Denver, Colorado

Braised Duck, Pullman Style

You'll only need to add a simple vegetable side dish to accompany the brown rice stuffing baked in this tender bird.

1 (5- to 6- pound) dressed duckling	1 large carrot, scraped
½ teaspoon salt	1 small onion
¼ teaspoon black pepper	1 cup water
¼ cup finely chopped onion	1 teaspoon all-purpose flour
⅓ cup butter or margarine, melted	1 cup chicken broth
1 cup long-grain rice, uncooked	⅓ cup dry red wine
2½ cups chicken broth	¼ teaspoon Dijon mustard
½ teaspoon salt	1 teaspoon Worcestershire sauce
1 large stalk celery	1 tablespoon red currant jelly
	Dash of ground red pepper
	1 large orange

Remove giblets from duckling; reserve for other uses. Rinse duckling thoroughly with cold water, and pat dry with paper towels. Prick skin with a fork at 2-inch intervals. Sprinkle cavity with ½ teaspoon salt and black pepper; set aside.

Cook chopped onion in butter in a large skillet over medium-high heat, stirring constantly, until tender. Add rice to skillet; cook, stirring constantly, until rice is lightly browned. Add 2½ cups chicken broth and ½ teaspoon salt to skillet. Bring mixture to a boil; cover, reduce heat, and simmer 20 minutes or until liquid is absorbed and rice is tender.

Stuff cavity with rice mixture. Close cavity with skewers, and truss; tie ends of legs together with string. Place duckling, breast side up, on a lightly greased rack in a roasting pan. Insert meat thermometer into thigh, making sure it does not touch bone. Place celery, carrot, small onion, and water around duckling in pan. Bake, uncovered, at 325° for 2 hours or until meat thermometer registers 180°, basting occasionally with pan juices.

Remove duckling to a serving platter, reserving juices in pan. Set duckling aside, and keep warm. Strain pan juices, discarding vegetables; skim fat. Return juices to roasting pan. Add flour, stirring until smooth. Gradually add 1 cup chicken broth to pan. Bring to a boil; reduce heat, and cook 20 minutes, stirring occasionally. Add wine and next 4 ingredients; stir until smooth. Cook until thoroughly heated, stirring occasionally.

Remove rind from orange; place rind in a small saucepan with water to cover. Bring to a boil; cook 5 minutes. Drain. Add rind to sauce, stirring gently. Section orange; arrange orange sections over duckling. Spoon ¼ cup sauce over orange sections. Serve remaining sauce with duckling. Yield: 4 servings.

West of the Rockies
The Junior Service League of Grand Junction, Colorado

Eastern Shore Roast Goose

The secret to preparing lean game birds is to add moisture and cook them covered.

1 (8-pound) dressed goose	2 cups water
1 cup chopped onion	1 tablespoon celery salt
1 cup chopped celery	1 tablespoon salt
1 cooking apple, quartered	1 teaspoon pepper
2 tablespoons dry red wine	

Remove giblets and neck from goose; reserve for other uses. Rinse goose thoroughly with water; pat dry with paper towels.

Place onion, celery, and apple inside cavity of goose. Truss goose, and place, breast side up, on a rack in a roasting pan. Pour wine over goose. Pour water into pan. Sprinkle goose with celery salt, salt, and pepper. Insert meat thermometer into thigh, making sure it does not touch bone.

Bake, uncovered, at 500° for 20 minutes. Reduce oven temperature to 350°; cover and bake 1 additional hour and 15 minutes or until meat thermometer registers 180°. Let stand 10 minutes before slicing. Yield: 6 servings.

Very Virginia: Culinary Traditions with a Twist
The Junior League of Hampton Roads
Newport News, Virginia

Deep-Fried Quail

Whole quail are tossed with an herb-kissed coating and deep-fried to a crispy golden finish.

12 quail
2 cloves garlic, crushed
1 cup all-purpose flour
1 tablespoon chopped fresh
   parsley
1½ teaspoons minced fresh
   thyme
1½ teaspoons minced fresh
   oregano

1½ teaspoons ground
   coriander
1 teaspoon dried crushed red
   pepper
1 teaspoon salt
¼ teaspoon pepper
Vegetable oil

Rinse quail thoroughly with cold water, and pat dry with paper towels. Rub quail with crushed garlic. Combine flour and next 7 ingredients in a large heavy-duty, zip-top plastic bag; add quail. Seal bag, and shake to coat.

Pour oil to depth of 5 inches into a Dutch oven; heat to 375°. Fry quail, 3 at a time, 15 to 20 minutes or until golden. Drain on paper towels, and keep warm. Repeat procedure with remaining quail. Yield: 6 servings.

Historic Spanish Point: Cooking Then and Now
Gulf Coast Heritage Association
Osprey, Florida

Salads

Fennel, Arugula, and Onion Salad with Oranges, page 266

Horseradish and Tomato Aspic

Even those of us who aren't aspic enthusiasts loved the sharpness of this horseradish and tomato marriage.

1 (3-ounce) package lemon-
  flavored gelatin
1¼ cups boiling water
1 (8-ounce) can tomato sauce
1¼ tablespoons white wine
  vinegar

2 tablespoons prepared
  horseradish
½ teaspoon salt
Dash of pepper
Lettuce leaves

Place gelatin in a medium bowl; add boiling water, and stir 2 minutes or until gelatin dissolves. Add tomato sauce and next 4 ingredients, stirring well.

Pour mixture into a lightly oiled 3½-cup mold. Cover and chill, at least 8 hours. Unmold onto a lettuce-lined serving plate. Serve immediately. Yield: 8 servings. Kathryn Jamison

Art in the Kitchen
Westmoreland Museum of Art Women's Committee
Greensburg, Pennsylvania

Frozen Fruit Salads

Served in individual cups, this frozen fruit salad with cherries, bananas, and pecans is a great make-ahead salad for any luncheon.

¾ cup plus 2 tablespoons sugar
½ cup sifted caked flour
¼ teaspoon salt
1 cup pineapple juice
3 tablespoons lemon juice
1 large egg, lightly beaten
1 cup whipping cream
1 (16½-ounce) can white
  cherries in extra heavy
  syrup, drained

1 (16-ounce) can sliced peaches
  in heavy syrup, drained
1 (8-ounce) can pineapple
  chunks, drained
1 medium banana, sliced
½ cup chopped pecans
¼ cup maraschino cherries,
  chopped
8 (8-ounce) paper cups
Green leaf lettuce (optional)

Combine first 3 ingredients in top of a double boiler; stir in pineapple juice and lemon juice. Bring water in bottom of double boiler to a boil. Reduce heat to low; cook, stirring constantly, 12 minutes or until thickened. Gradually stir a small amount of hot mixture into beaten egg; add to remaining hot mixture, stirring constantly. Cook over medium heat, stirring constantly, until candy thermometer registers 160° and mixture thickens (about 3 minutes). Remove from heat; let cool slightly. Cover and chill thoroughly.

Beat whipping cream at medium speed of an electric mixer until stiff peaks form. Fold whipped cream into chilled mixture. Stir in white cherries and next 5 ingredients. Spoon mixture evenly into paper cup-lined muffin pans. Cover and freeze at least 8 hours.

To serve, peel paper cup away from each individual salad. Serve on lettuce leaves, if desired. Yield: 8 servings. Opal Kendley

Saints Alive!
Ladies' Guild of St. Barnabas Anglican Church
Atlanta, Georgia

Oriental Cucumber and Rice Wine Vinegar Salad

Gomashio, a blend of black sesame seeds and salt, lends ethnic authenticity to this vinaigrette. You can buy gomashio at Asian food markets or substitute toasted regular sesame seeds.

2 medium cucumbers, unpeeled	2 teaspoons minced onion
1½ teaspoons salt	½ cup rice wine vinegar
3 cups shredded napa cabbage	1½ tablespoons sugar
½ cup shredded carrot	1½ teaspoons gomashio
1 green onion, thinly sliced	½ teaspoon seasoned salt

Thinly slice cucumbers, and place in a bowl with water to cover; stir in 1½ teaspoons salt. Cover and marinate in refrigerator at least 3 hours. Drain and rinse cucumber; pat dry.

Combine cucumber, cabbage, and next 3 ingredients. Combine vinegar and remaining 3 ingredients; pour dressing over salad; toss gently. Serve immediately. Yield: 6 servings. Chris Odt

Picnic in the Park
Atwood Community Center
Madison, Wisconsin

Olive and White Bean Salad

1 (15-ounce) can cannellini
  beans, rinsed and drained
1 cup pitted ripe olives
½ cup thinly sliced purple
  onion
⅓ cup diced tomato

2 tablespoons lemon juice
2 tablespoons olive oil
½ teaspoon dried basil
½ teaspoon dried thyme
½ teaspoon dried oregano
¼ teaspoon pepper

Combine all ingredients; toss well. Cover and chill at least 2 hours. Yield: 4 servings.   Phyllis Cusanelli-Lainis

Enough to Feed an Army
West Point Officers Wives' Club
West Point, New York

Sunshine Confetti Salad

Summer's harvest of tomatoes, cucumbers, and squash comes alive under a refreshing splash of red wine vinaigrette.

½ cup olive oil
¼ cup red wine vinegar
¼ cup chopped fresh basil
2 tablespoons chopped fresh
  parsley
2 tablespoons fresh lemon
  juice
1 clove garlic, minced
4 large tomatoes, chopped

4 medium cucumbers, chopped
2 medium yellow squash,
  chopped
1 medium onion, chopped
1 (6-ounce) can pitted ripe
  olives, drained
Freshly grated Parmesan cheese
Croutons

Combine first 6 ingredients in a small bowl; stir well with a wire whisk.

Combine chopped tomato and next 4 ingredients in a large bowl. Pour dressing over vegetable mixture; toss gently. Cover and chill at least 2 hours. To serve, top with Parmesan cheese and croutons. Yield: 11 servings.

Gourmet Our Way
Cascia Hall Preparatory School Parent Faculty Association
Tulsa, Oklahoma

Roast Pepper-Potato Salad

Broccoli, potatoes, and roasted peppers chill in a red wine vinaigrette.

2 medium-size sweet red peppers	2 tablespoons red wine vinegar
1 medium-size green pepper	1 clove garlic, minced
1 large red potato (about 8 ounces)	1 tablespoon minced fresh basil
1 cup broccoli flowerets	1 tablespoon minced fresh parsley
1 small tomato, seeded and chopped	¼ teaspoon salt
½ cup pitted ripe olives	Dash of pepper
	2 tablespoons olive oil

Wash and dry peppers; place on an aluminum foil-lined baking sheet. Broil peppers 5½ inches from heat (with electric oven door partially opened) about 5 minutes on each side or until peppers look blistered.

Place peppers in a heavy-duty, zip-top plastic bag; seal bag, and let stand 10 minutes. Peel peppers; remove core and seeds. Cut peppers into thin strips.

Peel and cube potato. Cook potato in boiling water to cover 10 minutes. Add broccoli, and cook 5 additional minutes. Drain well. Combine pepper strips, potato, broccoli, tomato, and olives in a bowl.

Combine vinegar and remaining 6 ingredients in a jar. Cover tightly, and shake vigorously. Pour dressing over vegetables, and toss well. Cover and chill 1 hour. Yield: 4 servings.

Presentations
Friends of Lied, Lied Center for Performing Arts
Lincoln, Nebraska

Bacon, Dill, and Onion Potato Salad

Thick slices of potato provide a hearty backdrop for bacon, dill, and onions–all in a creamy Dijon dressing.

2 pounds small round red
  potatoes, unpeeled
3 green onions, chopped
½ pound bacon, cooked and
  crumbled
1 green pepper, seeded and
  diced
1 hard-cooked egg, chopped

½ cup sour cream
¼ cup milk
3 tablespoons chopped fresh
  dill
1 tablespoon lemon juice
2 teaspoons Dijon mustard
½ teaspoon salt

Slice potatoes into ¼-inch-thick slices; place in a large saucepan; add water to cover. Bring to a boil; cover, reduce heat, and simmer 15 minutes. Drain.

Combine potato, green onions, and next 3 ingredients in a bowl; toss gently.

Combine sour cream and remaining 5 ingredients in a small bowl; stir well. Pour dressing over potato mixture; toss gently. Cover and chill. Yield: 12 servings.   Nina Geishecker

Seasonings
20th Century Club Juniors of Park Ridge, Illinois

Fennel, Arugula, and Onion Salad With Oranges

Fennel's licorice personality lures you to this showy salad of onion and orange.

1 cup fresh orange juice
2 tablespoons white wine
  vinegar
1 large shallot, sliced
⅛ teaspoon salt
⅛ teaspoon pepper
1 bay leaf
1 tablespoon extra virgin
  olive oil

1 large fennel bulb
4 (⅔-ounce) packages arugula,
  trimmed
½ medium-size purple onion,
  very thinly sliced
3 medium-size oranges, peeled
  and sectioned

Combine first 6 ingredients in a small saucepan. Bring to a boil over medium-high heat. Cook 14 minutes or until mixture is reduced to ⅔ cup. Let cool; remove and discard bay leaf.

Pour orange juice mixture and oil into container of an electric blender; process until smooth, stopping once to scrape down sides. Transfer mixture to a bowl. Cover and chill thoroughly.

Trim tough outer stalks from fennel. Cut bulb into thin slices. Combine fennel, arugula, and onion in a large bowl; pour dressing over salad, and toss well. Arrange salad on individual salad plates. Arrange orange sections around salads. Yield: 6 servings.

Creative Chef 2
Tourette Syndrome Association
Bayside, New York

Hearts of Palm Salad

1 clove garlic, minced
⅓ cup olive oil
2 tablespoons white wine
  vinegar
1 tablespoon Dijon mustard
½ teaspoon salt
½ teaspoon pepper
⅛ teaspoon dried tarragon

⅛ teaspoon dried basil
⅛ teaspoon dried thyme
6 cups mixed baby salad greens
1 (14.4-ounce) can hearts of
  palm, drained and cut into
  bite-size pieces
1 medium tomato, cut into
  wedges

Combine first 9 ingredients in a small bowl; stir with a wire whisk until blended. Cover and chill at least 4 hours.

Combine salad greens, hearts of palm, and tomato in a large bowl. Pour dressing over salad; toss well. Serve salad immediately. Yield: 6 servings.   Ann Thellefson

A Cook's Tour of Libertyville
Main Street Libertyville
Libertyville, Illinois

Autumn Salad with Spicy Walnuts

Sweet and spicy walnuts add crunchy contrast to the creamy feta cheese in this salad. The nuts are addictive, so you might want to double the recipe for munching.

2 heads red leaf lettuce, washed and torn
1 Granny Smith apple, cut into bite-size pieces
2 (4-ounce) packages crumbled feta cheese
3 tablespoons red wine vinegar
½ cup olive oil
1 tablespoon plus 1 teaspoon Dijon mustard
Spicy Walnuts

Combine lettuce, apple, and cheese; set aside. Combine vinegar, oil, and mustard; stir well with a wire whisk. Pour desired amount of dressing over salad, and toss gently. Add Spicy Walnuts to salad, and toss gently. Serve immediately. Yield: 10 servings.

Spicy Walnuts

3 tablespoons butter or margarine, melted
1 teaspoon salt
1 teaspoon ground cinnamon
¼ teaspoon ground red pepper
Dash of hot sauce
1¼ cups walnuts, coarsely chopped

Combine first 5 ingredients. Add walnuts, and stir well. Place walnuts on a baking sheet, and bake at 300° for 15 minutes.

Remove from oven, and let cool completely. Yield: 1¼ cups.

Gold'n Delicious
The Junior League of Spokane, Washington

Greek Tomato Salad

Mediterranean classics–olive oil, feta cheese, and kalamata olives–share a taste of the region in this tomato salad. A tip: Use a cherry pitter to remove pits from kalamata olives.

6 medium tomatoes, cut into
   ½-inch cubes
3 tablespoons olive oil
1½ tablespoons lemon juice
1 clove garlic, crushed
1½ teaspoons dried oregano
½ teaspoon salt

⅛ teaspoon pepper
2 (4-ounce) packages crumbled
   feta cheese
½ cup kalamata olives, pitted
2 (5-ounce) packages mixed
   baby salad greens

Combine first 9 ingredients in a large bowl, and stir well. Cover and chill at least 3 hours. To serve, add greens, and toss gently. Yield: 8 servings.
                                           Jeri Derscheid

A Cook's Tour of Gautier
Gautier Garden Club
Gautier, Mississippi

Walnut and Avocado Salad

⅔ cup vegetable oil
⅓ cup white wine vinegar
1 teaspoon salt
½ teaspoon lemon juice
1 clove garlic, minced

¼ teaspoon pepper
7 cups loosely packed torn
   romaine lettuce
1 large avocado, chopped
½ cup walnuts, toasted

Combine first 6 ingredients in a small bowl, stirring well. Cover and chill at least 8 hours.

Combine lettuce, avocado, and walnuts in a bowl. Drizzle with desired amount of dressing; toss gently. Reserve any remaining dressing for other uses. Serve salad immediately. Yield: 6 servings.

Generations
The Junior League of Rockford, Illinois

Chinese Coleslaw

Crinkly, delicate napa cabbage entertains the Asian flavors of sesame oil, ginger, and soy sauce.

5 cups coarsely chopped napa cabbage
1 cup shredded carrot
½ cup chopped green onions
1 (8-ounce) can sliced water chestnuts, drained
1 tablespoon sesame seeds, toasted
¼ cup vegetable oil

2 tablespoons sugar
2 tablespoons rice wine vinegar
1 tablespoon chopped fresh cilantro
1 tablespoon soy sauce
1 teaspoon dark sesame oil
½ teaspoon ground ginger
½ teaspoon salt
¼ teaspoon pepper

Combine first 5 ingredients in a large bowl, tossing well. Combine vegetable oil and remaining 8 ingredients; stir well with a wire whisk. Pour dressing over cabbage mixture; toss gently. Cover and chill 2 hours. Yield: 12 servings.   Katie Harvey

Gallatin Gateway School and Community Cookbook
Gateway School Support Group
Gallatin Gateway, Montana

Tortellini and Fresh Basil Salad

2 (9-ounce) packages refrigerated cheese-filled tortellini, uncooked
1 pound ripe tomatoes, seeded and chopped
3 cloves garlic, minced

⅓ cup chopped fresh basil
¼ cup chopped fresh parsley
¼ cup olive oil
3 tablespoons balsamic vinegar
½ teaspoon salt
½ teaspoon pepper

Cook pasta according to package directions. Drain and rinse with cold water; drain.

Combine tomato and remaining 7 ingredients; add pasta, and toss well. Cover and chill thoroughly. Yield: 8 servings.

The Tailgate Cookbook
National Kidney Foundation of Kansas and Western Missouri
Westwood, Kansas

Beef Tenderloin Salad with Creamy Blue Cheese Dressing

4 ounces crumbled blue
  cheese, divided
½ cup mayonnaise
¼ cup sour cream
Freshly ground black pepper
20 small new potatoes
1 large sweet red pepper
Vegetable cooking spray
1 large sweet onion, cut into
  ½-inch slices

2 tablespoons olive oil
1 (1½-pound) beef tenderloin
Freshly ground black pepper
12 cups mixed baby salad
  greens
2 large tomatoes, cut into
  ½-inch wedges
1 cup sliced fresh mushrooms
Chopped fresh chives

Position knife blade in food processor bowl; add half of cheese, mayonnaise, sour cream, and pepper. Process until smooth, stopping once to scrape down sides. Stir in remaining cheese. Chill thoroughly.

Cook potatoes in boiling water to cover 20 minutes or until tender; drain. Let cool, and chill thoroughly; cut into ½-inch slices.

Cut red pepper in half lengthwise; remove seeds. Place peppers, skin side up, on work surface; flatten with palm of hand. Set aside.

Coat grill rack with cooking spray; place rack on grill over medium-hot coals (350° to 400°). Place pepper halves, skin side down, on rack. Grill, covered, 20 minutes or until charred; remove from rack, and place in a heavy-duty, zip-top plastic bag. Seal bag. Place onion on rack; grill, covered, 5 minutes on each side or until soft, basting twice with olive oil. Remove from rack, and place in plastic bag with pepper halves; seal bag. Let cool completely; chill thoroughly.

Sprinkle tenderloin with ground pepper; place on rack. Grill, covered, 10 minutes on each side or to desired degree of doneness. Let cool; cover and chill thoroughly.

To serve, arrange salad greens on a large platter. Arrange tomato, mushrooms, potato, and grilled onion on greens. Drizzle with ½ cup dressing.

Peel and discard skins from pepper; cut into ¼-inch slices. Cut tenderloin into ¼-inch slices. Arrange pepper and tenderloin on dressing. Drizzle with remaining dressing. Sprinkle with chives. Yield: 6 servings.

Marcia Philipps Hyzer

Read'em and Eat
Middleton Public Library
Middleton, Wisconsin

Couscous Pork Salad

Shredded pork and a medley of fresh vegetables perk up this couscous salad. We recommend serving pita wedges alongside to provide an edible "scoop" to enjoy every morsel.

2 cups water
1 cup couscous, uncooked
2 cups shredded cooked pork
1 cup seeded, coarsely
   chopped cucumber
½ cup shredded carrot
½ cup thinly sliced radishes
⅓ cup sliced green onions

¼ cup chopped fresh parsley
⅓ cup olive oil
⅓ cup lemon juice
¼ teaspoon salt
¼ teaspoon ground cumin
¼ teaspoon curry powder
¼ teaspoon coarsely ground
   pepper

   Place water in a medium saucepan; bring to a boil. Stir in couscous. Cover, remove from heat, and let stand 5 minutes or until liquid is absorbed. Fluff couscous with a fork, and let cool 20 minutes.

   Combine couscous, shredded pork, and next 5 ingredients in a large bowl, stirring mixture well. Combine olive oil and remaining 5 ingredients in a small bowl, stirring well with a wire whisk. Pour dressing over couscous mixture, tossing to combine. Cover and chill. Yield: 6 servings.

Barbara Worcester

Grace Lutheran Church Family Cookbook
Grace Lutheran Church Women's Missionary League
Nashua, New Hampshire

Chicken-Wild Rice Salad

½ cup mayonnaise
1 tablespoon minced fresh dill
1 tablespoon lemon juice
1 teaspoon curry powder
3 cups chopped cooked
   chicken
2 cups cooked wild rice, chilled
½ cup frozen English peas,
   thawed
½ cup chopped carrot
¼ cup minced green onions
2 tablespoons diced pimiento,
   drained
½ teaspoon salt
¼ teaspoon pepper
⅛ teaspoon garlic powder
Green leaf lettuce leaves
Garnish: cherry tomatoes

Combine first 4 ingredients in a large bowl; stir well. Add chicken and next 8 ingredients; stir well. Cover and chill at least 1 hour. Spoon evenly onto individual lettuce-lined salad plates, and garnish, if desired. Yield: 6 servings.　　　　　　　　　　　　　　Sharon Huber

St. Aloysius Rosary Society Cookbook
St. Aloysius Rosary Society
Calmar, Iowa

Moma's Crab Salad

A bit of curry gives a distinct panache to this crab salad. The recipe makes enough for a luncheon, but it's easily divisible for fewer people.

6 to 7 pounds fresh lump
   crabmeat, drained
6 hard-cooked eggs, chopped
6 stalks celery, minced
3 cups mayonnaise
¼ cup plus 2 tablespoons fresh
   lemon juice
2 tablespoons curry powder
2 heads green leaf lettuce
Garnishes: hard-cooked egg
   halves, salad olives, paprika,
   radishes, pitted ripe olives

Combine first 3 ingredients; stir well. Add mayonnaise, lemon juice, and curry powder, stirring gently. Serve on lettuce leaves. Garnish, if desired. Yield: 18 servings.　　　　　　　　　　Rose Annette O'Keefe

Cooking on the Coast
Mississippi Gulf Coast YMCA
Ocean Springs, Mississippi

Grilled Corn and Shrimp Salad

Peppery watercress makes a leafy stage for this main dish salad as grilled corn and shrimp share the spotlight. Seed the jalapeño pepper if you'd like to mellow its supporting role.

2 bunches watercress
1 pound unpeeled medium-size
   fresh shrimp
6 ears fresh corn
Vegetable cooking spray
½ cup chopped purple onion
⅓ cup finely chopped fresh
   cilantro

1 large jalapeño pepper,
   minced
3 tablespoons fresh lemon
   juice
1 tablespoon white wine
   vinegar
¼ teaspoon pepper
⅓ cup olive oil

Remove coarse stems from watercress; wash and pat dry with paper towels. Set aside.

Peel shrimp, and devein, if desired.

Remove and discard husks and silks from corn. Coat grill rack with cooking spray, and place rack on grill over medium-hot coals (350° to 400°). Place corn on rack; grill, covered, 20 minutes or until corn is tender and slightly charred, turning every 5 minutes. Let cool.

Place shrimp in a grill basket, if desired; grill, covered, 3 minutes on each side or until shrimp turn pink. Let cool.

Cut corn from cobs, and place in a large bowl. Add shrimp, onion, cilantro, and jalapeño pepper.

Combine lemon juice, vinegar, and pepper in a small bowl. Gradually add oil in a slow, steady stream, stirring constantly with a wire whisk. Pour over corn mixture; toss well.

Divide reserved watercress evenly among four individual salad plates. Spoon shrimp mixture over watercress. Serve immediately. Yield: 4 servings.

Entertaining in Kingwood
Kingwood Women's Club
Kingwood, Texas

Banana-Poppy Seed Dressing

Spoon this creamy dressing over your favorite fruit. It's especially good with ripe melon.

1 ripe banana	1 tablespoon poppy seeds
1 tablespoon lemon juice	1 teaspoon dry mustard
1 (8-ounce) carton sour cream	¾ teaspoon salt
¼ cup sugar	

Mash banana with a fork in a small bowl; stir in lemon juice. Add sour cream and remaining ingredients, stirring well. Cover and chill at least 30 minutes. Yield: 1½ cups.   Shirley Crowe

Welcome Home
Thomasville Civic Center Foundation
Thomasville, Alabama

Governor's Mansion Dijon Salad Dressing

White and red wine vinegar lend extra tartness to the tangy Dijon in this salad dressing. Its easy preparation will get your vote, too.

¼ cup Dijon mustard	¼ teaspoon salt
3 tablespoons red wine vinegar	⅛ teaspoon pepper
1 tablespoon white vinegar	2 cloves garlic
1 tablespoon grated onion	2 drops of hot sauce
½ teaspoon dried basil	¾ cup vegetable oil

Combine mustard and vinegars in container of an electric blender; process until combined. Add onion and next 5 ingredients; process until smooth, stopping once to scrape down sides.

Turn blender on high; gradually add oil in a slow, steady stream. Cover and chill thoroughly. Serve dressing over salad greens. Yield: 1¼ cups.   Jean Carnahan

The Chancellor's Table
Friends of the Chancellor's Residence at
The University of Missouri-Rolla
Rolla, Missouri

Maple and Toasted Pecan Dressing

A salad of Boston lettuce, sliced apple, and Roquefort cheese plays the perfect host to this simply sweet dressing.

½ cup plain yogurt
½ cup pecans, toasted
⅓ cup pure maple syrup

¼ cup olive oil
2 tablespoons fresh lemon juice

Combine all ingredients in container of an electric blender. Cover and process until smooth. Serve over salad greens. Yield: 1⅓ cups.

Maine Course Cookbook
YMCA
Bar Harbor, Maine

Red Roquefort Dressing

Pungent Roquefort cheese adds spunky appeal to this ketchup-based dressing. A little goes a long way, so you may want to halve the recipe.

1 cup vegetable oil
½ cup firmly packed brown sugar
½ cup ketchup
½ cup water
½ cup white vinegar
1 tablespoon fresh lemon juice

2 teaspoons onion juice
½ teaspoon garlic powder
½ teaspoon salt
¼ teaspoon pepper
1 (3.5-ounce) package Roquefort cheese, crumbled

Combine all ingredients except cheese in small bowl, stirring with a wire whisk until blended. Add cheese; stir well. Cover and chill 3 hours. Serve over salad greens. Yield: 3½ cups.

Of Tide & Thyme
The Junior League of Annapolis, Maryland

Sauces & Condiments

Peach Preserves, page 286

Kahlúa Cream for Fresh Fruit

This billowy dip is short on ingredients and seductively enticing. Spunky Kahlúa enhances this easy fruit dipper.

1 (8-ounce) package cream
   cheese, softened
¼ cup Kahlúa or other
   coffee-flavored liqueur

2 tablespoons whipping cream
2 tablespoons chopped
   blanched almonds, toasted

Beat cream cheese at medium speed of an electric mixer until smooth; gradually add Kahlúa and whipping cream, beating well. Stir in almonds. Serve with strawberries, pineapple, or apple wedges. Yield: 1⅓ cups.

True Grits: Tall Tales and Recipes from the New South
The Junior League of Atlanta, Georgia

Praline Sundae Topping

Toasted pecans take a dip in a gooey ice cream topping kids of all ages will scream for.

¼ cup butter or margarine
16 large marshmallows
1¼ cups firmly packed brown
   sugar
2 tablespoons light corn
   syrup

Dash of salt
1 cup evaporated milk
½ cup chopped pecans, toasted
1 teaspoon vanilla extract

Melt butter in a large saucepan over medium heat. Add marshmallows and next 3 ingredients to pan. Cook over medium heat, stirring constantly, until mixture comes to a boil. Boil 1 minute. Remove from heat, and let cool 5 minutes. Stir in evaporated milk, pecans, and vanilla. Serve topping warm or chilled over ice cream. (Mixture thickens as it cools.) Store topping in an airtight container in refrigerator. Yield: 2¼ cups. Joy Engling

Home Cookin'
American Legion Auxiliary, Department of Wyoming
Torrington, Wyoming

Thick, Sweet Barbecue Sauce

½ cup chopped onion
1 clove garlic, minced
¼ cup vegetable oil
1 (8-ounce) can tomato sauce
¼ cup firmly packed brown
  sugar
1½ teaspoons grated lemon rind

¼ cup fresh lemon juice
2 tablespoons Worcestershire
  sauce
2 tablespoons prepared
  mustard
1 tablespoon chopped fresh
  parsley

Cook onion and garlic in oil in a medium skillet over medium-high heat, stirring constantly, until tender. Add tomato sauce and remaining ingredients. Bring to a boil; reduce heat, and simmer 20 minutes or until thickened, stirring often. Use as a basting sauce for burgers, chicken, or ribs. Yield: 1½ cups. Barbara Stewart

Carolinas Heritage
47th National Square Dance Convention
Charlotte, North Carolina

White Barbecue Sauce

Trade in tomato barbecue sauce for a fresh one that starts with mayonnaise. Temptingly spiked with tart partners–cider vinegar and fresh lemon juice–this sauce lends a new personality to grilled chicken.

⅓ cup mayonnaise
3 tablespoons cider vinegar
3 tablespoons fresh lemon
  juice

2 tablespoons sugar
1 tablespoon salt
1 tablespoon pepper

Combine all ingredients in a small bowl; stir well. Use as a basting sauce for chicken or ribs. Yield: ⅔ cup. Fran Farris

Briarwood Recipes to Crown Your Table
Women's Ministries of Briarwood Presbyterian Church
Birmingham, Alabama

Basil Cream Sauce

Fresh basil, toasted pine nuts, and garlic gild this cream sauce. Serve it over pasta, chicken, or fish.

1 **cup firmly packed fresh basil**	1 **cup half-and-half**
1 **tablespoon pine nuts, toasted**	½ **cup whipping cream**
2 **cloves garlic**	1 **cup freshly grated Romano cheese**
¼ **cup olive oil**	
¼ **teaspoon ground white pepper**	

Position knife blade in food processor bowl; add first 5 ingredients. Process until finely chopped, stopping once to scrape down sides; set aside.

Combine half-and-half and whipping cream in a medium saucepan. Bring just to a boil; gradually add basil mixture and cheese, stirring constantly with a wire whisk. Bring just to a boil; reduce heat, and simmer, uncovered, 10 minutes or until thickened. Serve over tortellini. Yield: 2 cups.

Sara Hackney

Simply Irresistible!
St. Monica Parish Home and School Association
Whitefish Bay, Wisconsin

Niki's Ham Sauce

This rich, creamy sauce resembles a hollandaise sauce, but without the butter. Fresh asparagus, eggs, and fish deserve its classy embellishment.

1 **cup whipping cream**	¼ **teaspoon salt**
¼ **cup sugar**	2 **egg yolks, beaten**
2 **tablespoons dry mustard**	¼ **cup cider vinegar**

Combine whipping cream and sugar in a small saucepan; cook over medium heat until sugar dissolves and mixture is thoroughly heated. Combine ¼ cup warm cream mixture and mustard in a small bowl, stirring with a wire whisk until blended. Add to remaining warm cream mixture, stirring well. Remove mixture from heat; add salt and egg yolks, stirring constantly. Cook over low heat, stirring constantly, until mixture comes to a boil and thickens. Stir in vinegar. Serve with broccoli or asparagus, or on a BLT. Yield: 1½ cups.   Hope Wigglesworth

Cooks by the Yard
Harvard Neighbors, Harvard University
Cambridge, Massachusetts

Joan Miro's Mystical Marinara Sauce

Intense dried tomatoes sharpen this thick tomato sauce.

8 ounces dried tomatoes
1 large sweet onion, coarsely chopped
5 cloves elephant garlic, chopped
1 teaspoon salt
¼ cup olive oil
2 (28-ounce) cans Italian-style tomatoes, undrained and chopped

1 (6-ounce) can tomato paste
3 tablespoons golden raisins
1 tablespoon sugar
1 cup fresh basil, coarsely chopped
Freshly ground pepper to taste

Combine dried tomatoes and boiling water to cover; let stand 5 minutes. Drain and coarsely chop.

Cook onion, garlic, and salt in olive oil in a large Dutch oven over medium-high heat until tender, stirring occasionally. Add dried tomato, canned tomatoes, tomato paste, raisins, and sugar; stir well. Cover and cook over medium heat 1 hour, stirring occasionally. Add basil and pepper; cover and cook 15 minutes, stirring occasionally. Yield: 11 cups.

Cuisine for Connoisseurs: Food Among the Fine Arts
Boca Raton Museum of Art
Boca Raton, Florida

Olive Oil Pesto

2 cups lightly packed fresh
   basil
4 sprigs flat-leaf parsley
4 cloves garlic
2 tablespoons pine nuts
2 tablespoons grated Parmesan
   cheese

2 tablespoons lemon juice
¼ teaspoon salt
½ cup extra virgin olive oil
Hot cooked spaghetti

Combine first 7 ingredients in container of an electric blender; process until smooth, stopping once to scrape down sides.

Turn blender on high; gradually add oil in a slow, steady stream. Process until combined. To serve, toss ½ cup Olive Oil Pesto with 4 cups spaghetti. Cover and store remaining ½ cup Olive Oil Pesto in refrigerator. Yield: 1 cup.   Elaine Curtis

H.E.A.L. of Michiana Cookbook: A Collection of Health Conscious Recipes
Human Ecology Action League of Michiana
Stevensville, Michigan

Lemon-Basil Butter

Lay a thick pat of fragrant basil butter atop warm fish or chicken, and allow it to melt lazily on its warm host.

2 cups butter, softened
½ cup chopped fresh basil
¼ cup grated lemon rind
½ cup fresh lemon juice

⅛ teaspoon salt
⅛ teaspoon ground white
   pepper

Beat butter at medium speed of an electric mixer until creamy. Add basil and remaining ingredients, beating until smooth.

Spoon one-third of butter onto a sheet of wax paper. Roll butter in wax paper, back and forth, to make a 6-inch log. Wrap log in wax paper. Repeat procedure twice with remaining butter mixture. Freeze logs at least 1 hour. Yield: 2 cups.   Byron McIntosh

Cooking with Class
Park Maitland School
Maitland, Florida

Angel of Death Garlic Mayonnaise

2 large heads garlic, unpeeled
2 tablespoons extra virgin olive
  oil, divided
1 cup mayonnaise
¼ teaspoon salt
⅛ teaspoon pepper

Cut off pointed end of garlic heads, leaving tight outer covering intact. Place garlic heads, cut side up, on a square of aluminum foil or in a garlic roaster. Drizzle with 1 tablespoon oil; wrap in foil or cover with lid.

Bake at 350° for 1 hour or until golden. Remove from oven, and let cool completely. Squeeze out pulp from each clove.

Position knife blade in food processor bowl; add garlic and remaining 1 tablespoon oil. Process until pureed. Stir in mayonnaise, salt, and pepper. Cover and chill. Yield: 1¼ cups. Alverta Fiscus

The Chancellor's Table
Friends of the Chancellor's Residence at
The University of Missouri-Rolla
Rolla, Missouri

Banana Salsa

Whoa! Habanero peppers light up the senses and turn on the heat in this four-alarm salsa. For tamer palates, substitute the milder jalapeño pepper.

5 firm ripe bananas, chopped
1 cup chopped sweet red
  pepper
1 cup chopped green pepper
¼ cup chopped fresh cilantro
1 to 2 tablespoons seeded and
  chopped fresh habanero
  pepper
1 shallot, finely chopped
1 tablespoon minced fresh
  ginger
2 tablespoons fresh lime juice
2 tablespoons brown sugar
1 tablespoon olive oil
½ teaspoon salt
¼ teaspoon freshly ground
  pepper

Combine all ingredients in a medium bowl; stir well. Serve immediately. Yield: 5 cups. Paul Malopolski

Pepper Lovers Club Cookbook, Volume I
Pepper Lovers Club of Virginia Beach, Virginia

Raspberry Vinegar

Fragrant homemade vinegars in decorative clear or colored bottles brighten any kitchen–yours or a friend's. Add a few sprigs of fresh herbs and some oil to this tangy-sweet vinegar, and you've got a salad vinaigrette in seconds.

4 cups cider vinegar
12 cups fresh raspberries, divided

2 cups sugar

Combine vinegar and 8 cups raspberries in a medium nonmetal container. Cover and let stand at room temperature 2 days. Pour mixture through a wire-mesh strainer into a large container; discard raspberries.

Combine vinegar mixture and remaining 4 cups raspberries in non-metal container. Cover and let stand at room temperature 2 additional days. Pour through a wire-mesh strainer into a medium saucepan, discarding raspberries; add sugar. Bring to a boil; reduce heat, and simmer, uncovered, 5 minutes, stirring often. Skim off foam with a nonmetal spoon. Let stand 10 minutes. Pour into a jar with a tight-fitting lid. Cover tightly, and store in refrigerator. Serve over salad greens. Yield: 4 cups.   Bertha H. Tyson and Margaret B. Walmer

Friendly Recipes
Religious Society of Friends (Quakers)
York, Pennsylvania

Red Onion and Apple Chutney

Chopped green apple, purple onions, and golden raisins drink up the essence of vinegar, honey, and cloves for a colorful condiment to savor with pork or chicken.

⅔ cup warm water
¼ cup cider vinegar
3 tablespoons honey
1 cup golden raisins
⅛ teaspoon dried mint flakes
⅛ teaspoon ground cloves
4 medium-size purple onions

3 tablespoons vegetable oil
2 tablespoons butter or margarine, melted
1 Granny Smith apple, cored and chopped
¼ teaspoon salt
⅛ teaspoon pepper

Combine first 6 ingredients in a small bowl; set aside.

Cut onions into quarters to, but not through, bottoms. Turn onions on sides, and thinly slice. Cover and cook onion in oil and butter in a large skillet over medium-low heat 15 minutes or until tender, stirring occasionally. Uncover and cook 30 minutes or until very tender, stirring often. Add raisin mixture and apple. Cook, uncovered, over medium heat 20 minutes or until liquid evaporates and apple is tender, stirring occasionally. Stir in salt and pepper. Let cool. Serve at room temperature. Yield: 2¼ cups.

Generations
The Junior League of Rockford, Illinois

Blueberry Jam

Discover the thrill of picking fresh blueberries. You can eat them by the handfuls for instant gratification, but we recommend "putting them up" with this simple recipe and enjoying the plump gems all year long.

6 cups stemmed blueberries, crushed
1 teaspoon grated lemon rind
2 tablespoons fresh lemon juice

7 cups sugar
2 (3-ounce) packages liquid pectin

Combine first 4 ingredients in a Dutch oven. Bring to a boil; cook until sugar dissolves, stirring occasionally. Boil 2 minutes, stirring often; remove from heat. Add pectin to mixture, and stir 5 minutes. Skim off foam with a metal spoon.

Quickly pour hot mixture into hot, sterilized jars, leaving ¼-inch headspace; wipe jar rims. Cover at once with metal lids, and screw on bands. Process in boiling-water bath 5 minutes. Yield: 8 half-pints.

Seasoned with Love
Mahoning County Foster Parent Association
Youngstown, Ohio

Peach Preserves

Relish summer's best pick of juicy peaches all year in this chunky preserves recipe deserving of any fluffy buttermilk biscuit.

3 pounds ripe peaches, peeled
  and quartered
4 cups sugar
¾ cup honey

½ medium-size orange,
  quartered and seeded
¼ teaspoon almond extract

Combine first 3 ingredients in a Dutch oven; stir well. Cover and let stand 45 minutes.

Position knife blade in food processor bowl; add orange quarters. Process until finely chopped, stopping once to scrape down sides; measure amount of orange.

Place orange and an equal amount of water in a medium saucepan. Bring to a boil; cover, reduce heat, and simmer 10 minutes or until orange rind is tender.

Bring peach mixture to a boil over medium heat, stirring until sugar dissolves. Increase heat to medium-high, and cook, uncovered, 15 minutes, stirring often. Add orange mixture. Bring to a boil; cook, uncovered, 20 to 25 minutes or until candy thermometer registers 221°, stirring often. Remove from heat; stir in almond extract. Skim off foam with a metal spoon.

Quickly pour hot mixture into hot, sterilized jars, leaving ¼-inch headspace; wipe jar rims. Cover at once with metal lids, and screw on bands. Process jars in boiling-water bath 5 minutes. Yield: 6 half-pints.   Mary Saunders Wood

Collard Greens, Watermelons, and "Miss" Charlotte's Pie
Swansboro United Methodist Women
Swansboro, North Carolina

Soups & Stews

Italian Sausage Chili, page 301

Cold Strawberry Soup

Fresh strawberries in their prime flaunt their sweet juiciness.

8 cups fresh strawberries, hulled
1 cup sugar
2 cups water
2 tablespoons Rhine wine
2 tablespoons grated orange rind (about 1 orange)
1 tablespoon grated lemon rind (about 1 medium lemon)
1 tablespoon fresh lemon juice
Garnish: whipped cream

Place strawberries in container of an electric blender; process 1 minute or until smooth, stopping once to scrape down sides. Place puree in a wire-mesh strainer over a bowl; press with back of a spoon against sides of the strainer to squeeze out juice. Discard pulp remaining in strainer. Chill puree thoroughly.

Combine sugar and water in a medium saucepan. Bring to a boil; boil 10 minutes. Let cool slightly; cover and chill.

Combine puree and sugar mixture in a large bowl, stirring well. Stir in wine and next 3 ingredients. Ladle soup into individual soup bowls. Garnish, if desired. Yield: 5 cups.

Add a Pound of Love
Geauga Humane Society
Chardon, Ohio

Creamy Swiss and Broccoli Soup

Cozy up to the fire with a bowl of this creamy broccoli and cheese soup. It's chock-full of ham chunks and shredded Swiss cheese.

1 cup chopped cooked ham
1 cup water
1 (10-ounce) package frozen chopped broccoli
2 cups milk
3 tablespoons all-purpose flour
2 cups (8 ounces) shredded Swiss cheese
½ teaspoon salt
Dash of pepper

Combine ham and water in a large saucepan; bring to a simmer, and cook 10 minutes. Add broccoli; bring to a boil. Cover, reduce heat, and simmer 5 to 7 minutes or until broccoli is crisp-tender.

Combine milk and flour, stirring until smooth; add to broccoli mixture. Cook, stirring constantly, 5 minutes or until thickened. Stir in cheese, salt, and pepper. Cook over medium heat until cheese melts. Yield: 5 cups.   Jo Ross

Seasoned with Love
Mahoning County Foster Parent Association
Youngstown, Ohio

Cheddar and Stilton Soup

Pungent Stilton cheese teams up with sharp Cheddar to deliver a full-bodied punch in a rich, creamy soup.

½ cup finely chopped onion
½ cup finely chopped carrot
½ cup finely chopped celery
1 teaspoon minced garlic
2 tablespoons butter or
    margarine, melted
⅓ cup all-purpose flour
2 teaspoons cornstarch
3 cups chicken broth
2 cups (8 ounces) shredded
    sharp Cheddar cheese

8 ounces Stilton cheese,
    crumbled
1 cup whipping cream
⅓ cup dry white wine
⅛ teaspoon baking soda
¼ teaspoon freshly ground
    black pepper
⅛ teaspoon ground red pepper
1 bay leaf
¼ cup chopped fresh parsley

Cook first 4 ingredients in butter in a Dutch oven over medium-high heat, stirring constantly, until vegetables are tender. Add flour and cornstarch to vegetable mixture, stirring well. Cook 1 minute, stirring constantly. Gradually add chicken broth and next 8 ingredients. Bring just to a boil; reduce heat, and simmer, uncovered, 10 minutes. Remove and discard bay leaf.

Ladle soup into individual soup bowls. Sprinkle each serving evenly with parsley. Yield: 7 cups.

Note: If you use canned chicken broth, we recommend the no-salt-added version.

Everybody Bring a Dish, Cooking in the Spirit of Shalom
Shalom United Church of Christ
Richland, Washington

Cream of Poblano Soup

Smoky seasoned chorizo sausage and roasted poblano peppers intensify this milky broth. Crispy tortilla strips, fresh cilantro, and shredded Monterey Jack echo the southwestern flavor.

4 (6-inch) flour or corn tortillas
Vegetable oil
½ pound chorizo, crumbled
3 poblano chile peppers
½ cup chopped onion
¼ cup diced carrot
2 tablespoons butter or
    margarine, melted
2 tablespoons all-purpose flour

4 cups water
2 cups chicken broth
¾ cup half-and-half
3 tablespoons finely chopped
    fresh cilantro, divided
1 teaspoon salt
1½ cups (6 ounces) shredded
    Monterey Jack cheese

Cut tortillas into thin strips. Pour oil to depth of 1 inch into a large heavy skillet. Fry tortilla strips in hot oil over medium-high heat until golden. Lightly crush strips, and set aside.

Brown sausage in a nonstick skillet over medium heat; drain well on paper towels. Set aside.

Wash and dry peppers; place on an aluminum foil-lined baking sheet. Broil 5½ inches from heat (with electric oven door partially opened) about 5 minutes on each side or until blistered. Place peppers in a heavy-duty, zip-top plastic bag; seal bag, and let stand 10 minutes. Peel peppers; remove core and seeds. Dice peppers.

Cook peppers, onion, and carrot in melted butter in a large heavy-duty saucepan over medium heat, stirring constantly, until tender. Add flour, stirring well. Gradually add water and chicken broth. Bring to a boil; reduce heat, and simmer, uncovered, 30 minutes.

Strain vegetables, reserving liquid. Place vegetables in container of an electric blender; process until smooth, stopping once to scrape down sides. Return vegetable mixture to pan; add reserved liquid, half-and-half, 1 tablespoon cilantro, and salt. Cook until thoroughly heated (do not boil).

Divide chorizo evenly among soup bowls. Ladle soup into individual soup bowls; sprinkle each evenly with crushed tortilla strips, cheese, and remaining 2 tablespoons cilantro. Yield: 7 cups.

Entertaining in Kingwood
Kingwood Women's Club
Kingwood, Texas

Butternut-Pear Soup

We didn't mind the long cooking time–the delectable result was worth the wait.

2 slices bacon	⅓ cup finely chopped celery
1 tablespoon olive oil	2 ripe pears, peeled, cored,
1 medium leek	and cubed
1 large butternut squash	2 cups chicken broth
(about 3 pounds)	2 cups water
3 cloves garlic, minced	1 cup whipping cream
½ cup minced onion	Minced fresh parsley

Cook bacon in olive oil in a Dutch oven until crisp; drain, reserving drippings in pan. Crumble bacon, and set aside.

Remove and discard root, tough outer leaves, and tops of leek to where dark green begins to pale; rinse well, and slice thinly. Peel squash; remove and discard seeds, and cut squash into 1-inch pieces. Set aside.

Cook leek, garlic, onion, and celery in pan drippings over medium-high heat, stirring constantly, until tender. Add reserved squash, pear, and chicken broth. Bring to a boil; cover, reduce heat, and simmer 50 minutes or until squash is tender, adding 2 cups water, if necessary, to keep from sticking.

Process soup mixture in batches in container of an electric blender until smooth, stopping once to scrape down sides. Return pureed mixture to pan. Bring to a boil; reduce heat, and stir in whipping cream. Cook, stirring constantly, until thoroughly heated.

Ladle soup into individual soup bowls, and sprinkle with crumbled bacon and parsley. Yield: 8 cups.   Matthew A. Wilson

Note: You can serve this soup warm or chilled.

Cooking with Faith
Faith United Methodist Church
Schenectady, New York

Onion Soup with Cheese Croutons

Slices of nutty-flavored Gruyère melted atop thick slabs of French bread float in a robust beef broth studded with caramelized onions.

2 to 3 sweet onions (about 2 pounds)
2 tablespoons vegetable oil
2 tablespoons butter or margarine, melted
1 clove garlic, minced
2 tablespoons all-purpose flour
5 cups beef broth, divided
1 bay leaf
¼ teaspoon dried thyme
¼ teaspoon salt
2 teaspoons lemon juice
Freshly ground pepper to taste
Cheese Croutons

Cut each onion in half lengthwise; cut crosswise into thin slices.

Cover and cook onion in oil and butter in a large Dutch oven over medium-low heat 20 minutes, stirring occasionally. Stir in garlic. Cook, uncovered, over medium heat 30 minutes, stirring often.

Sprinkle onion mixture with flour. Cook 2 minutes, stirring constantly. Add 1 cup broth. Bring to a boil; boil 1 minute. Add remaining 4 cups broth, bay leaf, thyme, and salt; stir well. Bring to a boil; reduce heat, and simmer, uncovered, 20 minutes. Stir in lemon juice and pepper. Remove and discard bay leaf.

Ladle 1 cup soup into individual soup bowls. Top each with a Cheese Crouton. Serve immediately. Yield: 4 cups.

Cheese Croutons

4 (¾-inch-thick) diagonally sliced French bread slices
1 clove garlic, crushed
2 ounces thinly sliced Gruyère cheese
2 teaspoons grated Parmesan cheese

Place bread slices on a baking sheet. Bake at 325° for 15 minutes or until golden.

Rub each slice of bread with garlic. Place Gruyère cheese on top of bread. Sprinkle with Parmesan cheese. Bake at 375° for 3 minutes or until cheese melts. Yield: 4 croutons.   Joanna Badger

Friends and Fellowship Cookbook
First Christian Church of Stow, Ohio

Baked Potato Soup

Loaded Baked Potato Soup describes this more accurately. The classic combination of crumbled bacon, shredded Cheddar cheese, green onions, and parsley tops off this chunky potato soup.

5 medium-size baking potatoes (about 2¾ pounds)
8 slices bacon
1 cup chopped sweet onion
⅔ cup all-purpose flour
6 cups chicken broth
2 cups half-and-half
¼ cup chopped fresh parsley
1½ teaspoons minced garlic
1½ teaspoons dried basil
1 teaspoon salt
1 teaspoon coarsely ground pepper
½ teaspoon hot sauce
1¾ cups (7 ounces) shredded Cheddar cheese, divided
1 cup sliced green onions, divided
¼ cup chopped fresh parsley

Wash potatoes; prick several times with a fork. Bake at 400° for 1 hour or until done; let cool. Peel potatoes, and slice crosswise.

Cook bacon in a large skillet until crisp; remove bacon, reserving drippings in skillet. Crumble bacon, and set aside.

Cook onion in drippings, stirring constantly, until tender; add flour, stirring well. Cook 1 minute, stirring constantly. Gradually add chicken broth; cook over medium heat, stirring constantly, until mixture is thickened and bubbly. Stir in potato, half-and-half, and next 6 ingredients. Bring to a simmer, and cook, uncovered, 10 minutes (do not boil). Stir in 1 cup cheese and ¼ cup green onions. Cook until cheese melts, stirring often.

Ladle soup into individual soup bowls. Top evenly with crumbled bacon. Sprinkle evenly with remaining ¾ cup cheese, ¾ cup green onions, and parsley. Yield: 12 cups.   Lee Foster Nix

Food for Thought
The Junior League of Birmingham, Alabama

Vegetable Borscht

Bright vermillion beets reign supreme in this traditional Russian recipe. Hearty vegetables mingle in the beets' shadows.

1 (15-ounce) can whole beets
½ cup finely chopped carrot
¾ cup finely chopped onion
¾ cup finely chopped celery
¾ cup finely chopped parsnips
2 cups water
1 cup shredded cabbage
1 (10¾-ounce) can tomato
  puree
2 (10½-ounce) cans beef
  consommé
4½ cups water, divided
1 tablespoon lemon juice
1 teaspoon salt
1½ teaspoons dried dillweed
½ cup sour cream
½ cup plain nonfat yogurt

Drain beets, reserving liquid. Shred beets, and set aside.

Combine carrot and next 4 ingredients in a Dutch oven. Bring to a boil; cover, reduce heat, and simmer 15 minutes. Add reserved liquid from beets, cabbage, tomato puree, consommé, and 2 cups water. Cook 20 minutes or until vegetables are tender. Add beets, remaining 2½ cups water, lemon juice, salt, and dillweed; cook 5 minutes. Combine sour cream and yogurt. Ladle soup into individual bowls. Top each with sour cream mixture. Yield: 12 cups.   Ilene Rubel

Hand in Hand, Heart to Heart
Sisterhood Temple Beth El
Allentown, Pennsylvania

Italian Sausage Soup with Tortellini

1 pound mild Italian sausage
1 cup coarsely chopped onion
2 cloves garlic, sliced
5 cups beef broth
2 cups thinly sliced carrot
2 cups peeled, seeded, and
  chopped tomato
1½ cups sliced zucchini
1 green pepper, cut into ½-inch
  pieces
1 (8-ounce) can tomato sauce
½ cup water
½ teaspoon dried basil
½ teaspoon dried oregano
1 (9-ounce) package
  refrigerated cheese- and
  basil-filled tortellini,
  uncooked
3 tablespoons chopped fresh
  parsley
½ cup freshly grated Parmesan
  cheese

Remove and discard casings from sausage. Brown sausage in a large Dutch oven over medium-high heat, stirring occasionally. Drain, reserving 1 tablespoon drippings in pan. Set sausage aside.

Add onion and garlic to drippings in pan; cook, stirring constantly, until onion is tender. Add sausage, beef broth, and next 8 ingredients, stirring well. Bring to a boil; reduce heat, and simmer, uncovered, 30 minutes. Add tortellini and parsley, stirring well. Bring to a boil; reduce heat, and simmer, uncovered, 10 minutes or until tortellini is tender.

Ladle soup into individual soup bowls. Sprinkle each serving with cheese. Yield: 10 cups. Ruth Longroy

Family Favorites
Allen County Extension Homemakers
Fort Wayne, Indiana

Chicken Soup with Lentils and Barley

Lentils and barley beef up classic chicken soup with surprising and flavorful results.

1 cup chopped leek
½ cup chopped green pepper
1 clove garlic, minced
1 tablespoon butter or
   margarine, melted
5 cups chicken broth
½ cup lentils, uncooked
½ teaspoon dried basil
½ teaspoon dried oregano
½ teaspoon dried rosemary
½ teaspoon pepper
1½ cups chopped cooked
   chicken
1½ cups sliced carrot
½ cup quick-cooking barley,
   uncooked
1 (14.5-ounce) can whole
   tomatoes, undrained and
   chopped

Cook leek, green pepper, and garlic in butter in a Dutch oven over medium-high heat until tender, stirring occasionally. Add broth and next 5 ingredients. Bring to a boil; cover, reduce heat, and simmer 20 minutes, stirring occasionally. Add chicken, carrot, and barley; simmer, covered, 20 minutes, stirring occasionally. Add tomatoes; cook until thoroughly heated. Yield: 8 cups. Trudy Kutter

Sampler Cookbook
Clarence Log Cabin Quilters
Clarence, New York

Spicy Thai Shrimp Soup

Tart lime, pungent red pepper, and sweet-hot ginger tease this chunky shrimp and mushroom soup with Thai flavors.

¾ pound unpeeled medium-size fresh shrimp
2 tablespoons minced fresh ginger
½ teaspoon dried crushed red pepper
2 tablespoons peanut oil
3 (14.5-ounce) cans chicken broth
1 tablespoon lime rind strips, cut into 1-inch pieces

⅓ cup long-grain rice, uncooked
6 large mushrooms, sliced
1 (13.5-ounce) can coconut milk
½ cup chopped onion
2 tablespoons fresh lime juice
Garnish: chopped green onions

Peel shrimp, and devein, if desired. Set aside.

Cook ginger and pepper in oil in a large Dutch oven over medium-high heat 1 minute, stirring constantly. Add broth and lime strips. Bring to a boil; stir in rice. Cover, reduce heat, and simmer 20 minutes. Add reserved shrimp, mushrooms, coconut milk, and onion to pan. Cook, uncovered, 3 to 5 minutes or until shrimp turn pink. Remove from heat. Add lime juice, and stir well. Garnish, if desired. Yield: 10 cups.

C. Norlic

What's Cooking at Chico State
Staff Council/California State University, Chico
Chico, California

Rosie's Best Creole Gumbo

1 pound unpeeled large fresh shrimp
8 cups water
1 (3½-pound) broiler-fryer, cut up
2 stalks celery, chopped
1 large onion, chopped
1 medium-size green pepper, chopped
1 cup chopped green onions
1 jalapeño pepper, minced
2 teaspoons salt
2 teaspoons black pepper
1 teaspoon ground red pepper
⅓ cup vegetable oil
¾ cup all-purpose flour
1 (28-ounce) can whole tomatoes, undrained and chopped
1 pound Polish sausage, sliced
1 (10-ounce) package frozen cut okra
½ pound fresh lump crabmeat, drained
2 tablespoons gumbo filé
Hot cooked rice

Peel shrimp, and devein, if desired. Set aside.

Combine water and next 9 ingredients in a large Dutch oven. Bring to a boil; cover, reduce heat, and simmer 40 minutes or until chicken is tender. Remove chicken, reserving broth and vegetables in pan. Let chicken cool to touch; skin, bone, and coarsely chop meat. Return meat to pan.

Combine oil and flour in a large heavy skillet; cook over medium heat, stirring constantly, until roux is caramel colored (about 13 minutes). Add roux, tomatoes, sausage, and okra to Dutch oven. Bring to a boil; cover, reduce heat, and simmer 15 minutes.

Add reserved shrimp and crabmeat to Dutch oven; cook 5 minutes or until shrimp turn pink. Stir in gumbo filé. Serve gumbo over rice. Yield: 21 cups.

Celebrating Our Mothers' Kitchens
National Council of Negro Women
Washington, DC

Moroccan Lamb Stew

Aromatic saffron permeates this robust Mediterranean fare.
Garnish with hard-cooked eggs, buttery almonds, and raisins.

3½ pounds lamb stew meat
2 tablespoons olive oil, divided
2¾ cups chopped onion
2 cloves garlic, chopped
⅓ cup chopped fresh parsley
2 whole cloves
1 teaspoon ground ginger
4 threads of saffron
2 bay leaves
1 tablespoon salt
1 teaspoon pepper

2 (14½-ounce) cans whole
    tomatoes, undrained and
    chopped
2 large onions, quartered
¼ cup butter or margarine,
    melted and divided
⅔ cup sliced almonds
¾ cup raisins
8 cups hot cooked rice
4 hard-cooked eggs, halved

Brown lamb in 1½ tablespoons olive oil in a large Dutch oven over medium-high heat. Remove meat from pan, reserving drippings in pan. Set lamb aside.

Add remaining ½ tablespoon olive oil, onion, and garlic to drippings in pan; cook, stirring constantly, until onion is tender. Add parsley and next 3 ingredients; cook 2 minutes, stirring constantly. Return meat to pan; add bay leaves and next 3 ingredients. Bring to a boil; cover, reduce heat, and simmer 1 hour and 30 minutes. Cook, uncovered, 20 minutes. Remove and discard cloves and bay leaves.

Cook quartered onion in 3 tablespoons butter in a large skillet over medium-high heat until golden, stirring occasionally. Set aside.

Cook almonds in remaining 1 tablespoon butter in a small skillet over medium-high heat until lightly browned, stirring constantly; stir in raisins. Set aside.

Serve stew over rice; top with cooked onion, almond mixture, and egg. Yield: 8 servings.   Hank and Lynn Hopeman

Our Favorite Recipes from Coast to Coast
Hopeman Brothers/Lofton Corporation/AWH Associates
Waynesboro, Virginia

Spicy Spanish Pork and Chorizo Stew With Creamy Polenta

1 pound chorizo
1 teaspoon ground cumin
1 teaspoon dried crushed red pepper
½ teaspoon salt
¼ teaspoon freshly ground black pepper
2¼ pounds pork shoulder, cut into 1-inch cubes
2 tablespoons olive oil, divided
2½ cups chopped onion
2 jalapeño peppers, seeded and chopped
3 cloves garlic, minced
1 large sweet red pepper, chopped and divided
2 (14½-ounce) cans diced tomatoes, undrained
1 cup chicken broth
1 tablespoon tomato paste
1 tablespoon chopped fresh parsley
1 tablespoon chopped fresh oregano
Creamy Polenta

Brown chorizo in a skillet, stirring until it crumbles. Drain. Combine cumin and next 3 ingredients in a zip-top plastic bag. Add pork. Seal bag; shake gently until coated. Brown pork in 1 tablespoon oil in a skillet over medium-high heat. Remove from skillet. Drain.

Cook onion and next 3 ingredients in remaining 1 tablespoon oil in skillet over medium-high heat until tender. Stir in pork, tomatoes, and next 4 ingredients. Bring to a boil; cover, reduce heat, and simmer 1 hour. Stir in chorizo; simmer 20 minutes or until pork is tender and mixture is thickened. Serve over Creamy Polenta. Yield: 6 servings.

Creamy Polenta

2½ cups milk
1 cup polenta
1 teaspoon salt
1 cup (4 ounces) shredded Manchego cheese

Combine first 3 ingredients in top of a double boiler; stir well. Cover and place over simmering water; cook 35 minutes or until very thick, stirring often with a wire whisk. Add cheese, stirring until it melts. Yield: 6 servings.

Divine Dishes
St. Mark's Episcopal Church
Southborough, Massachusetts

Green Chili from Allgood's

1¼ pounds lean boneless
    chuck roast, cubed
1¼ pounds ground pork
1¼ pounds ground beef
1½ cups chopped onion
1 tablespoon plus 1 teaspoon
    minced garlic
½ cup chopped fresh cilantro
½ cup butter or margarine,
    melted
4 (14½-ounce) cans chicken
    broth
1½ cups beer
5 pounds Anaheim chile
    peppers, chopped
2 medium tomatoes, seeded
    and chopped

¼ cup all-purpose flour
2 tablespoons chicken-flavored
    bouillon granules
2 tablespoons ground cumin
2 tablespoons granulated garlic
2 tablespoons hot sauce
1 tablespoon dried oregano
1 tablespoon dried parsley
1 tablespoon garlic powder
1 tablespoon onion powder
1 tablespoon pepper
½ cup butter or margarine,
    melted
½ cup all-purpose flour
Garnishes: shredded Monterey
    Jack cheese, sour cream

Cook first 3 ingredients in a large Dutch oven over medium heat until meat is browned, stirring until meat crumbles. Drain well; set aside.

Cook onion, minced garlic, and cilantro in ½ cup butter in a large skillet over medium-high heat, stirring constantly, until onion is tender. Add to beef mixture. Add chicken broth and next 13 ingredients. Bring to a boil; reduce heat, and simmer, uncovered, 30 minutes.

Combine ½ cup butter and flour, stirring well. Gradually add to chile pepper mixture. Bring to a boil; reduce heat, and simmer, uncovered, 30 minutes or until thickened.

Ladle soup into individual soup bowls. Garnish, if desired. Serve with tortillas. Yield: 17 cups.   Dick Allgood

Note: If you want to cut back on fat, decrease the butter by half when sautéing the vegetables.

Cookin' in the Canyon
Gallatin Canyon Women's Club
Big Sky, Montana

Italian Sausage Chili

Stewed tomatoes, black and red beans, and tomato sauce are added to hearty Italian sausage and a few fresh ingredients for a chili that's as easy as opening a can.

1¼ pounds mild Italian
    sausage
3 Anaheim chile peppers
¾ cup coarsely chopped green
    pepper
¾ cup coarsely chopped sweet
    red pepper
1 (15-ounce) can black beans,
    rinsed and drained

1 (16-ounce) can red beans,
    rinsed and drained
4 cups water
1 (14.5-ounce) can stewed
    tomatoes
1 (15-ounce) can tomato sauce
¼ cup chili powder
1 medium onion, coarsely
    chopped

Remove and discard casings from sausage. Brown sausage in a Dutch oven over medium heat, stirring until it crumbles; drain. Return sausage to pan.

Slice Anaheim peppers into rings; seed, if desired.

Add pepper rings, green pepper, and remaining ingredients to Dutch oven. Bring to a boil; reduce heat, and simmer, uncovered, 1 hour. Yield: 11 cups.

The Tailgate Cookbook
National Kidney Foundation of Kansas and Western Missouri
Westwood, Kansas

Chunky Chicken Chili

Cast off the winter blues with a brimming bowl of chili. Chunks of chicken and tomatoes warm you up along with the heat of the jalapeños.

Vegetable cooking spray
1½ cups chopped onion
1 cup chopped green pepper
3 jalapeño peppers, chopped
3 cloves garlic, minced
2 tablespoons chili powder
2 teaspoons ground cumin
½ teaspoon dried oregano
½ teaspoon ground red pepper
¼ teaspoon black pepper
4 cups cubed cooked chicken breast
1 (14½-ounce) can no-salt-added stewed tomatoes
1 (14¼-ounce) can no-salt-added chicken broth
1 (12-ounce) bottle chili sauce
1 cup water
1 tablespoon Worcestershire sauce
1 tablespoon Dijon mustard
1 (15.8-ounce) can Great Northern beans, drained
1¼ cups diced avocado
1¼ cups chopped purple onion
½ cup plus 2 tablespoons plain nonfat yogurt

Coat a Dutch oven with cooking spray; place over medium heat until hot. Add onion and next 3 ingredients; cook, stirring constantly, 5 minutes or until tender.

Stir in chili powder and next 4 ingredients; cook 2 minutes. Add chicken and next 6 ingredients. Bring to a boil; cover, reduce heat, and simmer 20 minutes. Add beans, and cook 5 minutes or until thoroughly heated.

Ladle chili into individual soup bowls; top each serving evenly with avocado, purple onion, and yogurt. Yield: 11 cups.

Dining with Duke Cookbook
Badger Association of the Blind
Milwaukee, Wisconsin

Vegetables

Lemon-Basil Green Beans, page 306

Asparagus with Cashew Butter

Lightly toasting the chopped cashews awakens their sweet flavor in the soft butter.

1½ pounds fresh asparagus
1 cup chicken broth
½ cup butter, softened

¼ cup chopped cashews, toasted

Snap off tough ends of asparagus. Remove scales from stalks with a vegetable peeler, if desired. Combine asparagus and chicken broth in a large skillet. Bring to a boil over medium heat; cover, reduce heat, and simmer 8 minutes or until crisp-tender. Drain.

Combine butter and cashews; stir well. Serve asparagus warm with cashew butter. Yield: 4 servings.   Marie Burge

Rainbow of Recipes, Volume I
The Dream Factory of Louisville, Kentucky

Asparagus Casserole

1½ pounds fresh asparagus
¼ cup butter or margarine
2 tablespoons all-purpose flour
2 cups milk
½ cup (2 ounces) shredded American cheese

¼ teaspoon salt
2 tablespoons butter or margarine, melted
¾ cup fine, dry breadcrumbs

Snap off tough ends of asparagus. Remove scales from stalks with a vegetable peeler, if desired. Cut asparagus into 1-inch pieces. Cook asparagus in boiling salted water to cover 6 to 8 minutes or until crisp-tender; drain and place in a lightly greased 11- x 7- x 1½-inch baking dish.

Melt ¼ cup butter in a heavy saucepan over low heat; add flour, stirring until smooth. Cook 1 minute, stirring constantly. Gradually add milk; cook over medium heat, stirring constantly, until mixture is thickened and bubbly. Add cheese and salt, stirring until cheese melts; pour over asparagus.

Combine 2 tablespoons melted butter and breadcrumbs in a small bowl, and toss well. Sprinkle crumb mixture evenly over sauce. Bake at 325° for 30 minutes. Let stand 5 minutes before serving. Yield: 6 servings.   Jean Kwandras

What's Cookin' from the "Young at Heart"
Douglas County Senior Center Nutrition Center
Gardnerville, Nevada

Savory Green Beans and Mushrooms

Sliced mushrooms and a warm herb vinaigrette release green beans from their ordinary existence.

1½ pounds fresh green beans, trimmed	1 tablespoon fresh lemon juice
½ pound fresh mushrooms, sliced	1 tablespoon chopped fresh parsley
1 tablespoon thinly sliced green onions	1 teaspoon dried savory or 2 tablespoons chopped fresh savory
3 tablespoons butter or margarine, melted	1 teaspoon sugar
⅓ cup vegetable oil	1 teaspoon salt
1 tablespoon white wine vinegar	⅛ teaspoon pepper
	4 slices bacon, cooked and crumbled

Cook green beans in boiling water to cover 10 minutes or until crisp-tender; drain.

Cook mushrooms and green onions in butter in a large skillet over medium heat, stirring constantly, 5 minutes or until vegetables are tender. Toss with beans.

Combine oil and next 7 ingredients in a small saucepan; bring to a boil. Pour over bean mixture. Stir to coat evenly; sprinkle with bacon, and serve immediately. Yield: 6 servings.

Gourmet Our Way
Cascia Hall Preparatory School Parent Faculty Association
Tulsa, Oklahoma

Lemon-Basil Green Beans

¼ cup chopped fresh basil
2 tablespoons lemon juice
1 tablespoon olive oil
1 clove garlic, finely chopped
¼ teaspoon salt
⅛ teaspoon pepper
1 pound green beans
Garnish: lemon wedges

Combine first 6 ingredients; cover and chill 1 hour.

Wash beans; trim ends, and remove strings. Cook in boiling water to cover 10 minutes or until crisp-tender; drain well.

Let marinade come to room temperature while beans cook. Pour marinade over beans. Cover and let stand at room temperature 45 minutes. Serve beans at room temperature. Garnish, if desired. Yield: 4 servings.

Virginia Fare
The Junior League of Richmond, Virginia

Jade Green Broccoli

A sugary glaze of garlic and soy sauce energizes stir-fried broccoli.

2 pounds fresh broccoli
1 tablespoon cornstarch
1 teaspoon sugar
⅛ teaspoon salt
½ cup chicken broth
2 tablespoons soy sauce
1 clove garlic, minced
¼ cup vegetable oil

Remove and discard broccoli leaves and tough ends of stalks. Wash broccoli thoroughly, and cut off flowerets; set aside. Cut stalks into ½-inch pieces; set aside.

Combine cornstarch, sugar, and salt. Add chicken broth and soy sauce, stirring until smooth; set aside.

Sauté garlic in hot oil in a wok or large skillet over medium-high heat until lightly browned. Add broccoli flowerets and stems; cook 2 minutes, stirring constantly. Cover and cook 2 additional minutes. Add broth mixture; cook, stirring constantly, 2 minutes or until sauce thickens. Yield: 6 servings.

Elaine Martin Barker

With Special Distinction
Mississippi College Cookbook Committee
Clinton, Mississippi

Brussels Sprouts with Bacon and Pecans

Shredded brussels sprouts burst with flavor when paired with crisp bacon and toasted pecans.

1 **pound fresh brussels sprouts**	⅛ **teaspoon nutmeg**
5 **slices bacon**	⅛ **teaspoon salt**
¼ **cup chopped pecans**	⅛ **teaspoon pepper**
2 **green onions, sliced**	

Wash brussels sprouts thoroughly; remove discolored leaves. Cut off stem ends; cut brussels sprouts vertically into thin shreds. Set aside.

Cook bacon in a large skillet until crisp. Remove bacon, reserving drippings in skillet. Crumble bacon, and set aside.

Add pecans to drippings; cook over medium-high heat, stirring constantly, until golden. Add brussels sprouts, green onions, nutmeg, salt, and pepper. Cook over medium heat 18 minutes or until brussels sprouts are tender, stirring often. Spoon brussels sprouts mixture into a serving dish; sprinkle with bacon. Yield: 4 servings.

Creative Chef 2
Tourette Syndrome Association
Bayside, New York

Ginger-Lime Carrots

3 **pounds carrots, scraped and**	2 **tablespoons fresh lime juice**
cut into ¼-inch slices	1 **tablespoon grated lime rind**
3 **tablespoons butter**	1 **tablespoon grated fresh ginger**
3 **tablespoons honey**	**Garnish: lime slices**

Arrange carrot in a steamer basket over boiling water. Cover and steam 10 minutes or until crisp-tender; drain.

Combine butter and next 4 ingredients in a medium saucepan; cook over medium heat until butter melts and mixture begins to boil. Combine butter mixture and carrot. Cook over low heat, stirring constantly, 2 minutes or until carrot is glazed; transfer mixture to a serving bowl. Garnish, if desired. Yield: 8 servings.

Around Our Table: California Cooks Kosher
Jewish Family Service of Los Angeles, California

Baked Cauliflower with Almond Sauce

Tender cauliflower flowerets ooze with elegance when crowned with a decadent cream sauce and crunchy almonds.

2 medium cauliflowers, cut
   into flowerets
¾ cup light sour cream
¼ cup mayonnaise
2½ teaspoons Dijon mustard
2 green onions, minced
2 teaspoons all-purpose flour
¼ teaspoon dried dillweed

½ teaspoon salt
¼ teaspoon pepper
⅓ cup chopped almonds,
   toasted
¼ cup fine, dry breadcrumbs
2 teaspoons butter or
   margarine, melted

Place cauliflower in a steamer basket over boiling water. Cover and steam 8 minutes. Drain well; rinse with cold water. Place cauliflower in a lightly greased 13- x 9- x 2-inch baking dish.

Combine sour cream and next 7 ingredients; stir well. Spread sour cream mixture evenly over cauliflower. Combine almonds, bread-crumbs, and melted butter; sprinkle mixture over cauliflower. Bake at 350° for 25 minutes. Yield: 10 servings.   Judy Bruemmer

Church of St. Anthony 75th Anniversary
Church of St. Anthony
St. Cloud, Minnesota

Corn Chili

Ignite your palate with this gutsy side dish of fresh, plump corn kernels and the fiery southwestern flavors of chili powder and jalapeño pepper.

4 cups fresh corn, cut from cob
   (about 6 ears)
½ cup water
1 medium-size sweet red
   pepper, diced
2 green onions, sliced and
   divided
3 tablespoons unsalted butter,
   melted

½ teaspoon chili powder
½ teaspoon salt
½ teaspoon freshly ground
   pepper
1 jalapeño pepper, seeded and
   minced
½ cup finely chopped fresh
   cilantro
2 dashes of hot sauce

Combine corn and water in a saucepan. Bring to a boil; cover and cook 3 minutes. Drain well.

Cook red pepper and half of green onions in butter in a medium saucepan over medium-high heat until tender, stirring occasionally. Add corn, chili powder, salt, and pepper; cook, stirring constantly, until mixture is thoroughly heated. Remove from heat; stir in remaining green onions, jalapeño pepper, cilantro, and hot sauce. Yield: 6 servings.   Jenny Johnsen

A New Taste of Yardley
Makefield Women's Association
Yardley, Pennsylvania

Corn Maque Choux

5 slices bacon	1 teaspoon ground red pepper
8 cups fresh corn, cut from cob (about 12 ears), divided	1 teaspoon black pepper
	½ teaspoon garlic powder
2 cups finely chopped onion	1 bay leaf
1 cup chopped tomato	1 cup chicken broth
1 cup finely chopped green pepper	1 cup milk
	1 teaspoon sugar
1½ teaspoons salt	1 teaspoon dried basil

Cook bacon in a Dutch oven until crisp; remove bacon, reserving ¼ cup drippings in pan. Reserve bacon for another use.

Cook 1 cup corn in drippings over medium heat, stirring constantly, 10 minutes or until corn is lightly browned. Remove corn from skillet with a slotted spoon; set corn aside. Add onion, tomato, and green pepper. Cook, uncovered, over medium-high heat 10 minutes, stirring often.

Stir in remaining uncooked corn, salt, and next 4 ingredients. Cover and cook over medium-high heat 5 minutes; uncover and stir well (a crust will have formed on the bottom of pan). Cook, uncovered, 5 minutes, stirring often to prevent burning; remove and discard bay leaf.

Add reserved corn, and cook, uncovered, 10 minutes, stirring often to scrape crust from bottom of pan. Add chicken broth, milk, and sugar. Cover, reduce heat, and simmer 15 minutes; add basil. Cover and cook 5 minutes, stirring occasionally. Yield: 8 servings.

Cajun Men Cook
Beaver Club of Lafayette, Louisiana

Glazed Leeks and Rhubarb

An unpredictable gathering of aromatic leeks and fruity rhubarb dances in the shower of a sweet-and-sour brown sugar glaze.

2 medium leeks
3 tablespoons butter or margarine, melted
2 stalks rhubarb, trimmed and cut into 1-inch-thick slices

½ cup firmly packed brown sugar
¼ cup malt vinegar

Remove and discard root, tough outer leaves, and tops of leeks to where dark green begins to pale. Cut leeks in half lengthwise; rinse well, and slice into 1-inch pieces. Cook leeks in butter in a skillet over medium-high heat until tender, stirring occasionally.

Add rhubarb, brown sugar, and vinegar; cover and cook 5 minutes. Uncover and cook 5 additional minutes. Serve immediately. Yield: 4 servings.

Sailing Through Dinner
Three Squares Press
Stonington, Connecticut

Baked Lentils with Cheese

Vegetarian fare is surprisingly unpretentious as a Middle Eastern staple shares its delightful ethnicity with familiar carrots, celery, green pepper, and tomatoes.

3 cups dried lentils
2 cups water
1 bay leaf, finely chopped
2 teaspoons salt
¼ teaspoon pepper
¼ teaspoon dried marjoram
¼ teaspoon sage
¼ teaspoon dried thyme
2 large onions, chopped
2 cloves garlic, minced
1 (14.5-ounce) can diced tomatoes, undrained

2 large carrots, scraped and cut into ⅛-inch slices
1 stalk celery, thinly sliced
1 medium-size green pepper, seeded and chopped
2 tablespoons chopped fresh parsley
1½ cups (6 ounces) shredded sharp Cheddar cheese

Sort and wash lentils; place in a lightly greased 13- x 9- x 2-inch baking dish. Add water and next 9 ingredients, stirring well. Cover and bake at 375° for 30 minutes. Remove from oven, and stir in carrot and celery; cover and bake 40 minutes or until vegetables are tender. Remove from oven, and stir in green pepper and parsley. Sprinkle cheese over top. Bake, uncovered, 5 additional minutes or until cheese melts. Yield: 6 servings.   Kathy Wolfe

Add a Pound of Love
Geauga Humane Society
Chardon, Ohio

Sour Cream Limas

Bacon and brown sugar transform dried limas into a baked homestyle classic sure to comfort the soul.

1 **pound dried large lima beans**	¼ **teaspoon salt**
1 **medium onion, chopped**	¼ **teaspoon pepper**
1 **(8-ounce) carton sour cream**	5 **slices bacon**
½ **cup firmly packed brown**	
sugar	

Sort and wash beans; place in a Dutch oven. Cover with water 2 inches above beans; let soak 8 hours. Drain. Return beans to pan; add water to cover. Bring to a boil; cover, reduce heat, and simmer 1½ hours. Drain well.

Combine beans, onion, and next 4 ingredients; stir well. Spoon into a greased 13- x 9- x 2-inch baking dish; top with bacon. Bake, uncovered, at 350° for 1 hour. Yield: 8 servings.   Joan Litchfield

Sharing Recipes
Hook & Ladder Association of
Holly Lake Volunteer Fire Department
Big Sandy, Texas

Mushroom-Spinach Crêpes

½ pound fresh mushrooms,
  chopped
1 tablespoon vegetable oil
2 cups chopped fresh spinach
½ cup chopped walnuts,
  toasted

3 cups (12 ounces) shredded
  provolone cheese, divided
16 Whole Wheat Crêpes

Cook mushrooms in oil in a large skillet over medium-high heat, stirring constantly, until tender. Add spinach; cook 2 minutes, stirring constantly. Stir in walnuts.

Sprinkle 2 tablespoons cheese and 1 tablespoon mushroom mixture down center of spotty side of each Whole Wheat Crêpe; fold sides over. Place crêpe, seam side down, in a lightly greased 13- x 9- x 2-inch baking dish. Sprinkle with remaining 1 cup cheese. Bake, uncovered, at 350° for 10 minutes or until cheese melts. Serve immediately. Yield: 8 servings.

Whole Wheat Crêpes

1½ cups whole wheat flour
½ teaspoon salt
1 cup milk
1 cup water

2 large eggs
2 tablespoons vegetable oil
Vegetable cooking spray

Combine first 4 ingredients, beating at medium speed of an electric mixer until smooth. Add eggs, and beat well; stir in oil. Chill batter at least 2 hours.

Coat bottom of a 6-inch crêpe pan or heavy skillet with cooking spray; place over medium heat until hot.

Pour 2 tablespoons batter into pan; quickly tilt pan in all directions so batter covers bottom of pan. Cook 1 minute or until crêpe can be shaken loose from pan. Turn crêpe over, and cook about 30 seconds. Place crêpe on a dish towel to cool. Repeat with remaining batter.

Stack crêpes between sheets of wax paper, and place in an airtight container, if desired. Refrigerate up to 2 days or freeze up to 3 months. Yield: 28 (6-inch) crêpes.   Andy and Christy Hoover

Friendly Recipes
Religious Society of Friends (Quakers)
York, Pennsylvania

Parsley Creamed Parsnips

1 pound parsnips, scraped and thinly sliced
1 cup water
1 teaspoon salt, divided
2 tablespoons all-purpose flour
½ cup skim milk
⅛ teaspoon pepper
1 tablespoon grated orange rind
2 tablespoons chopped fresh parsley

Combine parsnips, water, and ½ teaspoon salt in a saucepan; bring to a boil. Cover, reduce heat, and simmer 10 minutes or until tender. Drain, reserving ½ cup liquid. Set parsnips and liquid aside.

Combine flour and milk in pan; stir until smooth. Add reserved liquid, remaining ½ teaspoon salt, and pepper; cook, stirring constantly, over medium heat until thick and bubbly. Stir in rind and parsnips. Sprinkle with parsley. Yield: 4 servings.   Thelma Rickard

Rainbow of Recipes, Volume I
The Dream Factory of Louisville, Kentucky

Peas Pernod

A spritz of licorice-essence Pernod coaxes out the sassy horseradish and mint flavors in this chilled English pea side dish.

1 (8-ounce) carton sour cream
1 tablespoon chopped fresh mint
1 teaspoon prepared horseradish
½ teaspoon salt
½ teaspoon Pernod or anisette
2 (10-ounce) packages frozen English peas, thawed
3 green onions, chopped
1 Red Delicious apple, cored and chopped

Combine first 5 ingredients in a large bowl, stirring well. Pat peas dry on paper towels to remove excess moisture; add peas to sour cream mixture. Add green onions and apple; toss gently. Cover and chill thoroughly. Yield: 6 servings.   Helen Renzi

As You Like It
Williamstown Theatre Festival Guild
Williamstown, Massachusetts

Sweet and Hot Black-Eyed Peas

1 (16-ounce) package dried
  black-eyed peas
¼ cup unsalted butter
¼ cup water
2 cups chopped onion
1½ cups chopped sweet red
  pepper

2 cups chopped green pepper
1 small jalapeño pepper,
  seeded and chopped
2 cloves garlic, minced
1 teaspoon salt
½ teaspoon ground red pepper
¼ teaspoon black pepper

Sort and wash peas; place in a large Dutch oven. Cover with water 2 inches above peas; let soak 8 hours. Drain. Return peas to Dutch oven; add water to cover. Bring to a boil; cover, reduce heat, and simmer 30 minutes or until peas are tender. Drain peas, reserving 1 cup cooking liquid.

Combine butter and ¼ cup water in pan. Cook over medium heat until mixture comes to a boil. Add onion and remaining 7 ingredients; cook over medium heat, stirring occasionally, until tender.

Add peas and reserved liquid to pan; cover, reduce heat, and simmer 30 minutes. Uncover and simmer 15 additional minutes. Yield: 9 servings.

Diana Ellison

Holy Smoke
United Methodist Women of
Peachtree Road United Methodist Church
Atlanta, Georgia

Fabulous Four-Pepper Stir-Fry

2 tablespoons lemon juice
1½ tablespoons soy sauce
1 tablespoon honey
½ teaspoon chili oil
2 tablespoons thinly sliced
  green onions
1½ teaspoons minced garlic
1½ teaspoons minced fresh
  ginger
1½ teaspoons seeded, minced
  jalapeño pepper
2 teaspoons vegetable oil

2 medium-size sweet red
  peppers, cut into 1½-inch
  pieces
1 medium-size sweet yellow
  pepper, cut into 1½-inch
  pieces
1 medium-size green pepper,
  cut into 1½-inch pieces
1½ teaspoons cornstarch
1 tablespoon water
1½ teaspoons sesame seeds,
  toasted

Combine first 4 ingredients in a small bowl, stirring well. Set aside.

Stir-fry green onions and next 3 ingredients in 2 teaspoons vegetable oil 15 seconds. Add peppers, and stir-fry 2 minutes. Stir in lemon juice mixture; bring to a boil.

Dissolve cornstarch in water, and stir into pepper mixture. Cook 1 minute or until thickened. Sprinkle with sesame seeds. Yield: 6 servings.

Gold'n Delicious
The Junior League of Spokane, Washington

Mashed Potatoes with Shallots, Goat Cheese, and Herbs

Trendy mashed potatoes are no oxymoron. Upscale shallot, creamy goat cheese, and fresh herbs transform an old standby into a showy star.

¾ cup chopped shallot (about 4 large)
2 teaspoons olive oil
2½ pounds Yukon Gold or round red potatoes
1 cup milk
10 ounces soft goat cheese
1 tablespoon chopped fresh thyme
1 tablespoon chopped fresh parsley
1 tablespoon chopped fresh chives
¾ teaspoon salt
¼ teaspoon freshly ground pepper
Garnishes: fresh thyme sprigs, fresh parsley sprigs

Cook shallot in oil in a large skillet over medium heat 4 to 5 minutes or until tender and golden. Set aside.

Cook potatoes in boiling water to cover 30 to 35 minutes or until tender. Let cool 5 minutes. Peel and mash potatoes with a potato masher. (Do not use a food processor.)

Heat milk in a small saucepan until warm; add milk to potato. Stir in shallot, goat cheese, and next 5 ingredients. Spoon into a serving dish. Garnish, if desired. Yield: 10 servings.   Marge Eastman

A Culinary Tour of Homes
Big Canoe Chapel Women's Guild
Big Canoe, Georgia

Lauren's Cheesy
Broccoli 'n' Potatoes in Foil

5 medium-size baking
  potatoes, peeled and
  thinly sliced
  (about 2 pounds)
½ cup water
2 cups frozen broccoli cuts,
  thawed
1 medium onion, sliced

4 ounces American cheese,
  cubed
½ teaspoon salt
⅛ teaspoon pepper
¼ cup plus 2 tablespoons
  butter or margarine,
  softened

Combine potato and water in a 3-quart casserole. Cover with wax paper; microwave at HIGH 12 to 14 minutes or until potato is crisp-tender, stirring once; drain.

Cut one 22- x 18-inch piece of heavy-duty aluminum foil. Layer potato, broccoli, onion, and cheese on foil; sprinkle with salt and pepper, and dot with butter. Fold foil edges over, and crimp to seal securely.

Grill, covered, over medium coals (300° to 350°) 20 minutes or until potato is tender. Yield: 4 servings.   Peg LeRoux

Note: We used Velveeta for the American cheese because it melts so beautifully.

Fanconi Anemia Family Cookbook
Fanconi Anemia Research Fund
Eugene, Oregon

Restuffed Sweet Potatoes

Fashionably piped to puffy perfection, sweet potato shells serve as hearty vessels for the creamy, sherry-spiked potato stuffing.

12 small sweet potatoes
Vegetable oil
1 (8-ounce) package cream
  cheese, softened
¼ cup firmly packed brown sugar
¼ cup butter or margarine,
  softened

1 tablespoon sherry
1¼ teaspoons salt
½ teaspoon pepper
⅓ cup coarsely chopped pecans

Scrub potatoes thoroughly, and rub skins with oil; bake at 400° for 1 hour. Let cool to touch.

Slice skin away from top of each potato; carefully scoop out pulp, leaving shells in tact. Mash pulp. Add cream cheese and next 5 ingredients; mix well. Spoon filling into pastry bag fitted with large star tip; pipe into shells. Top with pecans. Bake at 350° for 30 minutes. Yield: 12 servings.

Note: You can prepare these potatoes up to 48 hours before serving. Remove from refrigerator, and let stand 30 minutes. Bake at 350° for 30 minutes.

Specialty of the House
Taylorville Business & Professional Women's Club
Taylorville, Illinois

Spaghetti Squash Fritters

1 (2½-pound) spaghetti squash	¾ teaspoon salt
½ cup all-purpose flour	½ teaspoon pepper
2½ tablespoons chopped	2 large eggs, lightly beaten
fresh dill	Vegetable oil

Wash squash; cut in half lengthwise. Remove and discard seeds and membranes. Place squash, cut side down, on a large baking sheet. Bake at 350° for 30 minutes or until crisp-tender. Let cool. Remove spaghetti-like strands with a fork. Cover and chill thoroughly.

Combine squash, flour, and next 3 ingredients; stir well. Add eggs, stirring well.

Pour oil to depth of 1½ inches into a large heavy skillet. Drop mixture by tablespoonfuls into hot oil. Fry over medium-high heat 5 minutes or until golden, turning once. Drain on paper towels. Yield: 20 fritters.

Kay Hutchinson

Emmanuel's Best in Cooking
Emmanuel Episcopal Church
Chestertown, Maryland

Mushroom Stuffed Tomatoes

8 medium-size ripe tomatoes
1½ pounds fresh mushrooms, sliced
½ cup butter or margarine, melted
1 (8-ounce) carton sour cream
1 tablespoon plus 1 teaspoon all-purpose flour
3 ounces Roquefort cheese, crumbled
¼ teaspoon ground oregano
1 teaspoon chopped fresh parsley
2 tablespoons dry sherry
½ teaspoon salt
¼ teaspoon pepper
¼ teaspoon paprika

Slice off top of each tomato, and carefully scoop out pulp. Reserve tomato pulp for another use. Invert tomato shells onto paper towels to drain.

Sauté mushrooms in butter in a large skillet over medium heat until mushrooms are tender and liquid evaporates. Set aside.

Combine sour cream and next 5 ingredients in a saucepan; cook over medium heat, stirring constantly, until thickened and smooth. Stir in mushrooms, salt, and pepper.

Spoon mixture into shells. Place in a greased 13- x 9- x 2-inch baking dish. Sprinkle with paprika. Bake at 375° for 15 minutes. Serve immediately. Yield: 8 servings.   Jeanne Mears and Nancy Myers

The Stoney Creek Recipe Collection:
A Treasury of Culinary Favorites and Historical Vignettes
Stoney Creek Presbyterian Foundation
Beaufort, South Carolina

Hot Vinaigrette Vegetables

2 cups broccoli flowerets
2 cups cauliflower flowerets
1 cup thinly sliced onion
6 cherry tomatoes, quartered lengthwise
½ small sweet red pepper, cut into very thin strips
½ teaspoon sugar
½ teaspoon salt
¼ teaspoon dried oregano
⅛ teaspoon pepper
1 tablespoon vegetable oil
1½ teaspoons lemon juice
1½ teaspoons raspberry vinegar
1 teaspoon sesame oil
1 small clove garlic, minced
1 teaspoon chopped fresh basil

Cook flowerets in boiling water to cover 30 seconds. Drain. Combine flowerets, onion, cherry tomato, and pepper strips in a large bowl.

Combine sugar and next 8 ingredients in a saucepan; bring to a boil. Remove from heat, and add to vegetable mixture; toss well. Sprinkle with basil. Yield: 6 servings.   Maureen Strauts

Seasonings
The 20th Century Club Juniors of Park Ridge, Illinois

Vegetable Sloppy Joes

Hearty pinto beans and an entourage of meaty vegetables such as eggplant, zucchini, and mushrooms create a mock sloppy joe sauce to rival any ground beef rendition.

1 cup cubed eggplant	1 (15-ounce) can tomato sauce
¾ cup chopped onion	3 tablespoons tomato paste
½ pound fresh mushrooms, chopped	1 teaspoon ground cumin
	1 teaspoon dried basil
½ cup chopped green pepper	1 teaspoon chili powder
½ cup chopped zucchini	Pinch of salt
1 clove garlic, minced	1 bay leaf
2 tablespoons olive oil	1 (16-ounce) can pinto beans, drained
1 pound fresh plum tomatoes, peeled and chopped	Whole wheat hamburger buns

Cook first 6 ingredients in oil in a large skillet over medium-high heat, stirring constantly, until crisp-tender. Add chopped tomato and next 7 ingredients to skillet. Bring to a boil; reduce heat, and simmer, uncovered, 30 minutes or until thickened, stirring occasionally. Add beans; simmer 5 additional minutes. Remove and discard bay leaf. Serve on hamburger buns. Yield: 11 servings.   Audrey Woods

Weymouth Township's Heritage of Recipes
Weymouth Township's Civic Association
Dorothy, New Jersey

Acknowledgments

Each of the community cookbooks listed is represented by recipes appearing in *America's Best Recipes*. Unless otherwise noted, the copyright is held by the sponsoring organization whose mailing address is included.

ABC of Cooking, McKean Elementary PTA, Inc., 5120 West Rd., McKean, PA 16426

Add a Pound of Love, Geauga Humane Society, 12513 Merritt Rd., P.O. Box 342, Chardon, OH 44024

Amazing Graces: Meals and Memories from the Parsonage, Texas Conference United Methodist Minister's Spouses Association, P.O. Box 3400, Palestine, TX 75802

Angel Food, St. Vincent de Paul School, 1375 E. Spring Ln., Salt Lake City, UT 84117

Another Taste of Aloha, Junior League of Honolulu, 1802-A Keeaumoku St., Honolulu, HI 96822

Appealing Fare, Frost & Jacobs, 201 E. 5th St., Ste. 2200, Cincinnati, OH 45244

Appetizers from A to Z, Christ Child Society, P.O. Box 15945, Phoenix, AZ 85060-5945

Applause! Oklahoma's Best Performing Recipes, Oklahoma City Orchestra League, Inc., 50 Penn Pl., R325, 1900 NW Expressway, Oklahoma City, OK 73118

Around Our Table: California Cooks Kosher, Jewish Family Service of Los Angeles, 6505 Wilshire Blvd., Ste. 614, Los Angeles, CA 90048

The Artful Table, Dallas Museum of Art League, 1717 N. Harwood, Dallas, TX 75201

Art in the Kitchen, Westmoreland Museum of Art Women's Committee, 221 N. Main St., Greensburg, PA 15601

As You Like It, Williamstown Theatre Festival Guild, P.O. Box 219, Williamstown, MA 01267

The Authorized Texas Ranger Cookbook, Texas Ranger Museum, P.O. Box 191, Hamilton, TX 76531

The Best of Wheeling, Junior League of Wheeling, Inc., 907½ National Rd., Wheeling, WV 26003

Beyond Brisket, Sisterhood of Temple Israel, 145 Hartford St., Natick, MA 01760

BMC on Our Menu, Baptist Medical Center Auxiliary of Volunteers, Taylor at Marion Sts., Columbia, SC 29220

Bountiful Blessings, St. Luke's United Methodist Church, % Karen Brown, 4851 S. Apopka Vineland Rd., Orlando, FL 32819

Briarwood Recipes to Crown Your Table, Women's Ministries of Briarwood Presbyterian Church, 2200 Briarwood Way, Birmingham, AL 35243

Cafe Oklahoma, Junior Service League of Midwest City, P.O. Box 10703, Midwest City, OK 73130

Cajun Men Cook, Beaver Club of Lafayette, P.O. Box 2744, Lafayette, LA 70502

Calvert Street School 1995 Cookbook, Calvert Street School, 19850 Deland St., Woodland Hills, CA 91367

Cane River's Louisiana Living, Service League of Natchitoches, Inc., 446 Jefferson St., Natchitoches, LA 71457

Canticle of Cookery, St. Irenaeus Church Music Ministry, 5201 Evergreen, Cypress, CA 90630

Carolinas Heritage, 47th National Square Dance Convention, Inc., 1223 Bearmore Dr., Charlotte, NC 28211

Celebrating California, Children's Home Society of California, 7695 Cardinal Ct., San Diego, CA 92123

Celebrating Our Mothers' Kitchens, National Council of Negro Women, Inc., 633 Pennsylvania Ave., NW, Washington, DC 20004

A Celebration of Food, Sisterhood Temple Beth David, 7 Clapboardtree St., Westwood, MA 02090

A Century of Cooking, Eden Chapel United Methodist Church, P.O. Box 441, Perkins, OK 74059

The Chancellor's Table, Friends of the Chancellor's Residence at the University of Missouri-Rolla, 506 W. Eleventh St., Rolla, MO 65401

Charlie Daniel's Angels Cook Book, Mt. Juliet Tennis Association at Charlie Daniels Park, 304 Anchor Dr., Old Hickory, TN 37138

Charted Courses, Child and Family Agency of Southeastern Connecticut, Inc., 255 Hempstead St., New London, CT 06329

The Christ Church Cookbook, Christ Episcopal Church, 7305 Afton Rd., Woodbury, MN 55125

Church of St. Anthony 75th Anniversary, Church of St. Anthony, 33 24th Ave. N., St. Cloud, MN 56303

Classic Connecticut Cuisine, Connecticut Easter Seals, 152 Norwich-New London Tpke., P.O. Box 389, Uncasville, CT 06382-0389

Collard Greens, Watermelons, and "Miss" Charlotte's Pie, Swansboro United Methodist Women, P.O. Box 771, Swansboro, NC 28584-0771

The Collection, Mountain Brook Baptist Church, 3631 Montevallo Rd. S., Birmingham, AL 35213-4299

Colony Club Concoctions, Colony Club, P.O. Box 1123, Ocean City, NJ 08226

A Continual Feast, St. Mary's Guild of St. Clement's Episcopal Church, 2837 Claremont Blvd., Berkeley, CA 94705

Cooking Around the Authority, Charlotte-Mecklenburg Hospital Authority, 1000 Blythe Blvd., Charlotte, NC 28232

Cooking Atlanta Style, Atlanta Community Food Bank, Longstreet Press, 2140 Newmarket Pkwy., Ste. 118, Marietta, GA 30067

Cooking from the Hip, Calvary Bible Evangelical Free Church, Mothers of Preschoolers, 3245 Kalmia Ave., Boulder, CO 80301

Cooking on the Coast, Mississippi Gulf Coast YMCA, P.O. Box 430, Ocean Springs, MS 39566

Cooking with Class, Park Maitland School, 1450 S. Orlando Ave., Maitland, FL 32794-1095

Cooking with Faith, Faith United Methodist Church, 811 Brandywine Ave., Schenectady, NY 12308

Cooking with Fire, Fairfield Historical Society, 636 Old Post Rd., Fairfield, CT 06430

Cookin' in the Canyon, Gallatin Canyon Women's Club, P.O. Box 160412, Big Sky, MT 59716

Cookin' with the Pride of Cove, Copperas Cove Band Boosters Club, % Rebecca Greenwood, 60035-1 MacMichael Cir., Ft. Hood, TX 76544

Cooks by the Yard, Harvard Neighbors, Harvard University, 17 Quincy St., Cambridge, MA 02138

A Cook's Tour of Gautier, Gautier Garden Club, % Anita Gallagher, 1720 MaryAnn Dr., Gautier, MS 39553

A Cook's Tour of Libertyville, Main Street Libertyville, Inc., 133 E. Cook, Libertyville, IL 60048

Cooper's Cookin' It Up!, Cooper Elementary School, 5143 S. 21st St., Milwaukee, WI 53221-3599

Creative Chef 2, Tourette Syndrome Association, Inc., 42-40 Bell Blvd., Bayside, NY 11361

Cucina Classica, Maintaining a Tradition, Order Sons of Italy in America, New York Grand Lodge Foundation, Inc., 2101 Bellmore Ave., Bellmore, NY 11710-5605

Cuisine for Connoisseurs: Food Among the Fine Arts, Boca Raton Museum of Art, 10586 Stonebridge Blvd., Boca Raton, FL 33498

A Culinary Concerto, Brick Hospital Association, 107 Brick Plaza, Brick, NJ 08723

A Culinary Quilt, Edison/Computech P.T.S.A., 555 E. Belgravia Ave., Fresno, CA 93706

A Culinary Tour of Homes, Big Canoe Chapel Women's Guild, 455 Big Canoe, Big Canoe, GA 30143

Delicious Developments, Friends of Strong Memorial Hospital, 601 Elmwood Ave., Box 660, Rochester, NY 14642

Des Schmecht Goot, St. Peter Christian Mothers, HCRI Box 81, Collyer, KS 67631

Dining by Fireflies: Unexpected Pleasures of the New South, Junior League of Charlotte, 1332 Maryland Ave., Charlotte, NC 28209

Dining with Duke Cookbook, Badger Association of the Blind, 912 N. Hawley Rd., Milwaukee, WI 53213

Discover Oklahoma Cookin', Oklahoma 4-H Foundation, Inc., 205 Poultry Science, Stillwater, OK 74078

Divine Dishes, St. Mark's Episcopal Church, 57 Main St., Southborough, MA 01772

Dock 'n Dine in Dorchester, Long Wharf Lighthouse Committee, P.O. Box 643, Cambridge, MD 21613

Dundee Presbyterian Church Cook Book, Dundee Presbyterian Church, 5312 Underwood Ave., Omaha, NE 68132

The Educated Palate: The Hamlin School Cookbook, The Hamlin School, 2120 Broadway, San Francisco, CA 94115

Emmanuel's Best in Cooking, Emmanuel Episcopal Church, P.O. Box 231, Chestertown, MD 21620

Emory Seasons, Entertaining Atlanta Style, Emory University Woman's Club, 849 Houston Mill Rd., NE, Atlanta, GA 30329

Enough to Feed an Army, West Point Officers Wives' Club, P.O. Box 44, West Point, NY 10996

En Pointe: Culinary Delights from Pittsburgh Ballet Theatre, Pittsburgh Ballet Theatre School, 2900 Liberty Ave., Pittsburgh, PA 15201

Entertaining in Kingwood, Kingwood Women's Club, P.O. Box 5411, Kingwood, TX 77345

Entertaining Recipes II, Madison Zonta Club, 3120-1 Creekview Dr., Middleton, WI 53562

Ethnic Delights, Our Lady of Perpetual Help Byzantine Catholic Church, 1210 Spotswood Ave., Norfolk, VA 23507

Evening Shade, Volume II, Evening Shade School Foundation, Inc., School St., Evening Shade, AR 72532

Everybody Bring a Dish, Cooking in the Spirit of Shalom, Shalom United Church of Christ, 505 Mac Murray, Richland, WA 99352

The Fabulous Footnotes' Cookbook, Sandy Paustian's Fabulous Footnotes, 849 N.E. Jensen Beach Blvd., Jensen Beach, FL 34957

Family Favorites, Allen County Extension Homemakers, Inc., 4001 Crescent Ave., Fort Wayne, IN 46815

Family Favorites, Optimist Clubs of Alabama/Mississippi District, 1925 Still Oaks Dr., Montgomery, AL 36117

Fanconi Anemia Family Cookbook, Fanconi Anemia Research Fund, Inc., 1902 Jefferson St., Ste. 2, Eugene, OR 97405

A Fare to Remember, Dublin Service League, 208 Huntington Dr., Dublin, GA 31040

Favorite Recipes, P.E.O. Chapter BC, 161 Birchwood Dr., Hendersonville, NC 28739

Favorite Recipes from Our Best Cooks, Senior Center of Ketchikan, Alaska, 1016 Water St., Ketchikan, AK 99901

A Feast for the Eyes, Cataract Care Center, 2020 S. Kingsboro Ave., Johnstown, NY 12095

Feast of Eden, Junior League of Monterey County, Inc., P.O. Box 2291, Monterey, CA 93942

Feeding Our Flocks, The Shepherd's Fund, 7 Ash St., Hollis, NH 03049

Feed My Sheep, Signal Mountain Presbyterian Church, 612 James Blvd., Signal Mountain, TN 37377

First Family Favorites, First Baptist Church of Orlando, 3701 L.B. McLeod Rd., Orlando, FL 32805-6691

Food for the Journey, St. Francis Xavier College Church Choir, 3628 Lindell Blvd., St. Louis, MO 63108

Food for the Spirit, St. Thomas Aquinas Home & School Association, 14520 Voss Dr., Hammond, LA 70401

Food for Thought, Junior League of Birmingham, Inc., 2212 20th Ave. S., Birmingham, AL 35223

Friendly Recipes, Religious Society of Friends (Quakers), 135 W. Philadelphia St., York, PA 17403

Friends and Fellowship Cookbook, First Christian Church of Stow, 3493 Darrow Rd., Stow, OH 44224

From Our Kitchens with Love, St. Mark Orthodox Church, 400 W. Hamlin, Rochester Hills, MI 48307

Gallatin Gateway School and Community Cookbook, Gateway School Support Group, 100 Mill St., Gallatin Gateway, MT 59730

Gardener's Delight, Ohio Association of Garden Clubs, Inc., 1934 Zuber Rd., Grove City, OH 43123-8970

Gaspee Days Cookbook, Gaspee Days Committee, P.O. Box 1772, Pilgrim Station, Warwick, RI 02888

Gathered at the Gables: Then and Now, The House of the Seven Gables, 54 Turner St., Salem, MA 01970

Generations, Junior League of Rockford, Inc., 4118 Pinecrest Rd., Rockford, IL 61107

Generations, Twilight Optimist Club of Conway, P.O. Box 1705, Conway, AR 72033

Global Feast Cookbook, Mystic Seaport Museum Stores, 47 Greenmanville Ave., Mystic, CT 06355

Gold'n Delicious, Junior League of Spokane, 910 N. Washington St., Ste. 228, Spokane, WA 99201-2260

Gourmet Our Way, Cascia Hall Preparatory School Parent Faculty Association, 2520 S. Yorktown Ave., Tulsa, OK 74114-2803

Gove County Gleanings: Recipes, Facts, and Photos Harvested from Gove County, Kansas, Gove Community Improvement Association, P.O. Box 155, Gove, KS 67736

Grace Lutheran Church Family Cookbook, Grace Lutheran Church Women's Missionary League, 125 Northeastern Blvd., Nashua, NH 03062

The Guild Cookbook, Volume IV, Valparaiso University Guild, Kretzmann Hall, Valparaiso, IN 46383

Hand in Hand, Heart to Heart, Sisterhood Temple Beth El, 1702 Hamilton St., Allentown, PA 18104

Happy Memories and Thankful Hearts: Traditions Kept and Blessings Shared, St. Christina's Catholic Church, Box 261, Parker, SD 57053

H.E.A.L. of Michiana Cookbook: A Collection of Health Conscious Recipes, Human Ecology Action League of Michiana, 4451 Cleveland Ave., Stevensville, MI 49127

Healthful Recipes from "Friends of Bear," Bear Necessities Pediatric Cancer Foundation, Inc., 271 Country Commons Rd., Ste. F, Cary, IL 60013

Heavenly Recipes, Rosebud WELCA, Lemmon Rural Lutheran Parish, HCR 82, Box 81, Lemmon, SD 57638-9217

Helpings of Hope, Franklin County Habitat for Humanity, P.O. Box 505, Louisburg, NC 27549

The Heritage Cookbook, St. George's Episcopal Church, Attn: Sylvia Hopkins, 905 Princess Anne St., Fredericksburg, VA 22401

Historically Delicious–An Almanac Cookbook, Tri-Cities Historical Society, 1 N. Harbor Dr., Grand Haven, MI 49417

Historic Spanish Point: Cooking Then and Now, Gulf Coast Heritage Association, Inc., 500 N. Tamiami Trail, P.O. Box 846, Osprey, FL 34229

History, Memories & Recipes, Fox River Grove Diamond Jubilee Committee, 408 Northwest Hwy., Fox River Grove, IL 60021

Holy Smoke, United Methodist Women of Peachtree Road United Methodist Church, 3180 Peachtree Rd., NE, Atlanta, GA 30342

Homecoming: Special Foods, Special Memories, Baylor University Alumni Association, 700 S. University Parks Dr., 2nd Floor, Waco, TX 76706

Home Cookin', American Legion Auxiliary, Department of Wyoming, 320 Linda Vista, Torrington, WY 82240-1739

In the Serving Tradition, Durham Woman's Club, Inc., P.O. Box 273, Durham, CT 06422

Irish Children's Summer Program 10th Anniversary Cookbook, Irish Children's Summer Program, 108 Glenwaye Dr., Greenville, SC 29615

Jewish Cooking from Here & Far, Congregation Beth Israel, 5716 Carmel Valley Rd., Carmel, CA 93923

Lake Murray Presbyterian Preschool Cookbook, Lake Murray Presbyterian Preschool Parents Organization, 2721 Dutchfork Rd., Chapin, SC 29036

Lakes Region Cuisine: A Centennial Celebration 1893-1993, Lakes Region General Hospital Auxiliary, 80 Highland St., Laconia, NH 03246

Lawtons Progressors, 50 Years and Still Cookin', Lawtons Progressors 4-H Club, 2093 Shirley Rd., North Collins, NY 14111-9746

The Legal Aid Bureau Cookbook, Recipes for Slaw and Order, Legal Aid Bureau, 14 E. Jackson Blvd., 15th Floor, Chicago, IL 60604-2245

The Lincoln Park Historical Society Cooks!, Lincoln Park Historical Society, 1335 Southfield, Lincoln Park, MI 48146

Literally Delicious, Friends of the Gates Public Library, 1605 Buffalo Rd., Rochester, NY 14624

Living off the Land: Arkansas Style, Howard County 4-H Foundation, 421 N. Main St., Nashville, AR 71852

Madison County Cookbook, St. Joseph Church, 607 W. Green St., Winterset, IA 50273

Maine Course Cookbook, YMCA, Mt. Desert St., Bar Harbor, ME 04609

Maine Ingredients, Junior League of Portland, 107 Elm St., Ste. 100R, Portland, ME 04101

Making a Memory, Hospice Circle of Love, 605 S. Monroe, Enid, OK 73701

Meals on Wheels, Meals on Wheels of Central Maryland, Inc., 515 S. Haven St., Baltimore, MD 21224

Minnesota Times and Tastes, Recipes and Menus Seasoned with History from the Minnesota Governor's Residence, 1006 Summit Avenue Society, 1006 Summit Ave., St. Paul, MN 55105

More Country Living, Waterloo Area Historical Society, P.O. Box 37, 9998 Waterloo-Munith Rd., Stockbridge, MI 49285

More Than Delicious, Erie Art Museum, 411 State St., Erie, PA 16501

The Museum Cookbook, Longport Historical Society, Old Borough Hall, 2300 Atlantic Ave., Longport, NJ 08403

A New Taste of Yardley, Makefield Women's Association, P.O. Box 163, Yardley, PA 19047

Not by Bread Alone, Catholic Committee on Scouting and Camp Fire for the Diocese of Lake Charles, 817 Azalea St., Lake Charles, LA 70605

Old Favorites from New Friends, Stillwater Newcomers Club, 1601 Wildwood Dr., Stillwater, OK 74075

Our Favorite Recipes from Coast to Coast, Hopeman Brothers/Lofton Corporation/AWH Associates, 435 Essex Ave., Waynesboro, VA 22980

Palette Pleasers, St. Luke Simpson United Methodist Women, 1500 Country Club Rd., Lake Charles, LA 70605

Paws and Refresh, Virginia Living Museum, 524 J. Clyde Morris Blvd., Newport News, VA 23601

Pepper Lovers Club Cookbook, Volume I, Pepper Lovers Club of Virginia Beach, P.O. Box 5043, Virginia Beach, VA 23455

Perfect Endings, The Art of Desserts, Friends of the Arts of the Tampa Museum of Art, 600 N. Ashley Dr., Tampa, FL 33602

Phi Bete's Best, Phi Beta Psi Sorority, Theta Alpha Gamma Chapter, 813 27th St., Bedford, IN 47421

Picnic in the Park, Atwood Community Center, 2425 Atwood Ave., Madison, WI 53704

A Place Called Hope, Junior Auxiliary of Hope, P.O. Box 81, Hope, AR 71801

Plain & Fancy Favorites, Montgomery Woman's Club, Inc., Box 42114, Cincinnati, OH 45242

Presentations, Friends of Lied, Lied Center for Performing Arts, 301 N. 12th, Lincoln, NE 68588-0151

Queen Anne Goes to the Kitchen, Episcopal Church Women of St. Paul's Parish, ECW of St. Paul's Parish, P.O. Box 278, Centreville, MD 21617

A Quest for Good Eating, Cape Cod Questers, 40 Conservation Dr., Yarmouth Port, MA 02675-1416

Quilters Guild of Indianapolis Cookbook, Quilters Guild of Indianapolis, 910 Tecumseh Pl., Indianapolis, IN 46201-1944

Rainbow of Recipes, Volume I, The Dream Factory of Louisville, Inc., 982 Eastern Pkwy., Louisville, KY 40217

Read'em and Eat, Middleton Public Library, 7425 Hubbard Ave., Middleton, WI 53562

Recipes and Remembrances, Newport Bicentennial Commission, 510 Linden Ave., Newport, KY 41071

Recipes & Reminiscences from the Oil Patch, West Kern Oil Museum, P.O. Box 491, Taft, CA 93268

Recipes from Colorado's Wine and Fruit Valley, Palisade Community Cookbook Association, 3560 G Rd., Palisade, CO 81526-9789

Recipes from the Heart II, South Suburban Humane Society Auxiliary, 228 Monee Rd., Park Forest, IL 60466

Recipes of Love, Alpha Delta Pi, Jackson Area Alumnae Association, 35 Sunline Dr., Brandon, MS 39042

Ribbon Winning Recipes, South Carolina State Fair, 1200 Rosewood Dr., Columbia, SC 29201

The Richmond Museum of History Cookbook, Richmond Museum of History, 400 Nevin Ave., P.O. Box 1247, Richmond, CA 94801

The Roaring Fork, Gloria J. Deschamp Donation Fund, 124 Mount View Dr., Grand Junction, CO 81501

Sailing Through Dinner, Three Squares Press, 17 Oak St., L.P., Stonington, CT 06378

Saint Louis Days, Saint Louis Nights, Junior League of St. Louis, 10435 Clayton Rd., St. Louis, MO 63131

Saints Alive!, Ladies' Guild of St. Barnabas Anglican Church, 4795 N. Peachtree Rd., Atlanta, GA 30338

The Sampler, Association for the Preservation of Tennessee Antiquities-Hardeman County Chapter, P.O. Box 246, Bolivar, TN 38008

Sampler Cookbook, Clarence Log Cabin Quilters, 4895 Kraus Rd., Clarence, NY 14031

Savor the Brandywine Valley, A Collection of Recipes, Junior League of Wilmington, Inc., 1801 N. Market St., Wilmington, DE 19802

Seaport Savories, TWIG Junior Auxiliary of Alexandria Hospital, P.O. Box 3614, Alexandria, VA 22302

Seasoned with Love, Mahoning County Foster Parent Association, 2801 Market St., Rm. 200, Youngstown, OH 44507

Seasonings, 20th Century Club Juniors of Park Ridge, P.O. Box 290, Park Ridge, IL 60068

Shared Recipes Among Friends, Junior Auxiliary of Russellville, P.O. Box 1011, Russellville, AR 72811

Sharing Our Feast, Holy Apostles Episcopal Church, 3185 Hickory Hill Rd., Memphis, TN 38115

Sharing Recipes, Hook & Ladder Association of Holly Lake Volunteer Fire Department, Rte. 1, Box 742, Big Sandy, TX 75755

Signature Edition, Junior Woman's Club of Green Bay, P.O. Box 12042, Green Bay, WI 54307-2042

Silver Selections, Catawba School Alumni, 1792 Sharonwood Ln., Rock Hill, SC 29732

Simply Classic, Junior League of Seattle, 4119 E. Madison, Seattle, WA 98112

Simply Irresistible, Junior Auxiliary of Conway, P.O. Box 10322, Conway, AR 72032

Simply Irresistible!, St. Monica Parish Home and School Association, 5635 N. Santa Monica Blvd., Whitefish Bay, WI 53217

A Slice of Orange: Favorite VOLS Recipes, University of Tennessee College of Human Ecology/Women's Athletics Dept., 110 Jessie Harris Bldg., 1215 W. Cumberland Ave., Knoxville, TN 37996-1900

A Southern Collection, Then and Now, Junior League of Columbus, 1440 2nd Ave., Columbus, GA 31901

Specialty of the House, Taylorville Business & Professional Women's Club, RR 2, Box 235, Taylorville, IL 62568

St. Aloysius Rosary Society Cookbook, St. Aloysius Rosary Society, 301 N. Maryville, Calmar, IA 52132

Stephens Remembered, Recollections & Recipes, Stephens College Denver Area Club, 117 S. Reed St., Lakewood, CO 80226

Sterling Performances, Guilds of the Orange County Performing Arts Center, 600 Town Center Dr., Costa Mesa, CA 92626

The Stoney Creek Recipe Collection: A Treasury of Culinary Favorites and Historical Vignettes, Stoney Creek Presbyterian Foundation, Inc., P.O. Box 1226, Beaufort, SC 29902-1226

Sunflowers and Samovars Recipe Collection, St. Nicholas Orthodox Church, 4313 18th Ave., Kenosha, WI 53140

Sun Valley Celebrity & Local Heroes Cookbook, Advocates for Survivors of Domestic Violence, P.O. Box 3216, Hailey, ID 83333

The Tailgate Cookbook, National Kidney Foundation of Kansas and Western Missouri, 1900 W. 47th Pl., Ste. 310, Westwood, KS 66205

Take Note! Band Boosters Community Cookbook, Pinconning Area Schools Band Boosters, 605 W. 5th St., Pinconning, MI 48650

Take the Tour, St. Paul's Episcopal Church Women, 101 W. Gale St., Edenton, NC 27932

Tasteful Treasures, Docent Guild, Bowers Museum of Cultural Art, 2002 N. Main St., Santa Ana, CA 92706

A Taste of the Past and Present, First Baptist and Pastor's Sunday School Class, 606 Church St., P.O. Box 45, Philadelphia, TN 37846

A Taste of Toronto: Ohio, That Is, Toronto High School Alumni Association, 102 N. Third St., P.O. Box 273, Toronto, OH 43964

Ten Years of Taste, An Adventure in Food and Wine, Adaptive Aquatics Center, 1800 Westwind Dr., Bakersfield, CA 93301

Texas Tapestry, Houston Junior Woman's Club, 12603 Barryknoll Ln., Houston, TX 77024

Of Tide & Thyme, Junior League of Annapolis, 19 Loretta Ave., Annapolis, MD 21401

Timeless Treasures, Junior Service League of Valdosta, P.O. Box 1582, 305 N. Patterson St., Valdosta, GA 31603

To Serve with Love, Christian Women's Fellowship of The First Christian Church, 916 W. Walnut, Duncan, OK 73533

Town Hill Playground Cookbook, Town Hill Playground Committee, RR 1, Box 71-5, Deerhill Rd., Whitingham, VT 05361

True Grits: Tall Tales and Recipes from the New South, Junior League of Atlanta, Inc., 3154 Northside Pkwy., NW, Atlanta, GA 30327

The Very Special Raspberry Cookbook, Carrie Tingley Hospital Foundation, 1127 University Blvd., NE, Albuquerque, NM 87104

Very Virginia: Culinary Traditions with a Twist, Junior League of Hampton Roads, Inc., 751-B Thimble Shoals Blvd., Newport News, VA 23606

Virginia Fare, Junior League of Richmond, 205 W. Franklin St., Richmond, VA 23220

Watt's Cooking, Oasis Southern Company Services, Inc., 64 Perimeter Center E., Atlanta, GA 30346

Welcome Home, Thomasville Civic Center Foundation, P.O. Box 1131, Thomasville, AL 36784

We Like It Here, Mukwonago High School, 605 W. School Rd., Mukwonago, WI 53105

West of the Rockies, Junior Service League of Grand Junction, 425 North Ave., Ste. B, Grand Junction, CO 81501

Weymouth Township's Heritage of Recipes, Weymouth Township Civic Association, P.O. Box 53, 45 12th and S. Jersey Ave., Dorothy, NJ 08317

What's Cookin' from the "Young at Heart", Douglas County Senior Center Nutrition Center, 2300 Meadow Ln., Gardnerville, NV 89410

What's Cooking at Allied, Allied Services Nurse Retention and Recruitment Committee, 1804 Bundy St., Scranton, PA 18508

What's Cooking at Cathedral Plaza, Cathedral Plaza, 1575 Pennsylvania Ave., Denver, CO 80203

What's Cooking at Chico State, Staff Council/California State University, Chico, 1st and Orange Sts., Chico, CA 95929-0160

What's Cooking in Delaware, American Red Cross in Delaware, 910 Gilpin Ave., Wilmington, DE 19806

With Special Distinction, Mississippi College Cookbook Committee, P.O. Box 4054, Mississippi College, Clinton, MS 39058

Years and Years of Goodwill Cooking, Goodwill Circle of New Hope Lutheran Church, 8555 4th Ave., NW, Upham, ND 58789

Community Cookbook Awards

The editors salute the three national, six regional, and two special merit winners of the 1996 Tabasco Community Cookbook Awards competition sponsored by the Walter S. McIlhenny Company, Avery Island, Louisiana.

- **First Place Winner:** *Stop and Smell the Rosemary,* Junior League of Houston, Inc., Houston, Texas
- **Second Place Winner:** *The Kansas City Barbecue Society Cookbook,* Kansas City Barbecue Society, Kansas City, Missouri
- **Third Place Winner:** *Main Line Classics II, Cooking Up a Little History,* Junior Saturday Club of Wayne, Pennsylvania
- **New England:** *Windows, A Tasteful Reflection of Historic Rhode Island,* Junior League of Rhode Island, Providence, Rhode Island
- **Mid-Atlantic:** *Rogers Memorial Library Centennial Cookbook,* Rogers Memorial Library, Southampton, New York
- **South:** *Sweet Home Alabama,* Junior League of Huntsville, Alabama
- **Midwest:** *Dawn to Dusk,* Junior Welfare League of Holland, Michigan
- **Southwest:** *Texas Sampler,* Junior League of Richardson, Texas
- **West:** *Cheyenne Frontier Days "Daddy of 'em All" Cookbook,* Chuckwagon Gourmet, Cheyenne, Wyoming
- **Special Merit Winner:** *The Sarah Booth Cookbook,* Friends of the Cyrenius H. Booth Library, Newtown, Connecticut
- **Special Merit Winner:** *The McClellanville Coast Seafood Cookbook,* McClellanville Arts Council, McClellanville, South Carolina

For information on the Tabasco Community Cookbook Awards or for an awards entry form send a self-addressed stamped #10 (legal size) envelope to
Tabasco Community Cookbook Awards
℅ Hunter & Associates, Inc.
41 Madison Avenue
New York, NY 10010-2202
For a free booklet about producing a community cookbook send a self-addressed stamped #10 (legal size) envelope to
Compiling Culinary History
℅ Hunter & Associates, Inc.
41 Madison Avenue
New York, NY 10010-2202

Index